WOMEN IN AND OUT OF PAID WORK

Changes across generations in Italy and Britain

Cristina Solera

This book has been published with a financial subsidy from the European University Institute

This edition published in Great Britain in 2009 by

The Policy Press
University of Bristol
Fourth Floor
Beacon House
Queen's Road
Bristol BS8 1QU
UK

tel +44 (0)117 331 4054
fax +44 (0)117 331 4093
e-mail tpp-info@bristol.ac.uk
www.policypress.org.uk

North American office:
The Policy Press
c/o International Specialized Books Services
920 NE 58th Avenue, Suite 300
Portland, OR 97213-3786, USA
tel +1 503 287 3093 • fax +1 503 280 8832 • e-mail info@isbs.com

British Library Cataloguing in Publication Data
A catalogue record for this book is available from the British Library.

Library of Congress Cataloging-in-Publication Data
A catalog record for this book has been requested.

ISBN 978 1 86134 930 9 hardcover

Cover design by The Policy Press
Front cover: image kindly supplied by Emmanouel Vantarakis
Printed and bound in Great Britain by the MPG Books Group

To my 'pillars', those friends who have unwaveringly
accompanied me over the years

Contents

List of figures and tables

Figures

Tables

Foreword

Chiara Saraceno

Changes in women's behaviour with regard to fertility and labour market participation are possibly two of the most important processes that have reshaped the overall societal framework in the developed countries in the second half of the 20th century and in the first decade of the 21st. On the one hand, together with increasing life expectancy, low birth rates have reshaped the demography both of society and of families and kin. On the other hand, women's, and particularly mothers', labour market participation has not only changed women's lifecourse patterns and resources; it has also changed the organisation of everyday life for families, men and children. The timing of these two processes, which are linked in complex and not univocal ways, has been different in the various countries. Furthermore, it has involved different social groups within as well as across countries, redesigning patterns of similarities and dissimilarities.

Cristina Solera's work focuses specifically on one of these two processes: changes in women's labour market participation. More specifically, it focuses on changes in the way in which women since the post-war years have or not combined over the lifecourse participation in paid work and constructing their families. For men in industrialised societies, these two life trajectories and 'careers' (in Elder's – 1994 – meaning of life career), in fact, have become increasingly mutually reinforcing. For women, by contrast, these trajectories have become mutually weakening, if not exclusive. So much so, that in public discourse, their possible compatibility is now framed in the terminology of 'reconciling' (paid) work and the family, thus alluding to some mythical golden age when working and having a family were easy to combine. Only in the late 20th century did the contraposition between raising a family and being in paid work begin to weaken. For an increasing proportion of women, the two life trajectories became intertwined, although not to the same extent and nor through the same mechanisms across countries and social groups. Furthermore, even at present, any analysis of the impact on the likelihood of a woman with a child aged under six of being in employment compared with a childless woman shows that, among men and women in the 25-44 age bracket, the impact is uniformly positive for men in the European Union, and almost uniformly negative for women (the exceptions being Slovenia), although ranging from −34% in the Czech Republic to −1% in Portugal. In Italy and the UK, the values are respectively −9% and −17%. As Solera documents in this study, the difference between these two specific countries is largely explained by two distinct factors: first, in Italy, marriage, rather than having a child, is still the main reason why women exit the labour force. Second, in Italy, women's activity and employment rates are not only lower overall than in the UK; they also involve a much more select group in terms of education and geographical residence:

the better educated and those living in the Centre-North. These women have comparatively better chances and resources to combine paid work with raising a family throughout their adult lifecourses, albeit within a low fertility model. In the case of low education, other reasons, mostly linked to the demand side, in addition to having a child, play a crucial role in determining whether or not a woman is in the labour market particularly in the Southern regions (see also Reyneri, 2009).

In analysing these and other differences between two countries, which for long have been considered respectively the liberal and the familialistic variants of the male-breadwinner model, Solera takes a long and multidimensional view. Setting her longitudinal micro data in the historical context, her analysis enables detection of at least some of the micro–macro mechanisms that underlie the changes delineated above. In this perspective, this study may be considered an important methodological and substantive contribution to the comparative analysis of social change. Through the lives and choices of Solera's four cohorts of women, whose family and paid work trajectories she monitors from the time they leave school to when they turn 40, she traces both the changing patterns of adult female biographies in the past 50 years and the changing organisation of social and individual time schedules. Through a carefully developed micro–macro perspective, Solera is thus able to contextualise cross-cohort and cross-country differences and changes with regard to the characteristics of the labour market and of policy frameworks, and of the changing sets of options incorporated in the characteristics of demand, but also in the incentives and disincentives offered in the interplay between labour market and social security regulations.

Solera's data do not enable her to enter fully into the preferences versus constraints debate. Yet, she offers valuable elements with which to go beyond simplistic sides-taking and theories. The cohorts of women in her study appear significantly responsive to the institutional and labour market context, which suggests that something more than preferences, or even nation-specific gender and family cultures, are at play. The higher fluidity and flexibility of British women in entering and exiting the labour market appears a response to the opportunities of a labour market that offers little security but many second chances, however marginalised. In contrast, the stronger labour market attachment of the, fewer, Italian women who enter the labour market seems a response to a rigid labour market, where, having exited, it is difficult to re-enter, even in a marginal position, and often only in the informal labour market. Furthermore, although in both countries all four cohorts of women have had to deal with a scarcity of childcare services for the under-threes, in Italy this scarcity has been and still is partly compensated to a larger extent by the care provided by grandmothers. In addition to a possible different perception of inter- generational obligations in the two countries, the higher availability of grandmothers in Italy is also facilitated by closer geographical proximity between the households of adult children and those of their parents.

Interestingly, convergence is taking place between the younger cohorts of the two countries in the very characteristics that made them more different in the past: education is becoming a factor of polarisation in women's chances and behaviour in Britain, as it has been traditionally in Italy. And, owing to increasing deregulation of the labour market, Italian women are also becoming more flexible in their labour market participation, going from one to another contract, and in the meantime 'fitting in' their family choices. Policy also matters, although probably less than one would expect. The more generous maternity and parental leave granted to regular employees in Italy compared to Britain probably absorbs (or substitutes) part of the fluidity that British working women have to manage on their own. The working wife penalty incorporated into British unemployment benefit was largely responsible for the paradox, particularly apparent in the older cohorts, of the wives of the unemployed being less in the labour market than the wives of the employed.

Women's decisions, however, are not only the mechanic outcomes of the structure of opportunities and constraints. They are also the outcomes of women's own agency, given the opportunity and constraints with which they are faced. In this perspective, women in both countries seem to have used improved access to education to change their options and their negotiating power with regard to family and work decisions. Education seems to have helped them become more individualised within their partnerships. This appears most clearly in the declining importance of the partner's education and occupation in determining the chances of the wife's permanence in the labour force, in favour of the increasing importance of the wife's own education. In the Italian case, this result emerged also from a study using a retrospective longitudinal data source different from that used here by Solera (Rosina and Saraceno, 2008): women's education seems to protect them against the negative (with regard to female labour force participation) impact of husbands' high education, in so far as the well-educated wives of similarly educated husbands have better chances of remaining in the labour force than do wives with lower educations than their husbands.

Women's agency beyond institutional and cultural constraints is also apparent in the fact that, although in both countries childcare, particularly for children under three, is still mostly a family affair, more mothers are in the labour market than one would expect on the basis of the number of childcare places. Women who want children and also want, or need, to stay in the labour market use all the means at their disposal to do so: a systematic use of grandmothers, particularly in Italy, but to some degree also in Britain (see, for example, Lewis et al, 2008, on the basis of data of the European Social Survey), an organisation of time schedules of both parents that allows the longest presence possible with children, recourse to the market and, particularly in Britain, part-time work.

Certainly, policies (leaves, services, family-friendly work schedules and so forth) could greatly improve this constant endeavour of patchworking, also reducing social inequalities in the options available. But those who design policies might also learn from this work, from the needs and concerns that it expresses, how to intervene more effectively.

Acknowledgements

Writing a book is like a long journey along innumerable paths and which proceeds with different resources and at different speeds, sometimes marked by fatigue, often by the pleasure of discovery. I wish here briefly to thank the so many people who, each in a different way, have accompanied me on this journey.

First, on the academic level, I thank Richard Breen and Chiara Saraceno, who supervised, with rigour, constancy and passion, my doctoral thesis written at the Department of Political and Social Sciences of the European University Institute, defended on 15 April 2005, and which has formed the basis of this book. They have been my 'teachers' in every respect. I am also grateful to Chiara for reading various parts of the book and furnishing me with interesting insights, and for agreeing to write its foreword. I also wish to thank Nicola Negri and Manuela Naldini, from whom I have learned a great deal when working with them, and for giving me all the time and space necessary to complete my book. I am particularly indebted to Manuela for her constant encouragement, her careful and critical reading of every part of the book, and the tenacity of a friendship fuelled by a rare combination of the 'public' and 'private'. My thanks also go to Serena Pattaro, a patient reader of the central chapters of the book and an old friend. I am grateful to the European University Institute, which provided me with a grant to publish this book. I am also grateful for being able to spend a month at the ISER as an ECASS visitor, during which time I familiarised myself with the latest waves of the BHPS and profited from seminars and informal exchanges with the ISER researchers, first of all with Chiara Pronzato. I would like to thank Rossella Bozzon, Ivano Bison, Carlo Barone and Simone Sarti for their guidance on the ILFI data. I would also like to thank all those who listened to me and commented on previous versions of the empirical chapters of this book, presented in Berlin during the midterm EQUALSOC conference in April 2008, and in Turin on the occasion of the IAFFE annual conference in June 2008. Finally, my thanks go to Adrian Belton, who has patiently and rapidly revised the English of my book.

On the personal level, the year and a half spent writing the book has been a novel blend of experiences, among *dolcetto d'alba*, *pasta alla zucca* and *salami al tartufo*, among cinema, politics and music, and amid heated discussion and idle conversation. I am profoundly grateful for these pieces of shared life and for the relationships arising from them to my long-standing friends who for years have continued to accompany me despite the geographical distances among us: Katia, Betta, Alessandra, Elisa, Mamadou; to my friends in Turin, above all Carmen, Florence, Vittorio, Stefano, Lorenzo, Chiara and Silvia; to Mau, who made the last month of my immersion in this book so special; to my parents for their constant and unstinting support, including financial; and to my numerous nephews and nieces simply for being children.

ONE

Introduction

The issue: for whom, when and where has women's labour market attachment increased?

In the second half of the twentieth century, rates of women's employment increased markedly in all the advanced countries. As much research shows, this increase was due mostly to the changed behaviour of married women and mothers. Indeed, work and family have everywhere become more compatible. Compared to their 'mothers' and 'grandmothers', women belonging to the younger generations have not only entered the labour market on a larger scale, but they have also reduced their exits or shortened their family-care breaks.

Several phenomena have contributed to this remarkable transformation. On the supply side, women have increasingly invested in education, closing the gender gap and in some cases even reversing it. This process has been partly the consequence of the general educational improvement that characterised the post-war cohorts – male and female. In the case of women, however, the democratisation of education had an impact not only on inter-generational/inter-cohort differences but also on gender differences. The feminist movements of the 1960 and 1970s – with their contestation of traditional gender roles and redefinition of gender norms and practices – may be read as both an outcome and an accelerator of this process. Higher investments in education have also increased the opportunity cost of not working, or of withdrawing from the labour force during the family formation phase (Bimbi, 1992; Saraceno, 1992, 1993; Blossfeld and Shavit, 1993; Blossfeld, 1995). In parallel, on the demand side, the growth of service sector employment has expanded women's labour market participation. It has indeed created 'women's jobs', with sometimes (for example in the public sector), but not always, family-friendly features, although it has produced gender segregation as well (Gornick and Jacobs, 1998; Mandel and Semyonov, 2006). In some countries, tertiarisation has been accompanied by an expansion of, often deregulated, part-time work, which for women with family responsibilities has offered a way of remaining attached to the labour market, albeit in a marginal and under-protected way. Finally, on the institutional side, the improvement of the social security conditions of part-time work and, above all, the extension of maternity and parental leave programmes and of childcare services, have importantly affected the chances of combining employment with family responsibilities (Sainsbury, 1994a; Gustafsson, 1995; Gornick et al, 1997; Esping-Andersen, 1999; Boje and Leira, 2000; Uunk et al, 2005).

Although these trends have occurred everywhere, differences across countries and within women have been marked. There is considerable variation across countries in the timing, degree and type of cultural, economic and institutional change, and in how much, when and for whom women's employment has increased. This variation has been widely documented and discussed. Yet most of the evidence for it is based on cross-sectional or time-series data. Few studies have used longitudinal analyses in order explicitly to explore changes across cohorts; or, when they have done so, few have gone beyond single-country or single-region analyses. Moreover, few studies have looked at the work career as a whole. Rather, the tendency has been to focus on specific crucial phases in female careers or on specific groups of women: that is, on labour market transitions around childbearing and on married women.

The aim of this book is to start to remedy these shortcomings. It compares two countries – Italy and Britain – and it uses event-history data and methods to investigate changes across four successive birth cohorts in women's work–family histories, from the time when they leave full-time education until they reach the age of 40. Specifically, the book addresses the following questions: *How much and for whom have continuous careers increased? What kinds of women, instead, tend to exit from paid work?* 'All' mothers or only poorly educated women with 'bad' jobs, or those married to lower-class men? If they interrupt, at what stage of the lifecourse do they do so? At the time of marriage, when they are pregnant or their first child is young, or when income needs are less impelling? *Who, once they have exited, tend to re-enter and when?* The highly educated? When all the children are grown up, as soon as care needs become less urgent? Or only if an extra family income is necessary? *How has all this changed across cohorts?* In particular, has the trade-off between employment and motherhood decreased? Have inequalities among women increased, diminished, or changed form?

These questions are crucial if one wants to grasp the 'degree' and 'type' of change behind the aggregated statistics. Indeed, the growth in women's employment since the 1960s may simply be a 'compositional effect'. It may be due to the fact that more women in younger cohorts have acquired those characteristics (such as high education, good jobs and childlessness) that have always been associated with higher levels of labour market participation and continuity. Conversely, it may be that women's involvement in paid work has become the norm, and that this norm has begun to apply to mothers as well, regardless of their educational and occupational profile. In both cases, crucial issues of 'agency' are involved. If successive cohorts of women increasingly invest in their human capital it is because they intentionally invest in a lifecourse strategy that includes participation in paid work alongside investment in family relations. If also women with low educations accept the 'adult worker' norm and develop strategies to conciliate it with family formation, this is not only because they passively adopt top-down social models. They are actors as well.

The 'agency' perspective in turn entails that of 'social inequality'. *Do heterogeneous behaviours in women's employment trajectories reflect different preferences or different abilities to overcome constraints and act upon preferences? Has heterogeneity assumed new forms over generations?* In other words, is heterogeneity today based more on education or on class? And on the husband's profile more than on that of the woman? Does differentiation emerge more in the decision on whether and when to start a labour market career, or to return to it once it has been started and interrupted, or on whether and when to interrupt in the first place? *What accounts for the differences between Italian and British women?*

The relevance

Answering the above questions is of substantive importance for both scientific and political reasons. In the latter half of the 20th century, profound changes came about not only in employment but also in family behaviour. The younger cohorts started to marry later, and to cohabit instead of or before marriage. They also had higher rates of marital instability, became parents at older ages and, in most countries including Britain and particularly Italy, of fewer children. Whatever perspective one is inclined to take on the causes of the new patterns of family formation, there is no doubt that employment, family and gender changes are closely interconnected, at least in their timing. As cross-national comparative research shows, there is also no doubt that their connection is institutionally embedded. Where good parenting policies and employee-friendly labour market opportunities are not available, women face a trade-off between employment and fertility (Sorrentino, 1990; Blossfeld, 1995; Oppenheim Mason and Jensen, 1995; Brewster and Rindfuss, 2000; Del Boca and Wetzels, 2007). This has crucial implications at both the individual and societal level. At the micro level, it entails lower household incomes and higher risks of poverty. Many studies show that women's attachment to paid work furnishes key insurance against poverty risk. First, it is important, although not always sufficient, if the husband becomes unemployed or has a low-paid job. Second, it is crucial in the event of divorce, because the post-divorce poverty risk for women and children largely depends on their previous economic dependence on husbands. At the micro level, the scarce institutional support given to work–family reconciliation also entails inequalities between men and women and among women themselves. At the macro level, the existence of a trade-off between employment and fertility raises issues of equal opportunities and gender equality, especially where domestic and childcare work has remained a female domain. It also affects macro-economic efficiency and sustainability. It may indeed give rise to a waste of human capital but, above all, to unsustainability of the economy and of society itself. The more women do not enter employment, or interrupt while children are young, the smaller the tax base with which to finance the welfare state. The fewer children women have, the more problematic in the future will be not only the financial viability of the welfare state but also the 'natural' generational replacement of society. This book therefore addresses a phenomenon that touches upon crucial economic, social and political issues in contemporary societies. By analysing women's employment over a long span of their lifecourses, and by comparing across both space and time, it shows how different institutional and normative configurations help or hinder work–family reconciliation and reduce or reinforce (gender, generational and class) inequalities. In turn, the book contributes, although indirectly, to the ongoing debate on welfare and labour market reforms.

The analyses in this book seek to answer the above questions by adopting an approach that is, in many respects, innovative. As mentioned earlier, unlike most previous research, this study is simultaneously longitudinal (over a long span of women's lifecourses), comparative (across two countries) and historical (across four subsequent generations). Moreover, whereas explanations to date have typically focused on one single factor or a few factors, this study uses a unified theoretical framework that, within a micro–macro lifecourse model, comprises the interconnection of the material, the institutional and the symbolic at the level of individuals, households and societies.

The analytical approach: comparing lifecourses between the micro and the macro

There are various theories that attempt to account for women's labour market behaviour. Some of them, put forward by standard economists and sociologists such as Hakim (2000), emphasise supply-side factors, namely human capital resources and work orientations. Others analyse women's labour supply within the context of the household or of the social stratification system. Segmentation theories focus on the demand side, while institutional-oriented sociologists and economists point to the importance of the welfare state and its interconnection with the family and the labour market. Finally, besides institutions, feminists stress the role of culture either by considering, at a macro level, institutionalised gender and care norms or overall gender-role attitudes; or by examining, at a micro level, women's own attitudes, or the negotiated moral and social views developed within their social networks. *In this study, I seek to build a unified conceptual framework by amalgamating insights from these various theoretical accounts into what I term 'a (gendered) institutional rational-action framework'.* This framework incorporates both micro and macro factors and both agency and structure. The concept of constrained choices is crucial: women's choices in the labour market reflect their preferences and their human capital, but they are embedded in an array of institutional, economic and cultural arrangements. These arrangements not only set the material opportunities and constraints within which women form their actions; they also define models of what is 'proper' and 'feasible' behaviour, thereby influencing individual attitudes, individual positive beliefs, and social views of normality.

As feminists point out, social reality is sexed. Gender, as well as class and age, is a key factor organising and ordering individual lives, the family, and society as a whole. It structures access to both material and symbolic resources, and the power to define and redistribute such access. It shapes identities, experiences, and the time structure of everyday life between work, family and leisure. Gender is also incorporated into institutions. By defining citizenship rights, family obligations and private/public boundaries and by delivering specific levels and types of supports between care, income and employment, in fact, institutions assume and produce different lifecourses, different interdependences and different roles and positions for men and women. Put differently, everyday micro relations within the family and close social networks, as well as macro–economic and institutional relations, 'do gender' (West and Zimmerman, 1987; Saraceno and Piccone Stella, 1996; Hobson et al, 2002; Risman, 2004). In order to explain changes in women's employment and in work–family articulations over the lifecourse, the prism of 'gender' is therefore indispensable. In this book I shall adopt this prism by integrating mainstream theories with feminist critiques and accounts. Then, the extent to which and how marriage and motherhood have become more or less compatible with paid work, and women have become more or less polarised, will depend on the concrete characteristics of all the various '*explanans*' underlined in the literature, on their relations, and on which of them have changed, and how, over time in the countries studied.

Although my data do not allow for the direct measurement of preferences and constraints, the analytical approach that I shall follow provides 'insurance' for the advancement of causal narratives on observed behaviours. This approach has three distinctive features.

First, *it is based on retrospective longitudinal data and on a very rich set of relevant individual and familial covariates*. As the majority of social scientists and statisticians now agree, empirical analyses per se do not prove causality. Causal inference is theoretically driven. However, there is broad consensus that longitudinal data, and in particular lifecourse data, provide a better basis than cross-sectional data for depicting social change and for drawing causal inferences. As lifecourse scholars have argued (Elder, 1985; Kohli, 2001; Mortimer and Shanahan, 2003), the lifecourse is both agency and structure. Individual lives are intentionally and actively constructed, but they are also socially patterned over time. An individual's own work trajectory is intertwined with their other trajectories (educational, marital, childcare, moral and so on) and with the trajectories of other individuals with whom they interact and negotiate their choices. An individual's own development path is also embedded in, and transformed by, conditions and events occurring during the historical period and geographical location in which their life unfolds. Longitudinal data can be fruitfully used to capture these micro–macro intersections because they make it possible to distinguish among individual time, generational time and historical time. In technical terms, they allow the measurement of age, cohort and period effects (Mayer and Huinink, 1990; Blossfeld and Rower, 1995; Price et al, 2000).

More specifically, the analysis conducted in this book draws on the British Household Panel Survey (BHPS) up to the 15th wave, dated 2005, and on the Italian Household Longitudinal Survey (ILFI) up to the fifth and last wave, also dated 2005. The latter is a very recent retrospective longitudinal survey, which began in 1997. It is an important innovation in Italy, where previously a good national longitudinal survey did not exist, and where, consequently, research was mainly based on cross-sectional data. What was known about female labour market transitions over the lifecourse derived from longitudinal data on a specific geographical area (Schizzerotto et al, 1995; Bison et al, 1996), on single cohorts of married women (Bernardi, 1999, 2001) or on a specific short time period (Del Boca et al, 2007; Pronzato, 2007). Since the ILFI data became available, lifecourse research in Italy has flourished. However, to date no research has explicitly analysed changes across cohorts in women's work histories. Studies based on ILFI have mainly looked at transitions into adulthood (Schizzerotto and Lucchini, 2002; Pisati, 2002; Bernardi and Nazio, 2005), at marital stability (Arosio, 2004), at occupational mobility (Pisati and Schizzerotto, 1999; Arosio, 2002) or at atypical employment (Barbieri and Sherer, 2008). When ILFI has been used to explore women's employment patterns, the attention has concentrated on the period around the birth of the first child (Saurel-Cubizolles et al, 1999; Bratti et al, 2004) or on married women and the interconnection between 'her' and 'his' careers (Bison, 2006; Lucchini et al, 2007) or on types of overall work trajcetories (Bozzon, 2008). Thus, the present study is the first to use this relatively new Italian dataset to examine different phases of women's labour market careers and transformations across generations.

Britain has a longer longitudinal tradition. Prior to the BHPS, which was launched in 1992, there was the National Survey of Health and Development, the Child Development Study, the Women and Employment Survey, and the Social Change and Economic Life Initiative. Compared to Italy, therefore, much more is known in Britain on women's labour force participation over the lifecourse. Yet, as in Italy, longitudinal research on women's employment has typically concentrated on mothers' labour force transitions (McRae, 1993; Joshi et al, 1996; Jacobs, 1997; Dex et al, 1998; Elliot et al, 2001; Vlasblom and Schippers, 2006). Moreover, few studies have explicitly addressed changes across cohorts (Joshi and Hinde, 1993; Jacobs, 1999).

Few studies, too, have looked at a wide span of women's adult lifecourses. When this has occurred, the focus has been on the effect of the partner, and consequently on married women (McCulloch and Dex, 2001), or on occupational mobility (Jacobs, 1995). By contrast, *in this book I shall explore women's employment dynamics over long periods of individual lives, from the time when women leave full-time education to age 40 (or at the time of the interviews with the youngest cohort)*. This widening of the observational window has important advantages. First, it makes it possible to depict overall trajectories and − when focusing on single transitions within them − to capture exits and re-entries occurring at later ages as well. Second, the relatively long window chosen makes it possible to avoid the problematic sample selection inherent in research that focuses on specific groups of women, such as studies that analyse transitions around childbirth. As Drobnic (2000) argues, since in these cases only women with children or women who are working during pregnancy are observed, it is not possible to distinguish the impacts of other factors that may affect all women similarly, regardless of their childbearing and marital status.

Moreover, I would add, it is not possible to determine how the effect of marriage and children has changed across cohorts and, particularly, to what extent and for whom the timing of interruptions has been postponed from the period around marriage to the period around childbirth. Finally, a wide window also allows for the better inclusion of information about the past history. This is important in order to deal with the problem of misspecification that occurs if initial conditions at entry into an episode are not taken into account.

The approach followed in this book is also *comparative across both time and space*. It compares four subsequent birth cohorts in two different countries. As Mayer (1997) points out, cross-national comparisons of lifecourses are necessary to bridge the micro and the macro, to combine individual-level dynamic models with macro explanations. The book contains large amounts of information on changes over time in Italy and Britain, both in women's work histories and in the economic, institutional and cultural arrangements in which they are embedded, and it links such information to previous empirical research and to existing demographic, economic and sociological theories. Thus, as said, the book sheds light on the role of welfare and labour market policies in shaping women's work–family combinations. In addition, it offers new insights into the ongoing debate, following Beck and Hakim, on individualisation and 'choice' in lifecourses. According to these narratives, in the 21st century, structural constraints have lost influence, giving way to personal lifestyles, values and preferences. With a decline of rigid normative prescripts and of both material and symbolic class conditionings, women's agency – it is argued – has increased. By first measuring the changing effect, *ceteris paribus*, of 'her' and 'his' class and education in pushing women in and out of paid work, and then by breaking down the figures for low- and high-educated women and for women married to lower- or upper-class men, I shall show whether and in which phase of the lifecourse women's employment paths still differ by 'classic' stratification factors. Although the relative weights of preferences and constraints are not directly detectable in my analyses – but also acknowledging that such calculation would be anyway problematic since, as many sociologists maintain, preferences are socially structured – my findings will add evidence on old or new forms of polarisation.

Selection of countries and cohorts

A cross-national comparative design is required in order to capture micro–macro intersections. In this book I adopt an individualising rather than universalising strategy for comparisons (Tilly, 1984), and a case-oriented rather than variable-oriented approach (Ragin, 1991). I thus focus on only two specific countries, namely Italy and Britain. Comparison between Italy and Britain is interesting because they differ greatly in their economic, normative and institutional configurations, and in how they have changed from the 1950s to the 2000s. Britain experienced a much earlier and more intense shift to a service economy, and in particular to part-time employment. The approval of new roles for women has also generally increased in Britain, although childcare is still defined and largely practised as a women's issue. In Italy, a general cultural shift has not come about: education still mediates approval of the involvement of women and mothers in paid employment. Moreover, whereas post-industrial Britain has moved sharply away from a relatively regulated, relatively unionised labour market, and a Beveridge type of welfare state, and towards a 'liberal' country, with a residualist welfare state and a deregulated economy, Italy has seen only minor changes in its institutional setting. It still has a quite closely regulated labour market in a minimalist welfare context, with highly segmented social protection, with the family playing a crucial role as welfare provider. De facto flexibility has been achieved (at least until the late 1990s) in a peculiar way through small firms, non-dependent labour and the informal economy. Finally, whereas in Britain, rates of divorce, cohabitation and procreation outside marriage have risen significantly, in Italy the standard nuclear family is still predominant, and continues to be a central and relatively stable institution.

Italy and Britain also differ importantly in their levels and patterns of women's labour market participation. Despite an increase in the past few decades, the activity rates of women in Italy are still among the lowest in Europe. When they work, Italian women have always done so on a full-time basis and continuously. By contrast, in Britain, women tend to drop out of the labour force when they have children and to return when the children are older, often on a part-time basis. This discontinuous pattern has changed during the last few decades, in that the time spent out of work has progressively shortened and the incidence of continuous careers has increased. Yet a break in the period around childbearing is still particularly common in Britain.

Comparison of the lifecourses of different cohorts of women is necessary in order to grasp the timing and type of change that has occurred in women's labour market participation. Indeed, as said, such comparison allows one to distinguish different components behind aggregated rates. First, it may be that changes have affected specific phases of the lifecourse and not others, and specific types of women and not others. Women may have increased both their first entry into paid work and subsequent permanence in it over family formation; they may have increased re-entries after having interrupted paid work; or they may have changed only one of these behaviours. Also, the profile of women pursuing continuous careers may have changed, and the family/work combination may have become more 'universal', cutting across education, class and region. Second, it may be that not only the 'quantum' but also the 'timing' of entries, exits and re-entries have changed. More generally, it is only by following different cohorts of women over the development of their lifecourses that age–period–cohort sources of individual and social change can be disentangled. Furthermore, comparison across generations confutes the assumption of linear change inherent in many 'evolutionary' accounts, and it enables actual observations of similarities and differences in the experiences of women who have been born and have grown up in different periods. In an age of high labour market and family instability, and of low protection for new entrants, the employment trajectories of the young women of today may be more similar to those of their 'grandmothers' than their 'mothers'. At the same time, with the weakening of male-breadwinner norms and policies, the family/work patterns of young and old generations may differ.

In cross-national studies, however, the selection of cohorts encounters three problems. First, changes in the relevant macro *'explanans'* vary between countries: that is, the beginning and duration of periods, for example of the so-called 'golden age' or 'post-industrial/post-Fordist' era (Esping-Andersen, 1999; Brückner and Mayer, 2005; Kohli, 2007), differ. Also different is the extent to which, and the period in which, such 'goldenness' starts to regard women as well, with questioning of the male-breadwinner configuration of the nuclear family, the labour market and the welfare state. In countries like Italy, with its North/South economic divide and its segmented welfare provision, the labels 'golden age' and 'post-industrial age' are disputable in themselves. Second, the age on entry into adulthood (entry into the labour market or into marriage and motherhood) varies greatly within cohorts and across countries.

In this study, therefore, I prefer to use birth cohorts instead of labour market entry cohorts or Fordist/post-Fordist cohorts. The choice of birth cohorts is also more consistent with the theoretical framework used, in which the material, the institutional and the cultural are intertwined. This last aspect, in particular, cannot be disregarded and cannot be confined to a 'period effect'. When women make their choices, they are guided by the normative and moral frameworks of both actual and past social contexts. Put differently, primary gender socialisation is also important. Moreover, I shall use the terms 'generation' and 'cohort' as synonyms. 'Generation' has two meanings. It is first and foremost a kinship concept referring to positions and relationships within the line of descent. Since the works of Ortega y Gasset (1933) and Mannheim (1952), 'generation' also refers to a group of people who share a distinctive culture or a self-conscious identity by virtue of having experienced the same historical events at roughly the same time in their lives. Although I am aware that cohort differences do not automatically imply the existence of generations – that is, the existence of a 'collective identity' – I shall use 'generation' in a soft sense as a group of people who have been born and have grown up in the same historical period. Accordingly, I shall examine four successive birth cohorts: 1935-44, 1945-54, 1955-64 and 1965-74. These birth cohorts have entered the labour market and built their families and careers in different decades. The first birth cohort grew up in the 1940s-1950s and became adult mainly in the 1960s, when the male-breadwinner order predominated. The second cohort entered adulthood mainly in the 1970s, when norms, policies and demand for labour became more women friendly. The third and fourth cohort spent their childhood and adolescence within less traditional gender models but built their work and family careers under a deregulation policy in Britain and under a stagnant economy and welfare policy in Italy. The last cohort has also been exposed to the late-1990s reforms, in the form of 'partial and selective' deregulation in Italy, and of 'make (male but also female) work pay' in Britain. Unlike older women, those in the fourth cohort were still in their family formation phase when these reforms were introduced. Specific hypotheses on how employment patterns have changed in these four birth cohorts can therefore be put forward through reconstruction of the normative, institutional and economic contexts in different decades in Italy and Britain and in light of the theoretical discussion on the micro and macro determinants of female lifecourses.

Outline of the book

The book is organised into seven chapters, including the present introduction. Chapter Two discusses various sociological, demographic and economic theories that focus on different dimensions and predict different effects on women's labour market participation. The chapter begins with theories addressing the role of education, wages and class by outlining human capital theory. It then moves to criticisms of that theory, in particular those highlighting instrumental and non-instrumental returns to education, class conditionings, and their institutional and cultural embeddedness. The chapter then directs attention to the debate on Hakim's preference theory, the social structuring of preferences and 'choices', the link between norms and behaviour, and the role of gender-role attitudes in explaining family and employment changes. Following this, theories on the gender division of labour within the family and on the effect of partner's resources are discussed: Becker's 'new home economics' theory and the criticisms made of it by bargaining models, social capital scholars, gender studies, and those highlighting the weight of economic necessity. The next section of the chapter examines institutional theories on the role of the welfare state in shaping gender relations and women's chances and outcomes in the labour market. It first outlines Esping-Andersen's influential typology of welfare regimes and the 'gendering' criticisms brought against it. Then, drawing on both mainstream and feminist analyses, the section specifies what dimensions of welfare state policies are relevant to the study of women's labour market transitions. It is argued that women's attachment to paid work is best supported by a 'defamilialising' and 'decommodifying' package of policies revolving around three pillars (income, time and services) providing universal and generous benefits (in terms of both levels of coverage and levels of wage replaced or integrated) and which promote the father's and not just the mother's involvement in childcare. The following section discusses theories on the effects of the overall demand for labour, of labour market structure and of regulation. In particular, it briefly sketches demand-side-driven labour market segmentation theory and then focuses on the accounts deriving from cross-national comparative researches, which show that the type of labour force divide existing in a given country and its gender profile also depend on institutional and cultural settings. The section identifies areas of labour market regulation with important direct or indirect implications for women's employment. Particularly important are employee- and parent-friendly flexibility measures and statutory working time regulations. Finally, the last section integrates these diverse theories into a (gendered) institutional–rational action approach as outlined earlier.

Chapter Three provides a descriptive reconstruction of how the potential '*explanans*' identified in Chapter Two have been concretely configured in Italy and Britain from the 1950s to the 2000s. After an introductory section, by referring to international aggregated employment data, cross-sectional micro-level studies, and findings from previous longitudinal analyses, the next section of the chapter illustrates changes in female activity rates, in the overall and sectoral distribution of demand, and in women's supply characteristics. Following this there is a brief overview of family change in Italy and Britain – that is, of trends in cohabitation, marriage, divorce and fertility, and of the explanations given for them. The subsequent two sections describe the main features of the institutional context in the two countries by looking at the welfare state and labour market regulation, and by reporting the findings in the literature on the impact of such features on women's labour market participation. The chapter then draws on empirical studies on gender-role attitudes and gender allocation of time between paid market work and unpaid domestic work to show how these have changed across cohorts in Italy and Britain. The chapter then concludes.

Chapter Four outlines the methods, data and hypotheses on which the empirical analyses set out in the rest of the book are based. The chapter starts with an illustration of the nature and strengths of longitudinal data compared to cross-sectional data, and of an event-oriented observation design compared with other types of longitudinal design. Particular attention is paid to the analytical and methodological virtues of a lifecourse perspective, and to the debate on notions of causality, and on the power of event-history data and methods in testing it. The chapter then briefly illustrates the transition rate models used in the empirical analyses, namely discrete-time logit models. It then addresses the problems of sample selection and unobserved heterogeneity and discusses the extent to which these problems exist in the models I have used in this book and how they have been tackled. Following this, the chapter describes the two datasets (BHPS and ILFI), the sample of women, and the variables used in the empirical analyses. The next section summarises Chapter Three on the changes that Italy and Britain have seen in their economic, cultural and institutional systems. On the basis of the theoretical accounts discussed in Chapter Two, hypotheses are formulated on their impacts on women's employment over the lifecourse. The chapter then draws to a close.

Chapters Five and Six present and discuss the empirical findings. Chapter Five uses the BHPS and ILFI first to give a descriptive overview of the entire work trajectory from the conclusion of schooling to age 40 and then to focus on distinct transitions within it. More precisely, it distinguishes five types of work histories ('never worked', 'continuous', 'one break, no return', 'one break, return', 'two plus breaks') and shows how the proportion of women pursuing continuous or discontinuous careers has changed over time, whether this proportion was and is different for mothers and non-mothers and for mothers with one or more children.

The chapter then uses event-history models to analyse changes across cohorts in the factors driving women out of and back into paid work. By estimating a single additive model for all cohorts and separate models for each cohort, the second part of this chapter addresses the 'compositional question' on the increase in women's employment rates since the 1960s. Particular attention is paid to the changing effects, *ceteris paribus*, of education and class, and of marriage and motherhood. In fact, this part of the chapter explores whether, in Italy and Britain, the labour supply of younger women still responds to family responsibilities, whether it responds more to childrearing than to marital responsibilities, with a progressive postponement of the timing of exits and anticipation of the timing of re-entries, and whether it responds more to age than to the number of children. It also highlights the nexus between class and education. It shows whether differences between highly and poorly educated women remain after controlling for class (and type of job and labour market experience), or whether class is more important, so that also women who have invested in education but are not in the primary labour market tend to interrupt their participation when they become mothers. Hypotheses put forward at the end of Chapter Four are resumed, and explanations based on different welfare, employment and attitudinal regimes are suggested. Since in Italy large numbers of women have never started a labour market career, especially in the past and in the South, first entry into the labour market is also modelled for Italy, and the extent to which education and region still mark a divide is analysed. The chapter then draws to a close.

Chapter Six explores the issue of stratification further. It estimates separate figures and models by education and cohort and, in doing so, shows how the effects of marriage, children and class differ between low- and high-educated women and how the difference has changed over time. It then adds information on the profile of the partner and examines how 'his' education and class divided and may still divide women's movements in and out of paid work. Thus, the chapter affords new insights into changing forms of polarisation in Italian and British women's work–family combinations.

Chapter Seven concludes with a summary of the main findings and with discussion of their policy implications. It re-opens the issue of individualisation and 'choice' in women's employment and, in the light of the persisting, although changed, stratification observed by education and class, it reflects on the weight of 'preferences' and 'constraints', and on their problematic distinction, given that preferences are endogenous to cultural and institutional models. Moreover, the chapter backtracks types of changes across generations and across countries through the lenses of 'linearity versus non-linearity' and 'convergence versus divergence'. It discusses how changes across generations and countries have been multifarious and irregular, so that the family/employment trajectories of young women are in some respects more similar to those of their 'grandmothers', and in other respects to those of their 'mothers'. Moreover, it outlines the extent to which and how the experiences of British and Italian women have grown more convergent. Finally, Chapter Seven resumes the issue of the micro–macro foundations of individual lifecourses and draws some policy conclusions, asserting the importance of social and labour market policies that combine decommodification with defamilialisation and which support, both materially and symbolically, a 'dual-earner/dual-carer society', giving more (income-protected) time for care and encouraging male time to care as well. The comparison between Italy and Britain suggests that only policies of this kind can sustain women's attachment to paid work without threatening levels of fertility, gender and class equality, and overall economic and societal sustainability.

TWO

Conceptualising influences on women's employment transitions: from various sociological and economic theories towards an integrated approach

Introduction

Women's labour market participation, marriage and fertility behaviour, and, generally, gender roles changed dramatically during the second half of the 20th century. Given their extent and their economic, social and also moral implications, such changes have dominated the academic and political debate and generated an enormous body of empirical and theoretical literature. Some theories focus on supply-side factors such as human capital resources and work–family orientations. Others analyse women's labour supply within the context of the household or of the social stratification system by looking at the effect of the partner's resources or women's class position. Yet others emphasise the institutional context that shapes women's and couple's choices by examining either specific policies or the overall welfare state or welfare regime. Other theories focus more closely on the labour market structure, opportunities and regulations. Further scholars point to the importance of culture, either at a macro level, by considering institutionalised gender and care norms, or overall gender roles and work attitudes in the society; or at a micro level, by looking at women's attitudes and at moral and social views negotiated with partners and within other social networks.

In this chapter I shall review these various theories, my aims being to identify the different potential micro and macro determinants of women's employment patterns, and to propose an integrated approach that considers the interplay among supply-side, demand-side, cultural, material and institutional factors. The extent and type of change across cohorts in women's work histories in the two countries studied will thus depend on the concrete characteristics of all these different '*explanans*', on their relations, and on which of them have changed over time and how.

The effects of education, wages and class

Human capital theory acts as a sort of benchmark in the study of women's labour market outcomes. It derives from the standard economic approach of rational choice and, like any 'standard', it has been used to explain many different phenomena. The theory has been widely discussed within economics, but also within sociology and politics where its influence has spread. This longstanding debate has produced several pro and contra arguments, several empirical tests, and it has given rise to more liberal rational-choice versions or to alternative accounts that emphasise non-instrumental rationality, non-monetary returns to education, the importance of class and of the institutional and cultural embeddedness of choices and outcomes.

Human capital theory and women's labour market outcomes

Women's involvement in paid work has been explained in terms of human capital investments and returns. Investments are time-consuming: each additional year of schooling or on-the-job experience, or, in the case of women, domestic and caring time, causes a postponement of earnings and a reduction in the duration of the working life for future pensions rights. Because of these costs, investment is made only if it raises the level of the deferred income stream (Mincer and Polachek, 1974). This calculation is linked to expectations. In a society where women are primarily responsible for family care, it is rational for them to invest in education, on-the-job training and work experience if they are career oriented and intend either to remain childless or to not fully commit to paid work (Becker, 1975, 1996). Given that depreciation is lower for general than for specific human capital, it is also rational for women to choose general human capital (Tam, 1997). Decisions on how much to invest in human capital, as regards both education and labour market experience, will also depend on the relative size of the depreciation and restoration effects and the probability of returning to work.

Following these arguments, human capital theory predicts that the greater a woman's investment in education, the lower will be her probability of leaving the labour market, and the higher her probability of returning.[1] The same prediction applies to the type of time commitment made to the labour market: women who work full time are less likely than those who work part time to interrupt their employment and, if they do, they are more likely to resume it rapidly.

Much research has shown that such human capital resources are indeed strong predictors of women's labour market behaviour (for reviews, see Killingsworth, 1983; Del Boca and Wetzels, 2007). Using the mainstream economic approach of maximisation of household expected lifetime utility under budget and time constraints, this research finds that female wages have a negative effect on fertility and a positive effect on participation, while male wages have the opposite effects. Demand for children and for paid work are interlinked: children affect wages because the time that they demand cannot be invested in education or on-the-job training. Hence, the relative investment in one or the other will depend on the opportunity cost and on the value of women's time, that is, on the extent to which women will substitute non-market time (children) with market time (used to acquire market goods). If only mothers' time and market goods are required for childrearing, the human capital model predicts that a wage increase will lead to an increase in labour supply at low wages, with substitution effects dominating over income effects and producing less demand for children and more demand for paid work. At higher wages, further wage increases produce a positive demand for children, without depressing women's labour supply (for a review, see Wetzels, 2007)

More recent studies have shown that wage and income elasticities, as well as the wage cost of motherhood, have changed over time and differ across countries. For example, Joshi et al (1996) and Dex et al (1998) find that in Britain the effect of the woman's own wage has strengthened over time, while the negative husband's income effect has declined. Income effects appear to be stronger in other countries (Bernasco et al, 1998). Gustafsson et al (2003) and Harkness and Waldfogel (2003) show that the variation in the pay gap between mothers and non-mothers is largest in the UK and smallest in Sweden, and that it is not primarily due to differential selection into employment or to differences in the wage structure. Institutional factors are important, as will be discussed in later in this chapter.

Recent studies also show that the link between participation and fertility has changed. Using the European Community Household Panel (ECHP) for 1994–99 and comparing different countries, Del Boca and Pasqua (2005), for example, find that education positively affects both the probability of working and of having children. This may be due to a preference effect or to an income over substitution effect for highly qualified women who can afford to buy childcare in the market. Other econometric studies show that women's education affects more the timing than the quantum of fertility, although postponement may also lead to involuntary childlessness. Using a framework more dynamic than the classic Beckerian theoretical model, these studies argue that, for better-educated women and/or women with greater tastes for work, the risk of interrupting or reducing their labour supply around childbirth is too costly in terms of both current opportunity costs (current wages) and future accumulation of human capital (career planning motive). Thus, highly educated women decide to become mothers when their predicted loss is minimal – probably when their current wages are high (consumption smoothing motive), which tends to happen later in the lifecourse given the steeper wage profile for high-skilled jobs (Gustaffson, 2001; Bratti, 2003). Moreover, these studies show that returns to education and, in turn, fertility and participation decisions are influenced by policies and norms affecting own wages, family incomes and time to care (Del Boca, 1993; Del Boca and Wetzels, 2007).

Beyond wages and instrumental rationality: education, class and culture

As seen, according to standard economic theory, people's choices concerning their working lives respond primarily to non-own income and own wages. Own wages are largely influenced by choices of education – level and type – and education is only or mainly seen as instrumental to the acquisition of goods and incomes. Moreover, as we shall see in more detail later in this chapter, labour market decisions are taken within couples on the basis of women's market and domestic productivities relative to those of their husbands. The assumptions are well known: instrumental rationality, perfect information, optimisation of time allocation between paid and unpaid work under budget constraint, the family as unitary with a joint utility function, and atomistic agents. In more dynamic and heterodox economic approaches, norms and institutions also play a role, and rationality is bounded; but the focus is still on monetary returns to education.

These assumptions and focuses have been widely criticised. As underlined by feminist scholars, but also by many rational-action sociologists, although preferences and constraints are key concepts, and although the optimal gender division of labour within the couple is considered to reflect both biological and social barriers, the mainstream economic approach is silent both on the origins and development of preferences and on the concrete set of opportunities and constraints faced by actors. Preferences are often treated as being stable, and constraints as exogenously given. One may consequently say that, within mainstream economic theory, the prediction concerning the effect of education on women's labour supply is 'additive': this effect is context-less and class-less, so that no conceptualisation and measurement is made of interaction between the woman's own education (and partner's resources), on the one hand, and the institutional and cultural context and the individual and family position in the stratification system, on the other.

Moreover, many authors argue that investments in education may have an important non-monetary dimension. In economics, education is seen as yielding reconciliation returns in the theory of wage-compensating differentials (Rosen, 1986) or in the literature on the sectoral allocation of female employment and on the cost of career interruptions. However, both strands of literature can be easily combined with the human capital explanation, which emphasises monetary returns to education: on a lifetime basis, stability protects human capital against depreciation; hence, lower hourly returns may still be compatible with maximum lifetime earnings. However, numerous studies suggest that the lifetime maximisation of income is only part of the story. The adverse impact of unemployment or precarious labour market positions on fertility is now well recognised (Adsera, 2005; Blossfeld et al, 2005; Conti and Sette, 2007). This inhibiting effect derives not only from low income but also from the overall uncertainty that surrounds future work (location, duration, working schedule, as well as earnings). As some studies on the work–family conflict show (Nazio and MacInnes, 2007; Sherer and Steiber, 2007), family-friendly jobs contribute to reducing the organisational effort and the psychological stress required to reconcile domestic and care activities with paid work. As argued by Solera and Bettio (2007), this reduction in uncertainty and in psychological and organisational costs is an independent non-monetary reason for investing in education, and it is especially strong in contexts where work–family reconciliation provisions other than in-job provisions are scarce or more costly.

Investments in education imply a non-monetary dimension also in terms of identities, values and agency. As recently reiterated by the literature on women's empowerment in developing countries (Kabeer, 1999; Robinson-Pant, 2004), education can transmit selected norms and values such as gender equality, autonomy and emancipation, thereby increasing not only resources but also agency and achievements. As underlined by Solera and Negri (2008), investment in education can reflect, both instrumental and cognitive rationality: it may be a way to acquire income for 'consumption' or it may stem from (and reinforce) a cultural model where work is central to a woman's identity and conception of welfare. Thus, what economists call 'taste for work' and take to be a prior factor influencing labour market choices is likely to be produced or reinforced by the process itself of acquiring education, and it may favour labour market attachment beyond strictly monetary returns. To borrow an old expression from Robinson and Bell (1978), education exerts an 'enlightenment effect'.

The socialisation-identity effect at the micro level also depends on the macro level: on welfare regimes, on gender arrangements and on rates of value change over time and structure (Lück, 2006). In particular, the differentiating effect of education is stronger in contexts where a general cultural shift in favour of non-traditional gender roles has not (fully) come about. These are also contexts where family policies do not support a dual-earner family, making some options more or less costly but also defining them as more or less morally appropriate (Sjöberg, 2004). As argued by Solera and Bettio (2007), in these contexts education may increase the 'legitimacy to work' beyond the power of earnings. Education exerts its countervailing influence by increasing the perceived economic advantages of a higher commitment to paid work, by acting as a *passepartout* to external approval of 'modern roles', by reinforcing preferences or simply by affording greater bargaining power to a woman with a greater taste for work.

As many sociologists and heterodox economists have pointed out, by offering an excessively voluntarist and static account of women's employment patterns, and by only (or mainly) focusing on the monetary and instrumental dimension, standard economic analysis falls short of recognising and explaining differences across countries and across cohorts. Choice is always constrained, so that actors do not always have access to the same resources in order to follow their preferences. As the next section discusses in more detail, preferences are also socially structured: they change over the lifecourse and differ across countries but also across classes, sexes and generations.

As argued by many authors, one important constraint on choices by women and men is (still) class. According to individuation scholars (Giddens, 1991; Beck,

1992; Beck and Beck-Gernsheim, 2002), social class has become obsolete in social explanations because of the decline of a traditional working class based on manufacturing and on identifiable patterns of lifestyles, values and expectations. In reflexive modern societies, these authors argue, identities have become linked less to paid work and to the productive sphere and more to lifestyles and consumption. Moreover, a 'disembedding' from prescribed social forms and commitments has occurred, so that individuals now have more choices and are the authors of their own biographies. However, much research has shown that class, defined in terms of occupation, is still a crucial channel of differential access to material but also symbolic rewards (Goldthorpe, 1996; Scott, 2000; Breen, 2004), and that it still strongly affects biographies and life chances (in terms of income, health, lifestyle and so on). Echoing Bourdieu (1972, 1979), other studies have also shown that class is associated with specific cultural and normative practices that themselves reproduce inequalities. These class cultures are not the product of 'heroic collective agency' but of everyday practices within families and social networks that shape habitus, form identities and influence choices (Savage, 2000; Lareau, 2002). These choices and practices are intertwined with structural and institutional constraints, being also affected by own economic resources and by the opportunities made available by state policies (Ball, 2003).

A far as women's employment is concerned, many authors show that class is an important determinant of attitudes and behaviours. McRae (2003), for example, examined the career paths of a sample of first-time mothers in the UK. She emphasised that, in a 'liberal' context like Britain, it is class that largely explains women's ability to overcome constraints (above all, a lack of childcare support) and to act on preferences. In line with Bourdieu's (1972, 1979) cultural theory of reproduction, and with the 'doing gender' perspective (West and Zimmerman, 1987), other scholars show that there are differences between middle-class and working-class women in mothering: how they combine employment and family responsibilities, how they divide labour with their partners and how they understand their children's needs. These differences are not necessarily responses to instrumental rationalities, that is, to individual self-maximisation and to different sets of opportunities and constraints affecting both actors' goals and their capacity to achieve them. They respond more to moral rationalities created at a micro-relational level through the development of careers as identities, and of moral and social views on what is proper behaviour negotiated with partners and within social networks (Irwin, 2003; Duncan, 2005).

Also, Crompton (2006) shows that the effect of motherhood on women's labour market attachment is shaped by class. Indeed, lower-educated, lower-class women tend everywhere to reduce working hours or to withdraw from the labour market when they have young children, compared with women with high educations and belonging to advantaged occupational groups. Moreover, individuals of lower occupational status are everywhere more traditional in their gender attitudes. This feature reflects material, institutional and cultural dimensions. People in different occupational classes have access to different economic resources, which affect their opportunity cost (current and lifelong) of leaving the labour market. High-class jobs are also more rewarding in terms of social recognition and self-esteem, so that women are more attached to them not only 'instrumentally' but also, *à la* Boudon (2003), 'cognitively'. As studies of class culture demonstrate, classes are also associated with specific habituses and identities created within the family and social networks and which contribute to building 'preferences' and to perpetuating material class inequalities. These class inequalities are also institutionally shaped, being stronger where policies in support of dual-earner families are weaker. This suggests that social structure still matters and that 'theories of individuation and "choice" in respect of women's employment have the effect of systematically removing from critical examination the embedded practices and institutions that reproduce inequalities' (Crompton, 2006, p 185).

The institutional and cultural embeddedness of the effects of education and class

In accord with Crompton, many authors have argued and demonstrated that the effect of education and class on women's employment patterns, as well as on many other behaviours and outcomes, is institutionally embedded. As will be shown in more detail later in this chapter, women's continuous attachment to paid work depends closely on welfare regimes, on their degree and type of decommodification and defamilialisation, or, less generally, on policy arrangements such as maternity and parental leaves, childcare provisions, tax systems and working-time arrangements. As many feminist economists stress, these policies change the relative advantage of paid work versus unpaid work. Welfare state scholars show that social policies not only affect time availability and economic resources but also class and gender stratification. Indeed, institutions mediate the effect of individual-level characteristics (such as education and class) and of the costs of employment interruptions, also producing less or more heterogeneity in the female population (Stier and Lewin-Epstein, 2001; Del Boca and Pasqua, 2005; Geist, 2005). For example, Stier and Lewin-Epstein (2001) find that countries furnishing high support for maternal employment minimise the monetary cost of taking breaks out of the labour force and of moving into part-time jobs. Similarly, Del Boca et al (2007) find that human capital (education, tenure, actual labour market experience) is far less important in determining mothers' wages in Denmark than in other countries. Denmark is a country with a generous and universalistic package of social policies and with a narrow wage distribution. Part-time work is viewed as temporary, and its divide with full-time work is small.

Institutions also define 'normality models' for the entire population, or for specific subgroups within it, making some choices more or less possible but also more or less desirable and socially legitimated.[2] In general, the effect of education and class is not only institutionally but also culturally embedded. As already noted, education exerts an 'enlightenment' or 'socialisation-identity' effect that produces or reinforces a woman's taste for work. This effect is context dependent, being stronger where gender-role norms have remained rather traditional. Class is also culturally constructed. In Bourdieu's (1972, 1979) terms, class conveys cultural capital; in the case of 'doing gender' theory, class shapes identities, moral careers, moral rationalities but also expectations and dispositions. That is to say, in rational choice terms, class shapes both positive and normative beliefs. As has been argued, these cultural and normative practices are strongly intertwined with structural and institutional constraints.

I shall now go more deeply into this debate on the effect of 'culture' on women's employment. I shall start from theories focusing on the micro level of preferences, in particular Hakim's (2000) preference theory, and then move on to those that emphasise social norms or moral rationalities. The topic of the effect of institutions will be resumed later in this chapter.

The effects of preferences, social norms and moral rationalities

The debate on Hakim's preference theory

The debate on the significance of structural constraints versus individual intentions has a long tradition in the social sciences. It has recently taken a further turn within sociology in response to Hakim's (2000) controversial 'preference theory'. Hakim challenges what she considers to be the dominant feminist view on women's employment patterns. Career breaks or part-time work, she argues, are not choices forced on women against their will because of their domestic responsibilities and the insufficient provision of childcare services. Rather, women's disadvantaged position in the labour market reflects the outcome of their varying work orientations. Hakim argues, in line with modernisation and individuation accounts, that women, as well as men, are agents in their own lives, so that 'self-classification as a primary earner or secondary earner is determined by chosen identities, rather than imposed by external circumstance or particular jobs' (Hakim, 2000, p 275).

More precisely, Hakim argues that part-time work is chosen voluntarily by women – called 'grateful slaves' – primarily devoted to the marriage career. These women have more traditional attitudes, which give priority to non-market activities; as a consequence, they prefer less demanding jobs. By contrast, 'self-made women', who are primarily oriented to market careers, choose highly demanding jobs and pursue a full-time, continuous lifecourse employment pattern similar to that of men (Hakim, 1991). In her latest work, Hakim presents a threefold typology of women's work preferences. In addition to the relabelled 'home-centred' and 'work-centred' women, she introduces the 'adaptive women'. This third group is the largest in each country and also the most diverse: it comprises women who want to combine work and family, as well as 'drifters' and 'unplanned careers'. Unlike 'home-centred' women, 'adaptive' ones prefer to work; but unlike 'work-centred' women, they do not totally commit to their careers. They are consequently the most responsive to employment and family policies, whose impact indeed differs among preference groups (Hakim, 2000).

With respect to the vast feminist literature on institutional constraints, Hakim's theory certainly has the merit of citing – as rational choice theorists and human capital theorists do – the role of sex-role preferences and work orientations. It also has the merit of stressing that women should not be treated as a homogenous group in regard to these preferences and choices. However, as many authors have pointed out, Hakim's preference theory has several faults. First, what she calls a 'theory' seems to be more a classification of female types based on observed participation patterns. Indeed, Hakim gives no explanation as to why women fall into a particular category, on where their preferences come from or if and why they differ across countries. Rather, she tends to use information on labour market behaviour as a proxy for inferences about preferences (Fagan and O'Reilly, 1998a; Crompton and Harris, 1998). But choices are constrained, so that attitudes and behaviour may not correspond. For example, a study by McRae (1993) on returning to work after childbirth in Britain, and based on a survey of women who had their first child in 1988, shows a non-negligible discrepancy between women's intentions during pregnancy and their labour market outcomes. Whereas for the 'reluctant returners' the main reason for resuming work was financial need, the motivations for the 'disappointed returners' were the inability to find a job, or a proper job in terms of hours and location, and the lack of (affordable) childcare. In a later study, which used the same sample of women who became mothers in 1988 and who were interviewed again in 1993 and in 1999 (that is, when their child was five years old and then 11 years old), McRae (2003) found that 90% of mothers had worked discontinuously, combining spells of full-time work, part-time work and housework in various ways. Yet women with different employment patterns had quite similar attitudes towards work and family. Hakim – McRae argued – had confused voluntary action with genuine or unconstrained choice.

Other studies have demonstrated not only that preferences do not determine outcomes completely but also that preferences are not stable over the lifecourse. For example, on the basis of qualitative interviews with female part-time workers in low-level jobs in Britain, Walters (2005) concludes that women's orientations respond much more to their age, their stage in the family lifecourse and to the availability of jobs where they live than to their employment status (part time or full time). Drawing on the BHPS, Kan (2007) tests some major contentions of Hakim's preference theory. He finds, in corroboration of Hakim's arguments, that women who have followed different employment trajectories differ in their gender-role attitudes, and that the effect of childcare responsibilities on these trajectories depends on their work/home-centred attitudes. However, by using recursive structural equation models with the graphical chain method, Kan also shows that preferences are endogenous: that is, the relationship between gender-role attitudes and women's labour market participation is reciprocal.

However, the main criticism brought against Hakim's preference theory concerns the role of constraints. One crucial structural constraint on women's choices about their career, family and working hours is the need to care for dependent children. Hence, policies supporting mothers' employment (and, as we shall see, family care by fathers) affect the extent to which women (and men) can combine paid work with family responsibilities. Family policy institutions also affect gender-role attitudes and preferences. As well explained by Sjöberg (2004), this may come about in two ways: institutions affect the options and alternatives available, and the perceptions of the rewards and the costs associated with them; at the same time, institutions define and assume the 'proper' roles of women, and they institutionalise family and gender models, thereby affecting orientations and attitudes directly. As noted earlier, institutions and culture also mediate the effect of another crucial constraint, namely class. Women in high-skilled occupations have more resources with which to indulge their preferences. They earn higher wages, and they are often married to higher-income men, so that they can afford private childcare and domestic help, if necessary or desired. When they work part time, they have better jobs; moreover, they typically have less traditional attitudes towards work and family responsibilities. However, class differences, in both attitudes and behaviours, are more marked where (as specified in later in this chapter) defamilialisation and decommodification are less advanced.

As several authors have pointed out (Crompton and Harris, 1998; Fagan and O'Reilly, 1998a), because Hakim's analysis offers an overly voluntarist and static account of women's employment patterns, it falls short of recognising and explaining differences across countries. Hakim suggests that agency is everywhere becoming more important than the social structure, and that similarities across Europe are far greater than the differences. However, as will be specified in more detail later in this chapter, comparative research shows that there are important cross-country differences among the supply characteristics of part-timers, especially in the link between motherhood and part-time work. There are also differences among the characteristics of part-time jobs in terms of employment conditions, contractual length and the predictability and regularity of working time and scheduling arrangements (Fagan and Rubery 1996; Fagan and O'Reilly 1998b). Part-time and full-time workers, moreover, are not homogeneous groups within the same country, nor even in the same occupational sector, in terms of work commitments and job aspirations (Walters, 2005; McDonald et al, 2006).

Hakim's difficulty in accounting for changes over time and for cross-country differences derives largely from her endorsement of the conventional human capital, rational choice theory, and of the main ideas put forward by individuation theory. Indeed, many of the criticisms made of Hakim's findings resemble those that sociologists and heterodox economists level against those two theories. Explaining changes and differences in women's employment patterns requires consideration to be made of other theoretical and empirical literatures. How do other sociologists and economists conceptualise the impact of norms? And, more specifically, what does research on gender-role attitudes say about their correlates and their role in explaining women's changed family and employment behaviours?

The influence of norms on behaviour: intrinsic or extrinsic motivation?

In the line of the sociology forged by classics, which has always been more institutional than voluntaristic, sociologists endorsing a rational choice perspective have moved away from overly unrealistic conventional economic models to theories that envisage different forms of rationality and the heterogeneity of preferences. They consider the effects of uncertainty, the impact of structural constraints, and the link between norms and intentional action. They have also discarded the extreme normative sociological conceptions typical of the functionalist and structural-functionalist tradition.

In the functionalist approach, social norms play a crucial role in the creation of social order and integration. Through socialisation and the internalisation of norms, people learn their 'proper' roles and behaviours so that a social system can control its members and reproduce itself. However, how this process works, why people believe what they believe and why such values and beliefs differ over time and across countries is unclear. In contrast with this functionalist conception, other authors propose an instrumental view of adherence to norms. Social norms affect behaviours through external motivation and a cost/benefit evaluation. The power of a social norm depends on its level of acceptance in the population, and on the formal or informal sanctions associated with its breach (Blossfeld and Prein, 1998a).

Many sociologists have contested this conception of norms as well, calling for a more extensive definition of rationality and, in turn, for integration between the internal and external views of norms. As Boudon (1998, 2001, 2003) argues, while some actions are goal directed, others derive non-instrumentally from values and beliefs. Contrary to what classical rational choice theorists tend to argue, values and beliefs are not necessarily self-interested. And contrary to functionalist contentions, as people follow their beliefs, they are not simply passive executors of internalised social norms. They actively interpret norms, and they perceive their action as meaningfully based on their beliefs. Following Boudon, Blossfeld and Prein (1998b) suggest that norm-guided behaviour and instrumental behaviour often coexist in real-life choice processes. Similarly, Marini (1992) and Kreps (1997) speak of intrinsic and extrinsic motivation. In some cases, an actor adheres to a norm because they believe it to be right, and thus acts according to intrinsic motivation. In other cases, an actor adheres to a norm because other people (family, friends, the community) believe in it, and because its breach might lead to a formal sanction or to disapproval and social ostracism. Here the motivation is extrinsic. In rational choice terms, this means that social norms may affect both preferences and constraints.

According to symbolic interactionists, and in particular to the 'doing gender' perspective, norms concerning proper behaviour are the result of neither intrinsic stable motivations nor extrinsic changing pressures. Rather, they reflect micro-relational processes, which generate, not simply preferences, but indeed identities and moral careers. For example, as seen earlier, Duncan (2005) argues that individuals act within the family or social networks, and a web of negotiated moral and relational commitments, which give rise to individual and social moralities. Moreover, she demonstrates that these moralities are neither classless nor contextless, but are instead socially, geographically and historically articulated. In the same vein, Finch and Mason (1993) argue that family responsibilities are not fixed. They do not simple follow from an abstract normative principle but are created through interactions over time, which develop commitments and build moral identities and careers as mothers, sisters, fathers and so on.

Regardless of the theoretical perspective considered, it is generally agreed that values, social norms and moral rationalities influence actors. This concerns nearly all types of actors' choices, including family and work choices by women. Nevertheless, the relationship between gender-role attitudes and women's behaviour has yet to be defined. The next subsection will address this issue.

Gender-role attitudes: do they lag or lead changes in women's behaviour?

Multivariate micro-level analyses of gender-role attitudes find consistency between current attitudes and current employment behaviour. Women who work are more in favour of new roles for women than are those who do not work. Also, men whose wives have paid jobs are more supportive of women working. Compared to those with part-time jobs, women who work full time are more likely to believe that a woman should work full time even when children are young (Alwin et al, 1992; Scott, 1999a, 1999b). Moreover, women with a preschool child are generally more favourable to maternal employment, not only compared to childless women but also to parents with older children.

However, the reason for this consistency between current attitudes and current behaviour is not at all clear: is it attitudes that determine behaviour or the other way round? Alwin et al (1992) suggest that the consistency is likely to result from a process of both selection and socialisation. That is to say, particular attitudes induce people to choose certain behaviours; but, at the same time, by experiencing certain behaviours, people develop attitudes in support of such behaviours. Yet, because these studies are based on cross-sectional data, they cannot empirically test the direction of the causality. It seems from the few studies that have used longitudinal attitudinal data that the reverse causation is at work. For example, Thornton (1985) uses data from 'The Study of American Families Panel' to show that a woman's attitude towards divorce in 1962 did not have a significant effect on her probability of divorcing between 1962 and 1977, but if she experienced a marriage dissolution during this period, her approval of divorce markedly increased. In his already-mentioned work based on the BHPS and on a series of recursive regression models, Kan (2007) shows that the relationship between gender-role attitudes and women's participation in the labour market is reciprocal.

Using rational choice-type arguments, Kan suggests that, by increasingly acquiring skills and resources from employment, women reinforce their work career orientations; while, at the same time, constraints on employment may discourage them from investing further in their labour market role and identity. The results of qualitative interviews conducted from different theoretical perspectives, but focused on negotiations with partners and with social networks, also suggest that 'preferences' and 'choices' change over the lifecourse in response to new experiences, new opportunities and constraints, and new perceptions of the costs and rewards associated with different outcomes. (Crompton and Harris, 1998; McRae, 2003; Duncan, 2005; McDonald et al, 2006).

Also at the macro level the evidence often does not support the idea that attitudinal changes come first and are the driving forces of demographic and employment changes. In Britain, whereas already in 1951 some 30% of women aged 20-64 were employed full time, in 1989 still 42% of women and 53% of men agreed that 'a husband's job is to earn the money, a wife's job is to look after the home and family' (Scott et al, 1996). In the US, public attitudes towards women's labour force participation remained negative for 20 to 30 years after such participation started to increase. As Oppenheimer (1994, p 311) writes, this suggests that 'attitudes were adjusting themselves (albeit slowly) to changing work behaviour rather than representing a major force in producing these changes'. This also suggests that there has long been a gap between the 'new' attitudes of some and those of the majority of the population. Indeed, many cross-sectional analyses reveal that gender-role attitudes differ importantly across cohorts and gender: all else equal, in most countries women are more supportive of female paid work than men, and younger generations more than older ones. Young women's preferences have evidently started to change despite a generally negative normative climate.

This evidence of a 'normative lag' contrasts with a large body of demographic literature that instead regards norms as having been the main force in producing post-war changes in marriage, fertility and divorce patterns. This cultural change is what Inglehart (1977) has called a 'silent revolution', and it stems from multiple sources: increased demand for quality and symmetrical gender roles in interpersonal relationships and in the public sphere; a liberalisation of sexuality and family forms; an emphasis on individual autonomy; anti-authoritarian and anti-conformist ideology; and advanced consumerism together with increased market orientations (Inglehart, 1977, 1990; Lesthaeghe, 1995; Moors, 2001).

However, whether the well-documented family and employment changes are mainly the outcomes of a cultural shift is controversial. Many authors propose alternative explanations. As we shall see, Becker (1981) views these changes as a female economic independence effect: the increases in women's labour market participation and in women's wages have led to reductions in gains to marriage (associated with specialisation), and to rising opportunity costs for women. In polemic with Becker, whose focus has been only on women, Oppenheimer (1988, 1994) argues that marriage formation is linked to the transition to adult economic roles and that recent delays have importantly to do with a deterioration in the labour market position of young men. Also, Easterlin maintains that marriage and fertility postponement results from more difficult labour market conditions, which thwart increasing consumption aspirations (Easterlin 1976; Easterlin et al, 1990).

Also, the empirical support for the modernisation theory on 'processes of individuation' seems weak. First, historians document that in the past, family behaviour was much more differentiated than assumed by modernisation theory. This heterogeneity seems to suggest that family behaviour was already responding not only to normative imperatives, but also to changing social and economic conditions (Laslett and Wall, 1972; Barbagli, 1988). Second, as noted earlier in this chapter, much comparative empirical research shows that individual lifecourses are still structurally and normative shaped, and that differences across countries are still substantial. Differences across countries are also apparent in gender-role norms, and they remain after controlling for such strong individual predictors as gender, cohort, education and labour force involvement. Plausibly, the unexplained has to do with the macro level, and therefore with variations in institutional, political and/or cultural contexts (Alwin et al, 1992; Scott, 1999a; Treas and Widmer, 2000; Knudsen and Waerness, 2001; Lück, 2006).

Hence, in contrast to modernisation theory, social structure still seems to be important. However, its link with norms and preferences is complex. As the previously described study by McRae (1993) reveals, the social structure may hinder the realisation of women's intentions: a need for money, a lack of childcare support and adequate labour market opportunities, or difficult bargaining within the family may induce a woman to work or to stay at home against her initial preferences. Moreover, as discussed earlier in this chapter, the social structure not only constrains preferences, it also shapes them. It also affects positive beliefs concerning the number and quality of choices available: that is to say, in this case, cognitive assessments of the circumstances that make women's employment more or less difficult or desirable. For example, childcare provisions and parental leaves may mitigate the conflict between work and family and thereby increase support for maternal employment. Or, conversely, the scarcity of part-time opportunities may induce people not to regard part-time employment as a viable option. In fact, in those countries where there is little part-time work available, relatively few people believe that mothers should work part time (Treas and Widmer, 2000). Gender-role attitudes also influence positive beliefs on own ability and chances of success. Breen and Garcia-Penalosa (2002), for example, put forward an explanation of the persistence of gender segregation in occupations based on prior beliefs about the probability of success in different occupations. To the extent that such prior beliefs differ between men and women, and are updated and transmitted to subsequent generations as posterior beliefs, men and women will continue to self-select in different occupations even when they have identical preferences.

The effects of the family

Unlike that of men, the labour market participation of women is strongly dependent on family circumstances and events. As widely documented, it is women, not men, who tend to adjust their supply when they get married or have children and/or when the partner's income is insufficient. Why this happens is controversial. Neoclassical economists explain it in terms of human capital differences and of a beneficial specialisation within the couple between household and market work. Resource bargaining models see the family as a negotiation set where each marital partner is self-interested and prefers to do less housework so as to have more leisure, and where relative wages affect whose interests prevail. However, several sociologists criticise explanations based on economic resources alone. Some emphasise that the partner's education and occupation produces not only income but also social capital, which may favour women's participation in the labour market. Others direct attention to the role of gender norms. In this section, I shall first illustrate Becker's economic theory of the family and then move on to the various criticisms made of it, and the alternative or complementary explanations put forward.

'New home economics'

'New home economics' is the most popular economic theory of the family. It has been extensively used in socioeconomic studies to explain the gender division of labour within the family and current demographic trends such as declining marriages and fertility. This theory shares with the neoclassical approach the basic assumptions of full information, rational maximisation of utility, and equilibrium. But it introduces an important novelty into economic studies: namely the idea that an individual's allocation of paid work in the market and unpaid work in the home is best understood within the context of the family. The unit of analysis becomes the family, in which the partners' utilities depend on each other and form a joint utility function. In this Beckerian family, resources are pooled and decisions are taken 'rationally' and 'efficiently' through maximisation of the joint utility function.

The most important decision to be taken within the couple concerns the distribution of time between paid market work and unpaid domestic work. As 'rational' actors, this decision is taken by weighing the advantages and disadvantages of each possible choice. In technical terms, the amount of time that husbands and wives will spend on market and domestic work is decided by comparing the husband's marginal productivity in market work and domestic work with the wife's marginal productivity in market work and domestic work. If the spouses' productivities differ either at home or in the market, both partners will be made better off by a division of labour. This efficient specialisation does not necessarily mean a complete division of labour, neither does it automatically apply to all couples. Women with high earning potential may choose a full-time continuous type of career. A woman whose husband's market productivity is equal or higher will instead tend to specialise in household work. Specialisation may be complete, consisting in withdrawal from the labour market after marriage or the birth of a child; or it may be partial, in terms of time because part-time jobs are chosen, or in terms of effort because jobs below the woman's skills level are accepted. In all cases, women suffer from an underutilisation and depreciation of their human capital which, in turn, increases the comparative advantage, while also making it difficult for them to re-enter the labour market in the future, or to improve their occupational positions.

But why is it typically the woman who specialises in domestic work? Becker (1975) answers this question in terms of human capital investment decisions. Yet the evidence shows the opposite. Since the 1960s, in nearly all advanced societies, gender differentials in levels of educational attainment have declined; and in some cases, they have been almost eliminated or even reversed (Blossfeld and Shavit, 1993). Human capital theorists have consequently shifted their attention from education to family formation and occupational decisions. The increase in levels of education raises women's earnings capacity and their labour market attachment, thereby reducing gains to marriage (gains conceptualised in terms of specialisation) and increasing the opportunity cost of motherhood. However, since almost everywhere the structure of the sex-specific division of labour still imposes domestic and childcare work on wives, women who intend to form a family expect to have discontinuous work histories. This expectation induces many women to rationally choose occupations less demanding in terms of time or effort, and in which pay levels, chances of career advancement, and opportunities to acquire labour force experience and additional educational resources are lower, but also in which, exactly because of these characteristics, the cost of leaving and returning is lower (Mincer and Polachek, 1974; Polachek, 1981).

Bargaining within the couple

Becker's theory of the family has been widely disputed, and on several fronts. A first set of criticisms has been directed against his assumptions concerning how the family functions. Many authors underline that spouses may have conflicting motivations and aspirations, different powers, and different levels of satisfaction and stress attached to the established division of labour. Moreover, in both the short and the long run, the contention that men and women gain equally from a gendered division of labour is questionable. The main outcome for the integrative mechanism of gender specialisation within the family has in fact been the economic dependence of wives on husbands. Even assuming that both spouses agree with the male breadwinner family model, in a post-Fordist world where labour market security and family stability have diminished, specialisation is no longer the more efficient strategy. Indeed, specialisation is risky for the nuclear family, which has been increasingly hit by unemployment and low wages, and for which a good second earner can act as insurance against poverty (Münch 1992;

England, 1993; Oppenheimer 1994). Specialisation is also very risky for women in the event of divorce (Sørensen, 1994).

Becker's assumption of a harmonious family has also been criticised by economists and sociologists, who adopt a game theory or exchange theory perspective to argue that partners have distinct and often conflicting utility functions, and that they bargain in order to get the most preferred allocation of time. Since it is assumed that both spouses prefer leisure and market work to household work, the outcome of the negotiation will depend on power differences. This power is based on the resources that each spouse can exchange and on the credible alternatives outside or inside the current relationship. Human capital and income – these authors argue – are the main sources of power because, in contrast to relation-specific investments such as children and marriage, they are easily transferable to other relationships or retainable for oneself. This makes the spouse with lower earnings less powerful and readier to grant concessions to the partner (Brines, 1993; Coltrane, 2000). In similar vein, other sociologists argue that what is exchanged within the couple is money and housework: the partner who earns more is assumed to transfer a part of their money, while the other is expected to respond with a higher share of housework. Hence, it is the degree of economic dependency that affects the gendered division of domestic and care labour (Sørensen and McLanahan, 1987).

Consequently, although bargaining models use a completely different logic, they reach the same conclusion as Becker's efficiency perspective: relative wages (or generally human capital resources and time availability) affect relative contributions to unpaid work. In turn, they predict the same effect of the husband's characteristics on the wife's labour supply: if the man has higher earnings (or earning potential), it is the woman who leaves the labour market or switches to a part-time job in order to allocate time to domestic and childcare work.

The role of gender norms and institutions

Contrary to what both the efficiency and bargaining models would predict, many studies show that gender-role attitudes seem to matter more, and that they induce individuals to take 'irrational' decisions with suboptimal results (Ferber and Nelson, 1993). Indeed, even women with earnings equal to or higher than those of their husbands appear to do the bulk of domestic and childcare work (Bittman et al, 2001; Halleröd, 2005). According to the 'doing gender' perspective, this is the outcome of attitudes and identities expressed and created in everyday practices and which concern both men and women. Both men and women are 'doing gender' when they allocate time. Husbands who are not the main breadwinners tend to conform with the norm of masculinity by not doing 'feminine' housework. For their part, higher-income wives tend to comply with 'good' gender roles by taking on most, if not all, domestic and childcare work.

Moreover, many studies maintain that actors' decisions are not affected solely by their own or their partner's earning power. The welfare state, kinship solidarity models and the regulation and functioning of the labour market are also important. For example, in a comparative study on welfare regime differences in the domestic division of labour, Geist (2005) demonstrates that the equal sharing of housework is rare in conservative countries, while it is more widespread in Scandinavian and liberal countries, regardless of individual relative resources, time availability and gender ideology. As Geist suggests in her conclusions, this may mirror both cultural and institutional dimensions. In societies where traditional gender roles are institutionalised, being promoted and legitimated in social policies, and where, in turn, attitudes are less equalitarian, it is more difficult to find not only women but above all men supportive of women's employment and of a more balanced share of housework.

However, Crompton (2006), in chapter six of her book, concludes that culture seems to outweigh institutions. Indeed, there is evidence that the relative contribution of fathers to childcare increases with the strength of provisions on leave, childcare and working time; but these policies have not been as successful as hoped. France, for example, has relatively short working hours, generous support for working mothers, but a gendered division of domestic work more traditional than in liberal or Scandinavian countries. France also exhibits a higher level of reported work/life conflict. Evidently, similar outcomes can spring from very different origins. In liberal regimes, the lack of external support may have compelled men to help their employed wives. In Nordic countries, men are institutionally encouraged to share housework, and they do more housework than men in Southern or Continental Europe, but not much more than those in liberal countries. In France, parenting policies are generous but, as argued also by Gregory and Windebank (2000), they have been designed and promoted to support employment and fertility more than gender equality, with the (unintended) effect of reinforcing norms on the care and domestic work obligations of mothers.

Partner's education and occupation as a social capital

A further criticism of the new home economics theory derives from social capital theory. As argued by Coleman (1990), actors' choices are not affected by financial resources alone; social relations are also important and may operate as a social capital. When the effect of the husband's and wife's resources on the allocation of paid and unpaid work is studied, conceiving relationships as social capital leads to interestingly different predictions. Whereas economists predict that a wife's employment and occupational status is negatively related to the employment and occupational status of the husband, social capital sociologists suggest that a husband's resources can enhance his wife's chances in the labour market. Indeed, the husband may transmit his occupational skills, competence and experience to his wife. He may also transmit his cultural capital, that is, how to behave in different situations. Moreover, he can provide information on job vacancies and form a bridge to remote social networks. The transmission of all these resources between spouses is very likely to happen, first because the spouses trust each other and are therefore willing to share, and second because each can probably benefit from the partner's increased occupational attainment (Bernasco et al, 1998; Bernardi et al, 2000).

As suggested by Bernasco et al (1998), instead of these two theoretical arguments being seen as producing contrasting hypotheses, they can be viewed as predicting different and simultaneous processes. Indeed, the economic and sociological theories focus on different kinds of resources. Economists consider financial resources obtained through participation in paid work, whereas sociologists focus on non-financial labour market resources, namely skills, knowledge, access to information, and attitudes in general. The two theories can thus be reformulated in terms of the different effects of different types of resources: a husband's financial resources negatively affect his wife's participation and outcomes in the labour market, whereas his labour market resources have a positive effect.

Indeed, many studies demonstrate that the resources of husbands may also encourage their wives' labour market attachment and career (Bernardi, 1999; Blossfeld and Drobnic, 2001). Transfers of the benefits of human and social capital within the home occur also from women to men. A husband can benefit from a well-educated wife, regardless of how she uses her human capital outside the home, because her high education may bolster his ambition and stimulation and enable her to provide effective information and advice on his career and useful social networks, although the latter may remain underdeveloped if the wife does not work. Moreover, a husband may be induced to invest more in a labour market career in order to off set his wife's loss of earnings potential, which is greater, the higher her education (Brynin and Schupp, 2000).

The effect of income and economic necessity

That family resources are also a crucial determinant of women's labour supply is well established. This determinant operates via the neoclassical income effect, although, as already mentioned, its effect has generally weakened over time in favour of the woman's wage effect. It also occurs in the reverse direction: women may be induced to work by the paucity of their husbands' incomes. Many studies show that unemployment of the husband increases the wife's labour supply. However, this also depends on the system of unemployment benefits: where these are means tested on the basis of family income, women may be discouraged from working (Cooke, 1987; Dex et al, 1995; Joshi et al, 1996; McGinnity, 2002). As stressed by Del Boca et al (2000), the predominance of an 'added worker effect' over a 'discouraged worker effect' also depends on the individual characteristics of husbands and wives, on labour market opportunities and on the associated positive beliefs about employability.

Economic necessity may arise not only from unemployment but also from low wages, especially when the couple has children. Indeed, since children 'consume' both income and time, the couple must find new strategies between paid and unpaid work. As argued by Solera and Negri (2008), such strategies depend closely on education level and on previous investment by women in the labour market, and they have important implications in terms of poverty. Where women's paid work is seen as a second-best solution within a preferred or practised male-breadwinner model and, where, in turn, family/work reconciliation is constructed as an ex-post strategy, women are more likely to move in and out of paid work and to have weak job positions. By contrast, where couples are dual earner from the outset, and not because of an ex-post adjustment to income needs, and thus where women become mothers already with an attachment to paid work, the family is much less vulnerable to poverty.

As shown by Uunk et al (2005) and Haas et al (2006), the incidence of male-breadwinner households is not solely a child support effect. Employment opportunities and general levels of economic affluence also play a role. Indeed, to use McRae's (1993) terminology, women may be 'reluctant returners' when they start working out of necessity or 'disappointed returners' when they do not restart working because of the lack of job opportunities. As demonstrated by Lück (2006), the economic pressure for women to furnish an additional household income also shapes gender attitudes. This economic necessity effect is particularly evident in economically weak countries, such as those of Southern and Eastern Europe. In these countries, actual household employment patterns and women's labour supply may not reflect preferences simply because the economies suffer from high unemployment. In these poorer contexts, the assumption that parents not in employment act as full-time carers is questionable, because women (and men) may be engaged in a mix of informal employment and subsistence production that are difficult to capture with survey data.

The effects of the welfare state

The welfare state, with its threefold function as the main employer of women, supporter of work–family reconciliation and regulator of employment conditions, performs a crucial role in facilitating and shaping women's integration into the labour force. This section looks at the debate on the nexus between the welfare state, gender relations and women's employment. More precisely, it starts with an illustration of Esping-Andersen's (1990) influential typology of welfare states and its implication for women's labour market participation. It then discusses the feminist accounts that have developed alternative or complementary gendered frameworks for the analysis of the welfare state. Finally, by drawing on both mainstream and feminist analyses, the section specifies what dimensions of welfare state policies are important in the study of women's labour market transitions.

Esping-Andersen's welfare regimes

Welfare state analyses have been considerably influenced by Esping-Andersen's (1990) work *The Three Worlds of Welfare Capitalism*. As the title suggests, Esping-Andersen distinguishes three regime types according to how countries cluster along three dimensions: state/market relations, patterns of class stratification and quality of social rights.

The *social democratic regime* is characterised by a universalism of social rights, a strong role for the state and a commitment to full employment and to equality through a virtuous integration of social and economic policy. Universal state provision creates cross-class solidarity and implies modest stratification and a high degree of decommodification.

The *liberal regime* is almost the reverse. In accordance with the liberal ideology that the state should intervene only in the event of market and family failure, the liberal regime relies relatively heavily on the market and typically upholds the commodity character of labour power and limits the scope of social rights to the working class and the poor. By mainly relying on means-tested assistance, the liberal regime does not pursue a high level of decommodification. Moreover, as long as social insurance mirrors employment histories and does not reduce work incentives, the commodity status of wage labour and, thus, a high degree of stratification, are maintained.

In the *conservative-corporativist welfare regime*, rights are linked to class and status, and the capacity to reduce income inequality is small. Moreover, with its commitment to the principle of subsidiarity, this regime relies heavily on the family and defends and maintains its traditional functions. This is reflected in the provision of social services only when the family is no longer able to cope. Here, conservatism has historically rejected commodification on moral grounds and has sought to combat it through corporatism and statism, and by protecting the family against the disruptive impact of the market. These two factors have given rise to moderate levels of decommodification.

On the basis of these different, historically developed institutional characteristics, Esping-Andersen distinguishes three 'path-dependent', post-industrial trajectories. As he has argued in subsequent works – where in response to feminist criticisms he expands his focus on male workers' decommodification to encompass concerns about women's employment and fertility (Esping-Andersen, 1999, 1996a) – the ability of women to combine childrearing responsibilities with paid employment is at the centre of post-industrial challenges.

The Scandinavian welfare states have strongly supported women's employment with generous parenting policies allowing for paid work to be combined with children, and they have also done so by employing large numbers of women in the state service sector. However, this has given rise to a highly segregated labour market and an extremely costly welfare state that is difficult to sustain in the face of globalisation and fiscal pressures. In the English-speaking countries, the strong emphasis on the private sector is also reflected in family policies. Parenthood and childhood are seen as 'individual private choices', so that it is not the state's responsibility to provide facilities and policies enabling women to combine family and paid work. Women enter paid employment, but they are not always able to purchase care services in the market or to rely on family help. Consequently, unlike in Scandinavian countries, women mostly interrupt work when children are young. Moreover, the workfare ideology, by pushing for commodification rather than education and training, may undercut investments in human capital and may consequently reduce the chances of good re-entry into the labour market. This goes hand in hand with strong deregulation, which has led, at least in the US and Britain, to a persistent downward pressure on low-skill wage levels likely to create poverty traps. Social exclusion and poverty are therefore the price paid for liberal policies. According to Esping-Andersen, the Continental regime is the one worst equipped to meet post-industrial challenges. Here, large-scale labour shedding instead of structural reforms in response to industrial crises in the 1980s – that is, high labour costs and high expenditure on passive income support instead of active labour market policies and social services – all contributed to maintaining a 'Fordist' employment regime and a male-breadwinner type of family. Strict regulation of employment relationships was undertaken to protect core dependent workers and family heads at a time when one-earner families and a manufacturing economy were prevalent. However, in the absence of adjustment to the new employment scenario where female labour supply and service jobs are crucial, such strict regulation has produced an insider/outsider structure that has particularly penalised young people and women. Moreover, in the absence of a policy supporting the new two-earner families, the combination of paid work with motherhood becomes problematic.

The paradigm of gendered welfare states

Esping-Andersen's typology has been much criticised by feminist scholars. His conception of citizenship, his focus on state/market relations and on only class stratification are based – they argue – on the typical male experience. In particular, the concept of decommodification does not accurately describe women's relationship with the welfare state since women's work is often non-commodified. Esping-Andersen ignores many earlier feminist studies that have addressed the issue of the gendered division of labour within the family, and between the state, the family and the market, and its link with women's oppression, emancipation and full participation as citizens in the public sphere (Balbo, 1978; McIntosh, 1978; Molyneux, 1979; Saraceno, 1984; Hernes, 1987; Pateman, 1988). Feminist scholars have consequently called for welfare state analyses to be gendered through the introduction of concepts and dimensions that are women sensitive (Lewis, 1992; Orloff, 1993; Sainsbury, 1994a; O'Connor, 1996). Some propose a critical review of mainstream concepts and dimensions, while others entirely reject mainstream analytical schemas.

Orloff and O'Connor are the main representatives of the former approach. Orloff (1993) directs attention to the consequences of women's historical exclusion from employment, and to their right to be commodified. She thus proposes that Esping-Andersen's framework should be augmented by consideration of the extent to which states promote or discourage women's employment. Yet the state should also guarantee a certain degree of individual decommodification, thereby enabling women to survive and support their children without being forced either to work or to marry, or to enter other potentially oppressive relationships. Orloff calls this second dimension the 'capacity to form and maintain an autonomous household' (Orloff, 1993, p 321). Similarly, O'Connor (1993) suggests the concept of personal autonomy. On the same lines, but on more empirical grounds, Gornick et al (1997) propose that mainstream welfare state research should be integrated with policies related to mothers' employment.

Instead of incorporating gender into mainstream analyses, Lewis and Sainsbury reject Esping-Andersen's analytical schema and propose alternative bases for typologies. More precisely, Lewis (1992) looks at the strength or weakness of the male-breadwinner model in terms of the traditional division of labour between the sexes and its implications for social entitlements. Drawing on Connell (1987) but with a more institutional emphasis, she also suggests using the concept of 'gender regime'.[3] Sainsbury (1994b) distinguishes between the individual and breadwinner models of social policy on the basis of a broad range of dimensions, such as family ideology, basis of entitlement, unit of benefit and contributions (the head of household or the individual), whether employment and wage policies are directed at both sexes or primarily at men, and whether the care is primarily private or public and paid or unpaid. Pfau-Effinger (1999, 2004) introduces the concept of 'gender arrangements' as specific interplays among culture, institutions, social structures and agency in relation to gender.

Millar and Warman (1996, 1997) propose a new approach to the aggregation of countries based on the type and degree of family obligations. They look at whether legal and normative obligations of care and income support are imposed on the nuclear family, on the 'extended' family or on the state. When addressing the role of the 'extended' family, they also criticise previous feminist research, which has typically focused on gender relations while neglecting generational ones. Naldini (2003) likewise underlines the importance of kinship solidarity networks in the definition of welfare regimes. Mediterranean countries differ from other countries not only in their emphasis on the principle of subsidiarity and the weight of the church (Leibfried, 1992), but also in their strong bias towards cash transfers and a high degree of particularism in both the delivery and financing of policies (Ferrera, 1996). They also differ in the way that the family, with its gender and generational structure, works and has been institutionalised.

The extent to which the family performs a crucial role as a welfare provider has also been captured by analyses on defamilialisation. First introduced by McLaughlin and Glendinning (1994), the concept has been adopted by Esping-Andersen in his subsequent work (Esping Andersen, 1999) as a parallel to the concept of 'decommodification'. While decommodification 'refers to the degree to which individuals and families can uphold a socially acceptable standard of living independently of market participation' (Esping-Andersen, 1990, p 37), defamilialisation means the degree to which individuals can uphold a socially acceptable standard of living independently of care responsibility and income support in the family. Caring responsibilities can be distributed in various ways within the welfare triangle of state, market and family: they may be mainly attributed to families, and to the nuclear or 'extended' family; they may be socialised through the extension of public care services; or they may left for market-driven service provisions to deal with. Defamilialisation' is a precondition for women becoming 'commodified' *à la* Orloff (1993) or setting up 'independent households'. As recently argued by Leitner (2003), there are a variety of forms of familialism or defamilialisation. Indeed, some policies, such as those in relation to elder care or childcare services, aim to unburden the family in its caring function, while others – such as time rights, direct or indirect transfers for caring (such as cash benefits and tax reductions) and social rights attached to care – seek to strengthen the family's caring role, with different gender implications according to the mix proposed and the way in which each single measure is designed and promoted.

The issue of care and of caring regimes obviously has a crucial bearing on women's employment patterns and gender relations. In their pioneering work, Anttonen and Sipilä (1996) analyse differences across 14 European countries in the coverage of elder care and childcare services. They conclude that it is legitimate to speak of social care regimes, with the Scandinavian countries constituting a very distinct cluster characterised by a universalistic and abundant service provision. Subsequently, Bettio and Plantenga (2004) extended the analysis beyond the level of social care services to include leave arrangements and financial provisions, and to consider both formal and informal care.

As underlined by Lewis (2002, 2006), care is crucial because it lies within the interstices of the relationship, not only between the family, the market and the state, but also between women and men, and between paid and unpaid work. However, care has never been the main focus of mainstream welfare analyses, nor of policy making. Its recent entry on the academic and political agenda has been mainly due to preoccupations with the issue of work–family reconciliation and with its implications in terms of fertility, ageing societies and child poverty. The debate on defamilialisation/familialisation also tends to suffer from the same bias: it focuses on the employment side of the employment/care equation and advocates the promotion of active welfare and women's labour market attachment. However, not all care can be commodified; so that scant attention to how care is valued and shared, at the macro and micro levels, risks reinforcing gender inequalities or producing new ones. In line with Bettio and Plantenga (2004), Lewis (2006) proposes a variety of policies encompassing time, money and services in order to enable both men and women to choose to engage in paid or unpaid work. These policies also imply a logical shift: if one follows Sen (1985, 1992, 1999) in adopting a multidimensional concept of welfare, not only money and economic life, but also time, care and political, social and family life, become important functionings. Defining the goal of the welfare state in terms of well-being, rather than only work and wages, means that policies should not focus only on the work–welfare relationship and on the commodification of women (and men); they should also address the distribution of time and the decommodification of men (and women) (Lewis, 2002)

This echoes Fraser's (1994) philosophical analysis of gender equity and welfare states. Fraser argues that neither the 'universal breadwinner model' nor the 'caregiver parity model' is appropriate for the achievement of gender equality. The former encourages full employment for both men and women simply by trying to help women fit into the traditional male arena. The latter, which gives economic rewards for domestic and childrearing work, but is unlikely to offer similar rewards for carers and workers, produces income inequality. It also tends to reinforce the gendered division of domestic labour. The solution is the sharing of both care and employment: that is, making men more similar to women, not the reverse. In the same vein, in her most recent book, Crompton (2006) proposes a continuum of models of the gendered division of labour. These range from the 'traditional male breadwinner/female carer' arrangement, through 'a male breadwinner/female part-time earner' model, and 'a dual-earner/state or marketised care' arrangement, to an idealised 'dual-earner/dual-carer' society. As argued by Gornick and Meyers (2003), these diverse models of the gendered division of paid and unpaid work imply different ideological perspectives on work, caregiving, family and gender relations. They require different packages of policies, and they have different family outcomes. Only the 'dual-earner/dual-carer' model is compatible with various ideological concerns: it is gender egalitarian both in the labour market and in the household; it values and rewards care work (although not only female care); and it emphasises child well-being. In order to achieve this model, a country must offer a flexible and composite package of social policies, which includes three crucial components: family leaves, working-time regulations and a public system of early childhood education and care. Among Western countries, the Scandinavian ones come closest to this 'dual-earner/dual-carer' model. They are also those with the best records in terms of family outcomes: parents spend more time with their children; mothers and fathers divide paid and unpaid work more equally; and children's well-being is better (low poverty, low mortality, moderate school achievement scores, low television consumption and low levels of teenage pregnancy).

Regardless of positions for or against Esping-Andersen's analytical framework, and the dispute on the number of welfare regimes (three or more?), this debate on 'gendering welfare states' has yielded important insights into the various dimensions of gender inequalities, and into the complex nexus among the state, the family and the market. In particular, it represents a valuable source of information with which to identify what dimensions of welfare state policies are important in the study of women's movements in and out of paid work.

Identifying welfare state policies affecting women's employment transitions

The concept of defamilialisation is crucial for the analysis of women's employment. Indeed, as previously mentioned, it is a precondition for the capacity of women to become commodified. In particular, the degree to which the family is released from its caring and welfare responsibilities, via either welfare state provision or market provision, affects women's labour market participation in two ways. First, on the supply side, the provision of extra-family care services enables women to combine paid work with children and thus favours continuous careers. Second, on the demand side, the externalisation of family goods and services contributes to the development of the service sector, which mainly attracts female labour, as discussed in more detail in the next section.

As Gornick and Meyers (2003), Bettio and Plantenga (2004) and Lewis (2006) point out, policies intended to defamilialise caring responsibilities and child costs should affect three dimensions: services, time and money. In turn, they should comprise childcare services, maternal and parental leave policies, income transfers to child families and working-time regulations. As other feminists have emphasised, the extent to which these policies support the commodification of women also depends on the extent to which they decommodify men. Hence, of crucial importance is how care responsibilities are distributed among the state, the market and the family, and whether, within families, they are defined and practised as being solely the mother's concern, or the father's as well. Moreover, these policies in themselves do not guarantee the continuous employment of women. Their effect depends on the degree and type of defamilialisation or familialism that they actually promote or produce. Crucial in this case is how the three pillars of income, service and time are individually designed, whether all are in place and how they are combined with each other. Also important is the degree of universalism: that is, how income and/or labour market history and position act to define eligibility and levels of support. As Orloff (1993) suggests, a mix of commodification and decommodification is necessary to reduce divisions (between men and women and among women) and to render women autonomous and free to choose.

There is broad consensus that childcare services are of great importance in supporting the employment of mothers and, more generally, the reconciliation between parenthood and employment. Indeed, there is a great deal of evidence that furnishing childcare services that are cheap, widely available, with long hours coverage and of good quality, increases women's labour supply (Gustafsson, 1994, 1995; Fagnani, 1996; Gornick and Meyers, 2003; Del Boca and Wetzels, 2007). For example, a recent study by Uunk et al (2005) on the impact of young children on women's labour supply finds that one third of the observed country differences in the 'child effect' is due to differences in public childcare. This is because childcare subsidies reduce the probability of exiting the labour market when children are young and potentially close the monetary cost of motherhood (and fatherhood). It also occurs because support for childcare time and costs increases the labour supply of low-earning potential mothers (Gornick et al, 1997).

Most empirical research on the link between childcare and the employment of mothers has focused on preschool children. Yet, as Gornick et al argue (1997), the working mothers of *school-aged children* may also encounter childcare problems. Indeed, in many countries, compulsory schooling has time schedules that incompatible with working parents: schools are open for only half the day, they do not provide lunch and their holidays only imperfectly correspond to parents' breaks from paid work. In the absence of affordable childcare alternatives, such public school schedules may hinder full labour market participation by women.

The relationship between maternal employment and *leave policies* is more controversial than that between maternal employment and childcare subsidies. Leave provisions are important because they provide basic income support for new mothers (and fathers) and prevent them from exiting employment following childbirth. The evidence shows that access to leave schemes facilitates continuous employment and, in the short run, reduces the wage penalty associated with motherhood (McRae, 1993; Joshi et al, 1996; Glass and Riley, 1998; Saurel-Cubizolles et al, 1999; OECD, 2001b; Pronzato, 2007). However, while childcare services enable mothers to spend more time working, leave enables working mothers (and fathers) to spend more time at home, thereby limiting career-enhancing opportunities. Indeed, the evidence shows that leaves are associated with an increase in women's employment in the short run, but with a reduction in the relative wages and in the quality of their jobs in the long run (Albrecht et al, 2000; Wetzels and Tijdens, 2002). As suggested by De Henau et al (2007), a vicious circle seems to operate: allowing a woman to take leave of absence, especially if for long time, further enhances unequal treatment in the labour market, causing human capital depreciation but also emitting negative signals to employers.

These effects obviously depend on the characteristics of maternity and parental leave programmes. As is widely acknowledged, of great importance are the levels of wage compensation and job protection, the duration of both paid and unpaid leave and the degree of flexibility in its use – that is, whether the leave can be taken on a part-time or full-time basis, and all at once or spread over a number of years, also when the child is a little older. Also crucial are the extent to which and how fathers are entitled to take leave. As Smith (2004) points out, the most decisive factor in fathers' time-off-work behaviour is the level of replacement income. It is also important for leave to be granted as an individual right not transferable between partners, because this allows for flexibility in terms of working-time reduction. Indeed, De Henau et al (2007) show that there is a positive correlation between parental leave supportiveness and the share of fathers in the overall period of leave taken by parents. Similarly, Smith and Williams (2007) show that father-friendly legislation is correlated with both absolute and relative levels of fathers' time spent caring for children. In general, policies that familialise or decommodify men – that is, which allow fathers to spend time caring for children with a low wage penalty – indirectly support maternal employment because they may favour a redistribution of caring responsibilities and may reduce the negative signalling effect on the part of women to employers (European Childcare Network, 1994; Gornick and Meyers, 2003; De Henau et al, 2007).

As already mentioned, *income transfers to child families* (child benefits, family allowances, child-related tax allowances) also affect maternal employment. However, their effects are mixed. On the one hand, income transfers to families with children may encourage labour market participation by reducing reliance on familial care. Indeed, they provide extra income that can be used to purchase care on the market. On the other hand, by raising family resources, they may depress a mother's participation. This is what neoclassical economists would predict in light of their 'income effect' theory. Generous child allowances, especially if not accompanied by equally generous provisions of services and time off to care, can also be seen as a form of 'housewife wage' – that is, as an income encouragement for full-time maternal care (Esping-Andersen, 1999; De Henau et al, 2007).

As well as these policies supporting maternal employment, there are social policies that generally affect the female labour supply. These include *income-tested transfers*, the *marginal tax rate* and the *tax treatment of spouses*. Income-tested transfers may discourage paid work among low-human-capital women, either married or single, because they determine benefit reductions associated with individual or family income and, often, create poverty traps (Staat and Wagenhals, 1996; Christofides, 2000; Saraceno, 2002). The recent emphasis in many European countries on activation policies, on 'making work pay', and, in particular, on reducing the 'welfare dependency' of lone parents, is also a way to tackle such poverty traps (Millar and Rowlingson, 2001). The effect of the tax system on women's labour market behaviour depends on whether taxation is levied on an individual or family basis: individual taxation of the husband's and wife's income favours a secondary earner, while joint taxation penalises him/her by taking his/her earnings at the joint higher marginal tax rate (Gustafsson, 1995).

As argued by many feminist scholars and as shown by many studies on differences across welfare regimes, what really matters are not single policies but packages of policies. The close attachment of Scandinavian women to the labour market is the joint outcome of a good childcare public system and job-protected, well-paid and relatively short maternity leaves, in combination with paternity and parental leaves and with universal cash benefits. In addition, low wage inequalities and 'employee-friendly' flexibility restricted to normal weekly working hours facilitate the conciliation of parenthood and employment. The next section examines these latter measures, which have more to do with labour market regulations.

Labour market effects

As labour market sociologists and heterodox economists have pointed out, individual outcomes in the labour market cannot be explained by the supply side alone: that is, by women's human capital, work–family orientations, family care demands and a partner's resources. The functioning, the structure and the level of demand of the labour market are very important as well. This section first presents demand-side-driven segmentation theory, with its explanation of the use of female labour and of non-standard employment. It then focuses on the criticisms arising from cross-national comparative research. These criticisms show that labour force divides are institutionally shaped and do not always follow gender lines and the part-time/full-time divide. Then, the section specifies the dimensions of labour market regulation relevant for the analysis of women's movements in and out of paid work.

What determines a country's labour force divides? Labour market segmentation theory and cross-national comparative research

Labour market segmentation theory assumes that the labour market is not a homogeneous entity but is instead segmented along lines that do not correspond to skill differentials because these respond to the need of firms to function more smoothly. Segmentation may arise between firms or within firms. It is mainly based on types of contracts, and tends to be patterned by gender because women are a particular attractive source of labour for flexible jobs, especially part-time ones (Fagan and O'Reilly, 1998b). However, a large body of empirical research shows that both the conceptualisation of part-time/atypical work as a marginalised form of employment and that of women as a flexible and malleable supply of labour is problematic. There is great variation both within and across countries in the extent and nature of atypical jobs. They differ in terms of their quality and security, and also in terms of those who hold such jobs and at what stage of the lifecourse. Further, atypical jobs may act as 'bridges' enabling women either to enter the labour market or to maintain continuous participation when they have young children. Or they may be traps and thus give rise to downward occupational mobility and create a secondary segment. The extent to which atypical work is a marginalisation or integration strategy varies both across countries and within countries, and then across sectors, occupations, geographical areas, cohorts and human capital profiles (Blossfeld and Hakim, 1997; Fagan and O'Reilly, 1998b; O'Reilly et al, 2000; Stier and Lewin-Epstein, 2001; Barbieri and Sherer, 2005).

The same across- and within-countries variation is observed in how women have been integrated into the labour market, and in the lines along which segmentation has come about. There is a great deal of evidence that the expansion of the service sector and the increase in female employment are associated. The job opportunities offered by tertiarisation, and in particular by the expansion of the welfare state, have been particularly attractive to women because they have offered favourable and convenient working conditions and required traditional feminine tasks, paying for those jobs that women have always done in the private sphere (Gornick and Jacobs, 1998). However, as argued by Mandel and Semyonov (2006), because this welfare state expansion still assumes that women are the main care providers, it has also reinforced the gendered division of labour. It has produced occupational segregation and, in particular, it has lowered and hardened the 'glass ceiling'. Moreover, tertiarisation has not always been driven by the state as it has typically been in the Scandinavian countries. In Britain, the market has prevailed, and the permanent mobilisation of female labour has been associated with reducing employment and pay protection in order to stimulate the growth of low-paid and female part-time employment. In Southern Europe, tertiarisation has arrived later and partially, and labour force divides have been created not only between public and private employment, but also between the informal and official sectors, between adult and young workers, and between small and big firms.

As underlined by many institutional-oriented sociologists and economists, the standard segmented labour market approach fails to explain differences across and within countries because of its too narrow focus on the productive system, and in particular only on employers' policies and practices. As already mentioned, the state also performs a crucial role. For example, the strength of the private/public divide and its education and gender distribution depend on the overall package of reconciliation policies. Where parenting policies are scarce, social protection is highly segmented, and entries and re-entries are made difficult by labour market rigidities, as in Italy, the chance of pursuing a continuous career depends closely on the sector and type of job. In such contexts, public jobs become particularly attractive to women, and especially to highly educated ones, not only because they prevent downward mobility and avert employment interruptions, thereby allowing lifetime income maximisation, but also because they offer psychological and organisational gains in terms of reconciliation. Besides reconciliation packages, also important are wage regulation and employment protection by government and trades unions – as the next subsection shows in more detail. Indeed, when labour law or collective agreements enforce equal treatment in job security and social security entitlements and payments, the gap between full-time and part-time workers is greatly reduced. Also, the existence of a minimum wage system reduces the scope for employers to use part-timers as cheap labour, and it may generally reduce class and gender inequalities.

As many feminists have emphasised, the failure of standard labour segmentation theory is also due to its disregard of processes of social reproduction and gender cultures (Bettio, 2008). When women assume the bulk of unpaid domestic and family care work, they are indeed an attractive source of labour supply for less demanding and 'deskilling' jobs, or for well-protected but 'segregating' public sector ones. If women are primarily seen as family centred and as secondary earners, and primarily define themselves as such, they may be prevented from re-entering the labour market once they have exited, unless the couple and the family needs an extra source of income (Bruegel, 1979; Humphries, 1983; Power, 1983; Rubery, 1988). Re-entries may also be prevented by a shortage of vacancies. As some studies show, there is a considerable reserve of discouraged workers consisting of (qualified) housewives (and students) who would enter the labour market if employment opportunities were better (Monteduro, 1998).

Apart from overall levels of female labour market participation and occupational segregation, and apart from types and explanations of tertiarisation and labour force divides, there is much evidence that relative risks of interruption are connected to the type of jobs that women have, not only in terms of class, as seen earlier in this chapter, but also in terms of contract, firm size and sector (McRae, 1993; Bernardi, 1999; Saurel-Cubizolles et al, 1999; Bratti et al, 2004). This is particularly true in those contexts where career opportunities and social protection have been segmented around firm size and employment status, as in Southern and Continental Europe. But in all countries, women working in primary segments have better employment conditions and better occupations. These make the cost of exiting from their jobs higher than those of women in secondary jobs or less protected sectors. The extent to which the employment patterns of these women differ over the lifecourse will depend on the strength of the segmentation, on how much occupation in secondary sectors is transitional, and the extent to which it is compensated or reduced by universal and generous social policies. As will be seen in Chapter Four, my models will include measures of social class and of working hours, but unfortunately not measures of other important labour market segmentation factors, such as the size of the firm, the labour market sector and the type of contract. This is because, unlike the ILFI, the BHPS makes such information available in the panel part of the survey, but not in its retrospective life history part. However, when commenting on my findings, I shall take previous studies that have taken such variables into consideration.

Identifying dimensions of labour market regulation affecting women's employment transitions

Unlike in the case of the welfare state, there are no specific theoretical frameworks that aim to explain the impact of labour market regulation on female employment. Indeed, while the feminist literature on women's engagement in paid work has typically focused on the role of the family and the welfare state, the debate on labour market (de)regulation has been mainly concerned with the link between labour market performance and the strictness of a country's employment regulations. Few studies have explicitly analysed the implications of labour market regulation for women (Cousins, 1994; Bettio et al, 1996; Bruegel and Perrons, 1998; Rubery et al, 1998; Purcell et al, 1999; Mosley et al, 2002). Only recently have feminist scholars started to address the role of labour market policies, calling for the explicit inclusion of working-time regulations in the reconciliation package (Crompton, 2006; Gornick and Meyers, 2003). Increasing attention has also been paid to company provisions in support of employees with family responsibilities, and to how they integrate with statutory provisions (Den Dulk, 2001; OECD, 2001b; Naldini, 2006; Ponzellini, 2006). Drawing on these studies and on the general debate concerning the nexus between labour market regulations and unemployment, this subsection singles out various areas of labour market regulation with direct or indirect implications for women's employment.

The typologies in the literature on labour market regulation have been constructed mainly in order to capture the factors believed to impact on labour market performance, especially in terms of unemployment. For example, Esping-Andersen (2000) draws on the debate about labour market flexibility to suggest that regulatory regimes generally contain three types of regulation. The first type of regulation is through welfare state benefits (mainly unemployment benefits, pensions and social assistance payments), which can raise the reservation wage, the cost of labour and the minimum wage floor. The second type of regulation consists of wage profile and bargaining. The third concerns employment protection, especially the cost of dismissals. Emerson (1988) likewise identifies the core features of a regulatory regime as the pay system, hiring and firing rules, income maintenance for people of working age, and basic social services.

All these general areas of regulation have impacts on labour costs and, in turn, on demand for the least productive workers, or those believed to be so (namely the lower skilled, young people and women). And they have indirect effects on women's movements in and out of paid work. Indeed, rigid labour markets with high labour costs tend to create insider/outsider segmentation, protecting those already employed and making it difficult for new entrants (into first jobs or into new jobs after a family-care break) to gain access to the labour market. In particular, highly protective legislation specifying the types of jobs for which women can be hired, and allowing generous maternity leaves to be paid out of contributions, increases the price of female labour and, in turn, may reduce the demand for female labour. Also, legislation on minimum wages or, more generally, wage regulations indirectly influence women's employment transitions, because they affect material class inequalities and the monetary returns to education. As shown by Stier and Lewin-Epstein (2007), gender wage inequalities in the labour market, together with a country's gender ideologies, are the strongest macro determinants of the division of housework.

Useful for identifying the dimensions of labour market regulation with more direct impacts on women's labour market participation are empirical studies on women's employment position with reference to the flexible labour debate. Bettio et al (1996) show that, in Europe, women and men are exposed to flexibility in different ways rather than to different degrees. While flexibility for men mainly takes the form of overtime and shift work, and it is usually remunerated, women predominate in atypical forms of employment, which usually pay less and may involve less predictable work schedules. Moreover, women are more likely to be involved in atypical employment during the core working years, when they have family responsibilities, while men are more likely to be involved at the beginning or end of their employment histories. Thus, statutory and collectively bargained regulations on temporary and part-time work are important in accounting for women's employment transitions. As Grubb and Wells show (1993), such regulations not only reduce the form of employment that is regulated, they also increase the forms of employment to which they do not apply. In Southern Europe, for example, the strict regulation of part-time and dependent employment at least until the late 1990s gave rise to other forms of flexibility, namely self-employment and irregular work. And the incidence of fixed-term contract work was reduced by restrictions on fixed-term contracting itself, and was increased by restrictions in another area, namely the dismissal of regular workers.

Also important are the policies on what Bettio et al (1996) call 'employee-friendly flexibility over the lifecycle' and which recognise that the working-time needs and preferences of women and men change over the lifecourse, according to the changing nature of care requirements and of their own preferences with regard to work, leisure and education. There are essentially three types of such policies that may be pursued either at the firm level or at the national level: leave arrangements (maternity and parental leave, leave for other family reasons such as sickness of children and visits to school, career break schemes); the possibility to reduce hours within an existing job when children are young; and standard working hours and the regularity or employee-chosen flexibility of working-time schedules and types of contract (such as contracts for weekly and annualised hours, and job-sharing, teleworking/working at home, term-time work, saving hours). As also emphasised by Gornick and Meyers (2003) and by Crompton (2006), statutory working-time regulations are important because they increase the time available to women and men for domestic and childcare work, doing so by means of two main mechanisms: first, the limit set to normal weekly working hours for all, which enables men to contribute more to housework and women to avoid the 'mummy track' of part-time or flexible work; second, the granting of vacation times, which can be spent with families and alleviate childcare strains when schools are closed. The types of work–family arrangements provided by firms are also important. These include, besides those indicated by Bettio (flexible working hours arrangements and leaves), extra-statutory childcare arrangements (workplace nurseries, childminding, childcare financial allowances, holiday play schemes and summer camps) and parenthood support schemes (work–family management training, employee counselling, work–family coordinators and research on employees' needs) (Den Dulk, 2001).

Obviously, the success of these employee- and parent-friendly flexibility policies over the life cycle depends on the nature of other types of policies – that is, as pointed out at the end of the last section, on overall packages of policies. For example, working-hours reduction schemes are successful in France and Sweden, where childcare services are numerous, cheap and with convenient opening hours; but this may not be the case in other countries where preschool care is limited and school days are short. Furthermore, if these policies are not nationally regulated but left to workplace negotiations, they may be introduced unevenly and consequently increase divisions within the female labour force.

Conclusion: towards an integrated approach

A variety of theories have been put forward to account for changing women's labour market participation. In that they point to different factors affecting women's labour market participation, these theories can be seen as being more complementary than mutually exclusive.

Economic theories have the merit of viewing labour market outcomes as the result of intentional choices. In the 'new home economics' version, they also have the merit of considering the family as the real decision unit of labour supply and product consumption. Women's choices in the labour market respond, these theories argue, to non-own income and own wage and to the comparative advantage of men and women's market and domestic work. Since wages are largely influenced by human capital investments, as rational actors seeking to maximise (or at least satisfy) their long-term economic well-being, women choose their type and level of education and on-the-job training according to their preferences, their perceived gendered division of labour, and therefore their expected future marital and childrearing path. Once women are married, it is convenient for the family, whose current and future labour productivity is generally lower, if women invest more in housework and choose less demanding jobs than their husbands. Among neoclassical economic theories, Hakim's preference theory emphasises gender-role preferences and work orientations and the heterogeneity of the female universe. However, both conventional economic rational choice theory and Hakim's preference theory pay insufficient attention to the influence of the macro context, to its interaction with individual preferences and to the origins and development of preferences and beliefs. By neglecting the role of norms, social policies and labour market structure and regulation, and/or without specifying what these concretely consist of at different times and in different countries, such theoretical models largely fail to explain differences across countries and changes across cohorts.

By contrast, sociological theories that, in the line of the sociology forged by classics, have always been more institutional than voluntaristic, focus more on contextual factors. More precisely, sociological rational choice theories recognise different forms of rationality, the heterogeneity of preferences, and they look at the impact of institutional and structural constraints, the link between norms and intentional action, and the effect of social class. In contrast with 'individuation' theories, they argue that social class still structures attitudes and material conditions, thereby shaping lifecourses. Other sociologists, mainly feminists, point to the role of culture, to how it affects individual preferences, rationalities and moral careers, but also to societal ideologies and gender welfare regimes. Contrary to what both Becker's efficiency perspective and bargaining models would predict, these feminist scholars also maintain that culture mediates the effect of wages, education and class, inducing some women to interrupt employment or assume most, if not all, of the housework even when their relative resources (time availability or earnings) are larger. Social capital theorists emphasise non-monetary dimensions as well. An individual's education and occupation determine not only income but also skills and knowledge, as well as access to information, social networks and attitudes that can also have positive influences on the partner's labour market supply and outcomes.

In addition to norms, many sociologists and institutional economists emphasise the role of the welfare state, kinship solidarity models, and the structure and regulation of the labour market. In particular, women's labour supply over the lifecourse is strongly influenced by more or less defamilialising policies supporting maternal employment (childcare services, family allowances, maternity and parental leaves) and by the regulation of atypical contracts and of working-time arrangements. The effects of these policies depend on their individual profiles in terms of costs, income support and coverage, and on their combination into an overall package. They also depend on the degree of decommodification of these policies: that is, the extent to which access to them is independent of a woman's labour market history and position, or of her family income. Finally, the effect of these policies is linked to definitions of fathers' rights and to incentives to share unpaid work. As feminist welfare state scholars emphasise, these policies also define models of 'proper' and 'feasible' behaviour concerning gender relations, women's involvement in paid work, care standards and children's needs. Put in rational choice terms, they also structure positive and normative beliefs. Finally, as has emerged from the debate on segmentation theory, women's decisions on exiting and re-entering the labour market are also affected by the level and type of tertiarisation, level and type of labour market segmentation (in terms of contract, sector, firm size and time commitment) and by their connection with gender role norms and with reconciliation policies.

Because these various theories focus on different '*explanans*' of women's labour supply and, more or less explicitly, predict different effects on women's transitions over the lifecourse, they can be viewed more as supplementary than alternative to each other. Indeed, their integration makes it possible to identify all the potential micro and macro determinants of women's employment history and, in turn, the factors able to explain changes across cohorts and differences among countries. In my analysis I shall adopt a (gendered) institutional/rational action approach, which, as shown in Figure 2.1, examines the interplay between supply-side, demand side factors, and institutional and normative factors. As Chapter Four shows in more detail, this approach is compatible with a lifecourse perspective. According to lifecourse scholars, the lifecourse is indeed agency: it is a sequence of events and transitions within interrelated trajectories that reflect individual choices over time. The lifecourse is also institutionally and culturally embedded. That is to say, choices reflect not only attitudes and preferences but also available opportunities and constraints. Moreover, as in the Weberian tradition, rationality has a subjective connotation and can assume the form of both a cost-benefit calculation and a cognitive-normative motivation. As many rational action sociologists argue (Blossfeld and Prein, 1998b), if the aim of the sociological analysis is not to predict individual behaviour (as is typical in economics), but to explain general empirical regularities, this 'soft' version of rationality is sufficient. Indeed, even a slight tendency of individuals to act rationally (that is, to make sense of their choices) generates stable patterns interpretable at the aggregate level. As Mayer (1997) emphasises, these aggregated distinctive patterns derive from individual lifecourses but have macro foundations: they vary systematically between societies because they are influenced by, and influence, 'political economies' – and, I would add, gender arrangements.

On Prein's (1998) distinction, constraints and opportunities can be either situational or structural/institutional. Situational constraints comprise the right-hand side of Figure 2.1: human capital, family situation, the position in the labour market. Clearly, these supply-side 'situations' are not exogenous but are also the

Figure 2.1: Framework for the analysis of women's labour market transitions

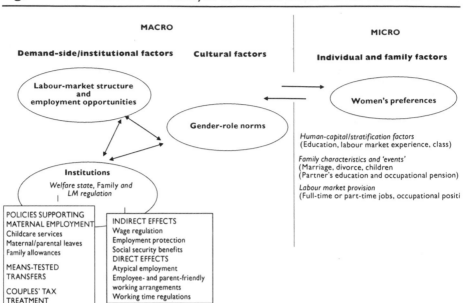

outcome of women's choices. Structural/institutional opportunities and constraints stand on the left-hand side of Figure 2.1: welfare state and labour market regulation, social norms and the demand for labour. Although it is analytically useful to distinguish them, all these micro and macro factors are, as discussed throughout the chapter, closely connected. In Crompton's (2006) terms, the material, the institutional and the symbolic are intertwined.

The importance of each of these factors in accounting for women's labour market transitions is an empirical question. In particular, the extent and type of change across cohorts observable in a given country will depend on the concrete characteristics of these different '*explanans*', on their relations, and on which of them have changed over time and how. In the next chapter I shall set out my two case studies – Italy and Britain – and I shall describe post-war changes in the labour market, in the family, in the welfare state and in gender attitudes and the division of labour. I shall then use individual longitudinal data to analyse changes across cohorts in the incidence of different types of work history and in the micro correlates of movements between employment and housework. As we shall see in Chapter Four, my models will include only supply-side factors together with an indicator of general demand for labour. Owing to a lack of data, direct measures of preferences, beliefs and constraints will not be made. As a consequence, it will not be possible to model and test individual choices. In technical terms, this means that the dependent variable will not be the probability of a choice itself, but the probability of a measurable event, namely exits from and (re)entries into paid work. However, as suggested by Prein (1998), I shall use the concepts of preferences and constraints within a micro–macro lifecourse model, and in particular, within a (gendered) institutional/rational action framework as delineated above, which enables better understanding to be gained of the relationships between observable variables. In my case, the possibility of offering explanations consistent with observed behaviours will be further supported by the use of retrospective longitudinal data with a very rich set of relevant covariates, and by a two-dimensional comparison across both time and space. The former, as argued more thoroughly in Chapter Four, provide a better basis than cross-sectional data for describing social change and drawing causal inferences. The latter, as discussed in Chapter One and throughout this chapter, enable light to be shed on the role of the macro context in shaping women's work–family combinations. Albeit with many caveats and in awareness that further research is necessary, such features represent my 'insurance' policy for advancing causal narratives based on observed behaviours.

Notes

[1] As we will see later in this chapter in the discussion of 'new home economics' – which can be regarded as an extension of human capital theory – the outcome of this education effect depends on the partner's educational and occupational resources.

[2] For example, in a study of women's labour market integration in Germany and Sweden, Theobald and Maier (2002) show that the divide for skills or classes is very low in Sweden. The reason is that, unlike in Germany, in Sweden women with any 'human capital' are able to remain in the labour market over family formation because both supply and demand are increased by the large provision of public services. Other studies underline that this close integration of Swedish women into the labour market is also the outcome of a longstanding emphasis, in both the practice and discourse of policies, on gender equality and on individualised rights. This has also been evidenced by studies on attitudes. In a comparative study on the role of family policy institutions in explaining gender-role attitudes, Sjöberg (2004) shows that, in countries where family policies support a dual-earner family, positive attitudes towards female employment are also widespread among the low educated.

[3] The concept of gender regime refers to institutionalised practices and gendered systems of domination that are constituted as social ordering principles in all societies.

THREE

The different Italian and British contexts: the link to women's employment patterns

Introduction

Italy and Britain differ greatly in the level, type and pattern of women's labour market participation, in their normative and institutional contexts, and in the way that these have changed from the 1950s to the 2000s. In this chapter, I shall look at changes in the potential determinants of women's employment behaviour, as specified in the previous chapter (Figure 2.1). More precisely, I shall start by describing trends in female activity rates, in the overall and sectoral distribution of demand and in women's supply characteristics. The description is based on international cross-sectional data and is intended to give 'snapshots' of the Italian and British situations, in comparison with other European countries, before my longitudinal empirical analyses begin. I shall then outline changing patterns of family formation, and the explanations given for them, focusing in particular on the Italian low participation/low fertility equilibrium. Subsequently, I shall discuss changes in welfare state policies and in labour market regulations, with specific reference to those dimensions affecting women's movements in and out of paid work, as discussed in Chapter Two. Finally, by drawing on the existing empirical literature, I shall illustrate how in Italy, Britain and other European countries, attitudes towards gender roles and behaviours with regard to the gendered division of domestic and care work have changed across cohorts. As usual, the last section summarises. The Appendix contains tables setting out the main characteristics of the various reconciliation measures implemented in Italy and Britain from the 1950s to the 2000s.

Trends in women's labour market participation

The growth of female activity rates: the demand side

During the second half of the 20th century, women's labour market participation increased markedly in all the advanced countries. However, the speed of change and the level of participation reached varied greatly across countries. As Figure 3.1 shows, the female activity rate in Italy increased later and more slowly, and it is still one of the lowest among advanced countries. Between 1970 and 2005, the rate rose from 33% to 51% in Italy, but in Britain from 51% to 69%. Moreover, whereas in Britain the trend was one of a steady increase, with peaks from the early 1970s to the late 1980s, Italy recorded an initial decline and then a slight growth, which was highest from the mid–1970s to the late 1980s. Further, unlike in Britain, in Italy the major component of the growth in women's labour market participation was unemployment (Bettio and Villa, 1996). As is evident in Table 3.1, whereas unemployment among men was, and is still, quite similar in the two countries, in Italy unemployment among women has been always more than twice that of the UK,[1] apart from in the mid–1980s, when the UK suffered from a severe recession.

Figure 3.1: Changes in women's activity rates in Italy, the UK and other selected European countries

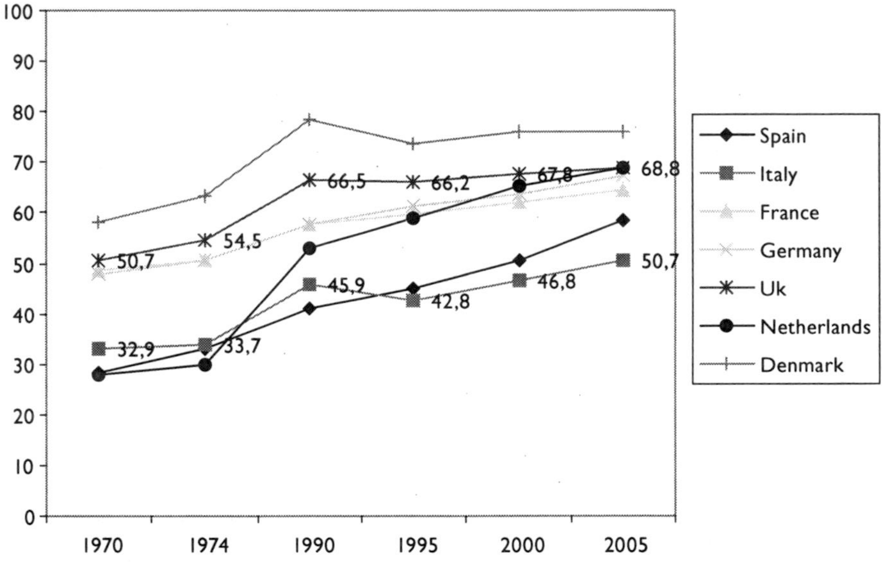

Notes: Data for Germany before 1991 refer to West Germany, after 1991 to Germany.
Source: OECD (2001a) for data from 1970 to 2000; OECD (2006) for data from 2005

As is widely documented, the pattern of female participation over time reflects the interplay between demand-side, supply-side and institutional factors. In Italy, the transition from a family- to a wage-labour system, which everywhere favoured married women's involvement in the labour market, had already taken place in the 1930s. However, the occupational and sectoral distribution of demand long prevented the emergence of these potential supplies. Because Italy was a latecomer to industrialisation, the decline in agriculture had a longer negative impact on women's employment rates. Only in the early 1970s, with the start of tertiarisation, did labour demand shift in favour of women. However, the increase in demand occurred while Italy, like many other countries, was undergoing a recession, and

Table 3.1: Changes in unemployment rates and levels of tertiarisation in Italy and the UK

	Unemployment rates		Distribution of total employment by sector			Distribution of female employment by sector		
	Women	Men	Agriculture	Industry	Services	Agriculture	Industry	Services
Italy								
1975	8.6	3.2	15.8	38.5	45.7	18.1	28.5	53.3
1985	13.1	5.6	11.0	33.5	55.5	11.5	24.5	64.0
1990	13.5	6.2	9.0	32.4	58.6	9.4	23.2	67.4
1995	15.4	8.6	6.0	30.9	63.1	5.8	20.7	73.5
2000	13.6	7.8	4.8	29.4	65.8	4.0	19.0	77.0
2005	10.1	6.2	4.2	28.8	67.1	3.2	16.1	80.7
UK								
1975	2.2	3.8	2.8	40.4	56.8	1.5	25.5	73.1
1985	10.7	11.6	2.4	34.7	63.0	1.3	19.5	79.2
1990	6.4	7.2	2.2	32.3	65.5	1.1	17.3	81.5
1995	6.8	9.9	2.0	23.3	74.6	1.2	11.5	87.3
2000	4.8	5.9	1.7	21.3	77.0	0.9	9.9	89.2
2005	4.3	5.2	1.5	18.2	80.3	0.0	7.6	91.6

Source: Eurostat (online database); European Commission (2000)

it went together with (and probably further encouraged) an increase in supply, which eventually outstripped demand. The result was that the burgeoning female supply clashed with the risk of unemployment or employment in the informal sector (Bettio and Villa, 1996; Reyneri, 2002). Female unemployment was a major factor in the rise of women's activity rates in the 1980s as well. Hence, when labour force surveys were revised in 1992, with a stricter definition being given to unemployment, the figures on activity rates dropped substantially.[2] Moreover, the increase in demand for female labour never reached the level of the UK and most other European countries: the growth of services was, and has been thereafter, slow to develop. Table 3.1 shows that from 1975 to 2005, the total employment share in the service sector rose from 46% to 67%, compared to 57% and 80% in the UK. Women's share of employment in services in 2005 was 81% in Italy, against 92% in the UK.

Indeed, in Italy and Britain, the transformation of the employment structure has differed significantly. Britain exhibits the typical pattern of the English-speaking countries whereby tertiarisation has been mainly driven by the market, and where a rapid and early phasing-out of manufacturing has been coupled with a strong expansion of employment in producer services (in rate) and in private social services (in size), while employment levels have been maintained in the traditional services (distributive and personal). The shift from full-time manufacturing jobs to service ones has particularly affected women, whose participation in the labour market has increased steadily since the 1960s, albeit mainly in part-time jobs.

This pattern exhibited by the English-speaking countries differs significantly from that of the Scandinavian ones, where tertiarisation has been driven by the state, and from Germany and Japan, where the decrease of employment in industry has been moderate, where manufacturing and producer services are closely linked and where social services are relatively scant. It also differs greatly from the Italian and Southern European model characterised by a relatively slow decline in agriculture, belated and limited tertiarisation and the development of a dualistic industrial economy both geographically (North–South) and in terms of firm sizes (combining islands of mass industry with a large presence of small- to medium-sized firms surviving in the market through artisanal capacity, economic cooperation networking, and the use of personal and family labour, especially in the Centre and North-East – the so-called 'Third Italy') (Castells, 1996; Bettio and Villa, 1998; Crouch, 1999; Esping-Andersen, 1999; Reyneri, 2002). Hence, Italy, and especially the South, never had a fully proletarised working class engaged in manufacturing, and later a developed service sector, as did many other countries. Rather, it experienced a moderate development of the public sector and a marked development of informal and irregular employment, and of self-employment, especially in family firms (Mingione, 1995; Chiesi, 1998). The distribution of these various employment positions has assumed a clear gender profile whereby men are overrepresented among the self-employed while women predominate in the public sector or in the informal economy – with the associated penalties in terms of income and employment protection (Bettio and Villa, 1998).[3]

As argued by many authors, tertiarisation in Italy and the other Mediterranean countries has not reached the point of most European countries because it has received strong impetus neither from the market, as in Britain, nor from the welfare state, as in Sweden. Rather, it has been constrained, as said, by a persistent geographical dualism, which has particularly affected producer services. It has also been limited by a family-centred welfare regime, which by relying on the family to provide crucial welfare services (such as childcare, elder care, mortgages, small loans and financial assistance) has inhibited the 'externalisation' of female-intensive goods and services, constraining the development of both personal services (such as cleaning, catering and domestic work) and public or private social care services (Bettio and Villa, 1998).

As we shall see later in this chapter, the growth of family firms, self-employment and the underground economy was closely linked with the type of 'Fordist' labour market regulation promoted by the Italian trades unions and governments. This type of regulation also restricted the number of atypical jobs at least until the late 1990s. As Table 3.2 shows, in Italy in 1990, part-time employment accounted for only 5% of total employment, and for 10% of female employment. There is a similar incidence of fixed-term contracts among all and, to a lesser extent, female employees. The deregulation policies introduced in the late 1990s and early 2000s had the effect of pushing the part-time share up to 13% of total employment in 2005, and to 25% of female employment, although these were still far from the levels recorded in Britain.

Table 3.2: Changes in the share of part-time and fixed-term employment in Italy and the UK

	% part-time share of			% fixed term contracts share of		
	Total employment	Female employment	Male employment	Total employees	Female employees	Male employees
Italy						
1975	–	–	–	–	–	–
1985	5.3	10.1	3.0	4.8	7.0	3.6
1990	4.9	9.6	2.4	5.2	7.6	3.9
1995	6.6	13.1	3.0	7.2	9.2	6.0
2000	8.8	17.4	3.9	10.1	12.2	8.8
2005	12.8	25.6	4.6	12.3	14.7	10.5
UK						
1975	–	–	–	–	–	–
1985	21.2	44.8	4.4	7.0	8.8	5.7
1990	21.7	43.2	5.3	5.2	7.0	3.7
1995	24.1	44.3	7.7	7.0	7.8	6.2
2000	25.3	44.4	9.1	6.8	7.7	5.9
2005	25.4	42.7	10.4	5.7	6.2	5.2

Notes: – indicates no data available.
Source: Eurostat (online database); European Commission (2000)

In the UK, by contrast, already in 1985, part-time employment accounted for 22% of total employment and 45% of female employment, and it remained quite constant until 2005. Fixed-term work was, and still is today, much less widespread. However, as mentioned in the previous chapter and detailed later in this chapter, the development of a large female part-time sector has been part of a deregulation strategy linked to cost advantages to employers, lack of employment protection, uneven patterns of demand, and tasks that require limited qualifications and limited hours to complete. Thus, part-time employment in Britain has acted as the main channel for women's integration into the labour market, but it has also contributed to producing or reinforcing gender (and class) inequalities (Rubery, 1988; Cousins, 1994).

Education, motherhood and employment: the supply side

In addition to demand-side and institutional factors, in all the advanced countries, the increase in women's labour market participation has been closely linked with changes in supply-side factors. The most important of these changes has been increasing investment in human capital. In the 1960s, women began to acquire more educational and professional qualifications, and converted these investments into better jobs and career opportunities. As Künzler (2002, table 8.5) shows, across cohorts, both British and Italian women increased their educational levels much more than did men, and they nearly closed the gender educational gap, especially so in Italy. As data from 2000 from the Organisation for Economic Co-operation and

Development (OECD) reveal, levels of tertiary education increased in Italy from 40% in the 55-64 age group to 55% in the 55-64 age group. The corresponding figure for the UK was 36% and 47% (OECD 2002, table 2.3).

Although education has expanded everywhere, there are still marked differences across countries in women's labour market integration by level of education. As Figure 3.2 shows, Italy has not only one of the lowest total female employment rates but also one of the highest rate gaps between high- and low-educated women. The difference is 43 percentage absolute points, followed by roughly 36 in the UK, Spain and the Netherlands, as against 21 points in Denmark. As Chapter Two argued, the differing effect of education is institutionally and culturally embedded and, as illustrated empirically in Chapter Six, it may concern first entry, or subsequent exits and re-entries over family formation. In Italy, weak tertiarisation and a general lack of employment opportunities (especially in the South), coupled with still quite traditional gender and childcare norms, and with scarce reconciliation policies, have all inhibited female labour market participation, especially first entries (and re-entries after an interruption) and especially by low-educated women (Bettio and Villa, 1996, 2000). In the UK, female entries into paid work were already high in the 1950s, but education and class have always conditioned subsequent patterns of movements in and out of paid work during family formation. However, over time, the divide has moved from whether and when to re-enter paid work after interruption due to marriage or childbirth to whether and when to exit in the first place (Joshi and Hinde, 1993; Davies and Joshi, 2001)

Figure 3.2: Women's employment rates by education in Italy, the UK and other selected European countries (late 1990s)

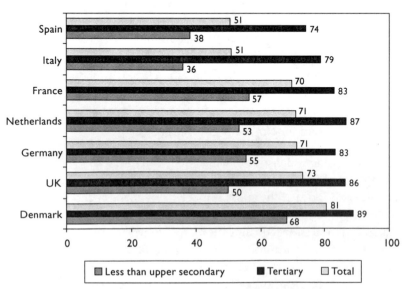

Notes: Data refer to 2000 and are calculated as percentages of the population aged 25 to 54 years old.
Source: OECD (2002, table 2.2)

Differences across countries in female employment rates are strongly associated with differences in the links between education, motherhood and participation. Everywhere, the main post-war increase in female labour supply has been due to the behaviour of married women and mothers. However, their level and type of labour market participation vary significantly across countries. In 1991, in the UK, three out of five married women aged 25-50 worked, while in Italy one out every two did so. By contrast, in the UK, mothers aged 20-39 had activity rates of 31 percentage points lower than those of non-mothers, while in Italy the motherhood effect was less marked, being 22 percentage points less. Moreover, whereas in the UK mothers were five times more likely than non-mothers to work part-time, in Italy they were less than twice as likely to do so (Fagan and Rubery, 1996).

Not only do countries differ in the ways in which mothers and non-mothers engage in full-time work, part-time work or housework over the lifecourse; they also vary in the 'type' of motherhood effect – that is, in their behaviour according to the age and the number of children. As Figure 3.3 shows, in the UK it is the age of the youngest child rather than the number of children that most affects women's participation. In the late 1990s, mothers with children aged under three had employment rates of 23 percentage points below those of mothers with school-age children. The gap was equally wide in Germany, somewhat smaller in France and much smaller – almost non-existent – in Italy, Spain and the Netherlands. In Italy, indeed, it is more the number of children that reduces participation, although the reduction is no higher than in most European countries: 11 percentage points, as in Spain and the Netherlands, slightly lower than in France, and markedly lower compared to the UK and Germany. In Denmark, as generally in the Scandinavian countries, there is almost no difference in employment rates between mothers and non-mothers, regardless of the number and age of their children.

Cross-sectional differences in employment rates by education and number and age of children reflect differences in patterns of labour market participation over the lifecourse. Findings from previous longitudinal research confirm that, in Britain, discontinuous employment around childbearing has always been the typical pattern: 67% and 69% respectively of the 1930-45 and 1946-55 birth cohorts had discontinuous histories (Kempeneers and Lelievre, 1991). The discontinuous pattern also prevails for younger cohorts, but women have increased their labour market attachment by reducing exits, returning to work more often between births and more quickly after childbearing (Davies and Joshi, 2002). By contrast, Italy (like most Southern European countries) can be described as exhibiting an 'opt in/opt out' participation pattern, rather than a universal model of discontinuous participation as in Britain, or of continuous or curtailed participation as in Scandinavia and Germany, respectively. In 1996, one in every four/five married women aged 20-50 had never entered the labour market, and only one in every four/five had re-entered it after an interruption (Bernardi, 1999). At the same time, a considerable subset of women had had

Figure 3.3: Married women's employment rates by number and age of children in Italy, the UK and other selected European countries (late 1990s)

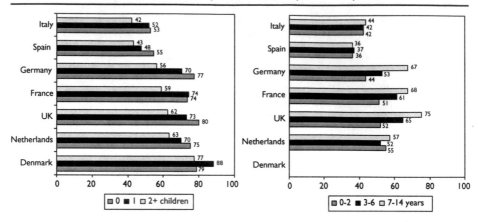

Notes: data for number of children refer to 2000 and are calculated as a percentage of population aged 25 to 54 years old; data for age of children refer to 1996 and are calculated as a percentage of couples with at least one child aged 0-14 (data for Scandinavian countries not available).
Source: OECD (2002, table 2.4); Smith (2005, table 1)

full-time continuous careers lasting as long as those of men (Schizzerotto et al, 1995; Bison et al, 1996).

Chapters Five and Six will return to changes across cohorts in the incidence and correlates of women's employment patterns over the lifecourse, when the findings of my analyses based on the ILFI and the BHPS will be discussed.

Family change: trends in marriage, divorce and childbearing

During the second half of the 20th century, patterns of family formation in industrialised countries changed so markedly as to induce talk by social scientists of a 'second demographic transition' (Van de Kaa, 1987). In contrast to the early ages at marriage of the immediate post-war period in most countries, entry into marriage had been postponed for both men and women. In the meantime, young people had started to experiment with new arrangements such as single living, living with friends and cohabiting with partners. Despite increasingly delayed marriages and increased education, mean ages at first sexual experience continued to decline. With the adoption of efficient contraception at early ages, and with the overall postponement of parenthood, this resulted in an increase in the number of years between first sexual intercourse and parenthood. But it was not only the 'tempo' of fertility that changed, with a clear decline in childbirths prior to age 30; since the catch-up of postponing cohorts was limited, the 'quantum' also changed: overall, total fertility rates declined. Finally, marital instability and extra-marital births increased (Oppenheim Mason and Jensen, 1995).

Although these family changes took place everywhere, their extent, timing and speed differed markedly across countries. Roughly speaking, the leads and lags followed a North–South axis, with the Nordic countries starting to change in the 1960s, and the Mediterranean ones a decade later. Yet, it was not only a matter of timing. Whereas in the North, new living arrangements became widespread and started to 'weaken' the institution of marriage, in Southern Europe the family continued to be a relatively cohesive and stable institution. Changes occurred 'from within'. Although women tended to postpone the formation of families, marriage and children within marriage remained the norm. Only very recently, in the 1990s, have cohabitation and extra-marital births started to increase; yet the great majority of cohabitations, especially after a child, turn into marriages. Other living arrangements, such as unmarried cohabitation and living alone are still very rare. Indeed, home leaving and residential independence come relatively late, typically upon marriage. Moreover, marriage in the Mediterranean countries exhibits a stability unknown elsewhere (De Sandre 1991; Lesthaeghe, 1995; Kaufmann et al, 1997; Naldini and Jurado, 2008). This North–South divide is also evident when Italy is compared with Britain.

The 'golden age' of marriages in Britain began in the late 1930s, when people began to marry more and at earlier ages, and had children relatively soon, regardless of socioeconomic background. It was particularly in the 1970s – that is, with the 1940s cohort – that the marriage and fertility rates reached their peaks (Table 3.3). Cohabitation and remaining celibate or childless was relatively uncommon. Strong social norms seemingly governed the demographic behaviour of this 'Fordist' cohort. From the 1970s onwards, in common with many European countries, the pattern was once again of later and less frequent marriages. In 2005, the marriage rate was 2.28 points lower than in 1960 (Table 3.3). New forms of union emerged in the stead of marriage. Cohabitation, which before the 1970s had been practised by specific and small groups (those unable to obtain divorces under strict legislation, very poor ones, and the *avant garde*), became widespread. And as it grew more common, socioeconomic or cultural backgrounds lost importance in distinguishing those who started and ended cohabitation (Kiernan and Lelievre, 1995; Ermisch and Francesconi, 2000).

In Britain, not only the timing and the rate of marriages but also their stability changed in the post-war decades. After peaking after each world war, divorce declined steeply in the 1930s and 1950s, when families enjoyed unprecedented stability. But since the mid-1960s divorce rates have increased rapidly. Like the risk of ending cohabitation, the strongest predictor of divorce has become the age of the woman, while social class, religion and length of previous acquaintance count for less (Ringen, 1997; Ermisch and Francesconi, 2000).

After fertility declined towards replacement levels in the 1930s and 1940s, Britain experienced an exceptional 'baby boom' between the early 1950s and the late 1960s. This was partly a result of younger ages at marriage and of the increased popularity of marriage. Like divorce, fertility behaviour also started to change from the mid-1960s onwards. The fertility rate fell from 2.7 in 1960 to 1.8 in 1985, and then remained fairly constant until the late 1990s (Table 3.3). Indeed, during the 1980s and the 1990s Britain experienced neither the Scandinavian

Table 3.3: Changes in marriage, divorce, and childbearing in Italy and UK

	Crude marriage rate	Crude divorce rate	Crude fertility rate	Share of births outside marriage	Female mean age at 1st marriage	Female mean age at 1st childbirth
Italy						
1960	7.72	0.0	2.41	2.4	24.8	25.7
1975	6.74	0.2	2.21	2.5	23.7	24.7
1985	5.27	0.3	1.42	5.4	24.5	25.9
1990	5.64	0.5	1.33	6.5	25.5	26.9
1995	5.10	0.5	1.19	8.1	26.6	28.0
2000	4.99	0.7	1.26	9.7	27.4	–
2005	4.23	0.8	1.32	15.4	–	–
UK						
1960	7.51	0.5	–	5.2	23.3	–
1975	7.66	2.1	1.81	9.0	22.5	24.2
1985	6.95	2.8	1.79	18.9	23.9	25.1
1990	6.56	2.7	1.83	27.9	25.0	25.5
1995	5.55	2.9	1.71	33.5	26.2	26.1
2000	5.19	2.6	1.64	39.5	27.5	26.5
2005	5.23	2.6	1.78	42.9	–	26.9*

Notes: – indicates no data available; *data refers to 2003.
Source: Eurostat (online database); Council of Europe (2004, table T2.3 and T3.4)

rise in fertility, nor the continuing decline of the Mediterranean countries, nor the chronic low fertility of Germany. Rather, after a 'quantum' shift due to a fertility decline at all ages, a 'tempo' shift occurred. After the 1970s, the decline was concentrated mainly among 15- to 29-year-old women, while older women began to catch up. In the mid-1980s, the postponement started earlier and led to partial recuperation at ages above 30. At the same time, with an increasing incidence of teenage pregnancy, the decline in childbirths at young ages came to a halt. Overall, the reduction of total fertility rates in Britain during the 1980s and 1990s was very modest (Lesthaeghe, 1995; Lesthaeghe and Moors, 2000).

The total fertility rate started to decline in the late 1990s, and reached an all-time low of 1.63 for England and Wales in 2001. However, it increased every year thereafter, and in 2006 reached 1.87, its highest level since 1980 (Office for National Statistics, 2007). Sobotka (2004) has recently suggested that England and Wales may, together with the Northern European countries, France and Ireland, form a 'high fertility belt' within Europe. However, as also concluded by Sigle-Rushton (2008), unlike in the other high-fertility countries, this has occurred despite the government's reluctance to implement policies to encourage childbearing. The effect has been a marked polarisation by educational level and occupational class: in other words, it has been the fertility of teenagers and low-educated women that has helped keep fertility rates stable in recent years. The high frequency of teenage pregnancy together with that of cohabitation have given rise to a relatively high proportion of out-of-wedlock births: their share of total births was 33% in 1995 and 43% 10 years later, compared to only 9% in 1975 (Table 3.3).

The family system has changed much less in Italy than in Britain and most other European countries. Cohabitation, out-of-wedlock births and premarital home leaving are still relatively rare, especially in the South of Italy. After an increase due mainly to a law enacted in 1987 that reduced the requisite years of separation prior to divorce from five to three years, the crude divorce rate rose from 0.2 per 1,000 inhabitants in 1975 to 0.5 in 1990, rising further to 0.8 at the beginning of the 2000s (Table 3.3). Hence, during the 1980s and 1990s, the Italian family model seems to have been still based on the 'old' married couple. Other kinds of family formation and living arrangements laboured to emerge. Only after 1995 did the frequency of cohabitations and legal separations accelerate, especially in the Centre-North (Castiglioni and Dalla Zuanna, 2008). Consequently, the share of out-of-wedlock births rose from 8% in 1995 to 15% 10 years later (Table 3.3). However, the continuing late departure from the parental home, which is a distinctive feature of Mediterranean countries (Billari et al, 2001), has meant that cohabitation is practised more by young adults (aged 25-34 and older) than by youth people (aged 15-24).

Nevertheless, important changes have occurred within the still 'strong' institution of marriage: young Italians have continued to delay and reduce family formation. As in the rest of Europe, after the post-war 'baby-boom', fertility began to fall in Italy, although it did so one decade later, in the mid-1970s. However, unlike in Northern and Continental Europe, fertility in Italy continued to decline during the 1980s and until the mid-1990s. This decline consisted more of a reduction of second and third children than of an increase of childlessness (Santini, 1997). Furthermore, because children were (and still are) normatively regarded as a post-marriage step, the decline in fertility was linked to postponement and reduction of marriages and to limited recuperation after age 30. Since the 1980s, Italy has had one of the lowest birth rates in the world (Lesthaeghe, 1995; De Sandre et al, 1999; Lesthaeghe and Moors, 2000). Only after the mid-1990s did fertility start slightly to increase, especially in the Centre-North, where the total fertility rate rose from 1.1 children per woman in 1995 to 1.35 in 2005. In the South, fertility decline slowed down.

Although important, postponement of entry into marriage and the low level of alternative forms of union cannot fully account for the declining Italian birth rate. The decline is observed also within marriages, in fact, and it has occurred despite the continuing tendency of Italians to place high value on family and parenthood, and to declare their intention to have children (Palomba, 1995; Jones and Brayfield, 1997). As discussed in previous chapters, crucial roles are played by economic and opportunity costs, and the extent to which they are publicly reduced. Indeed, it is women- and family-friendly policies that have helped reduce the inhibiting effect of paid work on fertility, and they largely account for the reverse of the country-level correlation between female labour force participation and total fertility rate, a correlation that was negative in the 1960s and 1970s but turned positive in the 1980s and 1990s (Brewster and Rindfuss, 2000; Engelhardt et al, 2001; Del Boca, 2002).

As mentioned in Chapter Two, opportunities in the labour market are also important. Unemployment and precarious jobs inhibit fertility not only because they lower actual and future expected incomes but also because they create general uncertainty concerning actual and future location, duration, rights and working schedules. The economic recession of the 1990s and the deregulation policies of the early 2000s, coupled with the long absence of institutional mechanisms able to reduce insecurity, have hindered the transition to adulthood in Italy (Schizzerotto, 2002b; Bernardi and Nazio, 2005).

However, also in Britain, where wage polarisation and labour market flexibility are strong and institutional protections are scant, the economic prospects of women and men are often insecure. Moreover, work–family reconciliation policies are similarly inadequate, and the compensation for them provided by the extended family is weaker. There are therefore additional factors that account for the low Italian fertility rate. Bettio and Villa (1998) point to the importance of economics and the ethics of the family. As discussed earlier in this chapter, while elsewhere the weakness of the welfare state has encouraged the growth of market substitutes for traditional family services, in Italy no market substitution has occurred so that the family has maintained the burden. Supported by a strong ethic of mutual assistance extending beyond the boundaries of the nuclear family, and by a strong normative belief that parents are responsible for their children well beyond their twenties until they have reached equal or higher standards of living, Italian families have resisted the externalisation of service activities. In a context where labour demand is weak and universal unemployment benefit non-existent, these family obligations have also pushed up the cost of children. Moreover, although less acknowledged, unsuccessful job searches produce discouraged housewives who tend to reject their identification solely with the 'mother role' and bear as few children as working women do. The result is a low participation/low fertility equilibrium.

In similar vein, although taking a more cultural approach, Livi Bacci (2001) suggests that it is familialism that has contributed to very low fertility in Italy. The strong interdependence between generations has led to the prolonged dependence of young people on their parents, and to their consequent postponement and reduction of long-term responsibilities and commitments. Other authors have focused on gender relations rather than familialism. For example, McDonald (2000) contends that low fertility in Southern Europe is linked to the preservation of a traditional gender system in a context of expanding labour force opportunities for women.

Besides the strong ethic of mutual assistance and the normative obligations to support children until they are well established, there is another cultural factor that makes the cost of children particularly high in Italy: perceptions on what children's needs are, and how children should be cared for and by whom. Data from the Multipurpose Survey conducted by ISTAT show that nearly half of mothers who do not use public childcare services for under-threes prefer family care arrangements. Moreover, about one in three mothers who use public services declares that they would prefer to rely on care by a family member or a relative if it were available (Saraceno, 2003b). Although this depends on age and education, many younger parents, too, believe that family care is the best solution for very young children. Scott et al (1996), in a cross-country comparative study on gender-role attitudes based on International Social Survey Programme (ISSP) data, find that in 1994 only 27% of Italians disagreed with the statement 'All in all, family life suffers when the woman has a full-time job', against 51% in Britain and the US, and 38% in Ireland and the Netherlands.

The welfare state

Italy and Britain differ widely in their institutional systems, and how they have changed since the post-war decades until the early 2000s. Whereas post-industrial Britain has moved away from a relatively regulated labour market and a Beveridge-type welfare state, becoming a 'liberal' country with a residualist welfare state and a deregulated economy, Italy has seen few changes in its institutional setting. It still has a highly macro-regulated labour market in an unbalanced welfare context, where the extended family plays a crucial role as both an income and a care provider, and where, at least until the mid-1990s, de facto flexibility has been achieved in a distinctive way through small firms, non-dependent labour and the informal economy. This section describes the main features of the welfare state in the two countries, focusing on defamilialising policies as defined in Chapter Two.

Italy

The position of Italy, like those of the other Mediterranean countries, is controversial in the debate on welfare regimes. In the post-war decades, Southern Europe developed a political economy organised around the male-breadwinner worker similar to the conservative-corporatist model in Continental Europe. In particular, male breadwinners were protected by relatively generous social insurance schemes and strict labour market regulation. Further, the subsidiarity principle led to scant provision of defamilialising care services, thereby reinforcing the male-breadwinner-family model. However, Southern Europe had a backward and distinctive model of capitalist development, and it built a welfare regime that differed from the continental model in various respects: a role for 'kinship and intergenerational solidarity', which extended well beyond the boundaries of the nuclear family; fragmentation of its income maintenance system; low development of family policy; and clientelism in the distribution of welfare benefits (Mingione, 1995; Ferrera, 1996; Jurado-Guerrero and Naldini, 1996; Negri and Saraceno, 1996, Naldini, 2003; Saraceno, 2003a). Moreover, the regime has subsequently resisted changes and reforms: although some new measures have been recently introduced, 'post–industrial' institutional arrangements in Italy differ little from the post–war 'Fordist' ones.

The corporatist and familistic profile of the Italian welfare state is also evident in the income maintenance system. In Italy, income transfer schemes are fragmented along occupational lines and targeted on a small number of risks linked to the 'Fordist' order. While pensions, sickness and unemployment benefits for (male) unionised industrial workers are generous, general unemployment benefit, universal child or family allowances and a national minimum income scheme are non–existent. *Family allowances* were first introduced during the fascist regime as a measure to reduce poverty among large families of dependent workers, but also to encourage fertility and a male-breadwinner type of family. During the 1950s, 1960s and 1970s, family allowances were progressively extended to other sectors and occupational categories, but their management and treatment were still fragmented and uneven. In 1988, family allowances departed further from universal and generous coverage. Despite the increasing incidence of family poverty and of women's labour market participation, family allowances were calculated not only according to employment and family status but also to proven need. Moreover, their amounts were neither increased nor adjusted to the cost of living: from 1988 to 1994 their real value decreased by 38% (Commissione di Indagine sulla Povertà e'Emarginazione, 1995). As Saraceno (2003a) points out, in the absence of other types of income support (general 'safety net' schemes and universal child benefits), and given their low amount and their mixed nature as social insurance and social assistance, Italian *'Assegni per il nucleo familiare'* have proved inadequate both as an anti-poverty measure and as a pro-working parent one.

In Italy, only during the 1990s did the inadequacy of support for the cost of children and, more generally, the problem of work–family reconciliation fully enter the public discourse and agenda. In the late 1990s and early 2000s, the centre-left government increased the amount of family allowances, reformed parental leave schemes and introduced a five-month maternity allowance for non-insured women (*'Assegno di maternità'*) and a specific extra allowance for families with more than two children (*'Assegni per il nucleo famigliare con 3 o più figli minori'*). In 1998, a minimum income scheme was also piloted for two years in a small number of municipalities. However, after two further years of trials, the newly elected centre-right government decided against its refinancing and extension.

In the second half of the 1990s, the value of *Tax Reliefs for Dependent Children* was also slightly increased. As summarised in Table A3 in the Appendix, a form of general support for the cost of children has been provided indirectly in Italy since 1977, when individual-based taxation was introduced. However, tax reliefs for dependent children have never represented significant supplementary income. At the outset, their amount was very low, and throughout the 1980s and early 1990s it was not index linked. In the late 1990s and early 2000s, their amount was increased, but never reached the level of child benefits in Continental or Northern European countries. Instead, the dependency of a spouse received stronger support: until the mid-1990s, tax reliefs for dependent spouses were much higher than those for dependent children. What effects they had on wives' labour supply are debatable. On the one hand, an individual-based tax system favours the secondary wage earner; on the other, generous treatment of the traditional one-earner male-breadwinner family skewed towards lower income brackets may discourage women from taking official paid jobs when both the husband's income and the wife's earning capacity are very low (Negri and Saraceno, 1996; Saraceno, 2003a).

Behind this weak and fragmentised income support system have lain specific institutional definitions of the role of the family, and of its gender and generational structure (Bimbi, 1992; Saraceno, 1994; Bettio and Villa, 1998; Bettio and Plantenga, 2004). As discussed in Chapter Two and in previous sections of this chapter, the type and degree of family solidarity assumed and practised is one of the most distinctive features of the Mediterranean welfare regime, and it contributes largely to explaining its low participation/low fertility equilibrium. Indeed, unlike in Continental Europe – where social insurance prevails, social services are scarce but universal family allowances, general unemployment benefits or national minimum income schemes also exist – in Italy defamilialisation is low because also decommodification is left to the family. The latter is expected to provide support to family members out of the labour market or weakly positioned within it. Moreover, in Mediterranean countries it is the extended family more than the strict nuclear family that is considered the relevant and proper locus of social aid (Millar and Warman, 1996; Millar, 1999; Naldini, 2003; Saraceno, 2003a). This is reflected in expectations and behaviours but also in legal obligations. For example, Italian family allowances are paid to breadwinners also for their parents, siblings and parents-in-law with no income.

As many Italian female sociologists (Bimbi, 1997, Trifiletti, 1999; Naldini, 2003) have pointed out, in Italy familialism has prevailed over the male-breadwinner model. In other words, the system has been based more on inter-generational dependency than on dependency between husbands and wives. This pattern has a long economic and cultural history: it derives from the rural economy, Catholic family norms and 19th-century legal definitions of family and kin obligations. It is also linked to Italy's distinctive model of capitalist development. Indeed, as described in earlier in this chapter, Italy's late and partial industrialisation and the divide between North and South have prevented the full achievement of a male-breadwinner model because the strong protection granted to male wage-workers (and subsequently to public employees) has never been extended to broader sections of the population. In the agricultural and unemployed South particularly, there was often no 'Fordist' breadwinner through whom support could be channelled. Rather, families had to activate survival strategies based on supplementing the few (often only one) secure wages of the men in the extended family who had regular, stable jobs, with (where possible) 'breadcrumbs' from the women earning from the irregular or self-employed market, the state and the voluntary sector.

Extended familialism is also evident in the support for maternal employment, which largely offsets the lack of appropriate public reconciliation policies. Leave provisions are relatively generous in Italy, but, until recently, and as in many other Western countries, they have covered only mothers, not fathers, only dependent employees, and only for infants. The provision of services for preschool children is also generous, although opening hours are awkward for working parents. By contrast, the availability of formal childcare services for the under-threes has always been scarce. Nevertheless, as mentioned earlier in the chapter, a considerable subset of working women in Italy do not exit the labour market when children are young. A large body of research shows that this combination of family and work responsibilities is largely based on informal help, especially from grandparents. ISTAT data document that about two thirds of couples with children and half of lone parents are helped by relatives. While non-working married mothers mainly receive income transfers, and working married mothers receive help mainly in the form of childcare services, lone parents receive both kinds of help (Saraceno, 2003a). A more recent ISTAT survey on women who became mothers in 2002 showed that 54.5% of those who then returned to work used 'grandmothers or fathers' as the main form of childcare during the week, 22.4% used childcare services, while 11% relied on private childminders (ISTAT, 2006) In their comparative study on caring regimes, Bettio and Plantenga (2004) calculate an

Figure 3.4: Formal child-care coverage in Italy, Britain and other selected European countries (late 1990s)

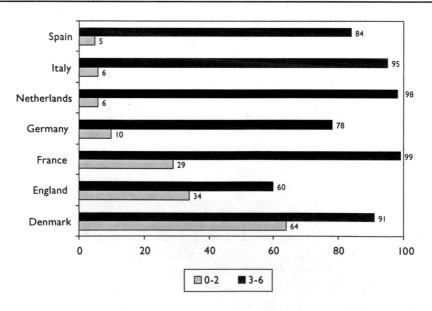

Notes: Formal childcare includes: group care in child-care centres (nurseries, kindergartens, play-schools); residential care; child-minders; non-family member carer frequently living in with the family. For Britain only data for England are available.
Source: OECD (2001b, table 4.7)

index of 'informal care intensity' by combining two indicators: the number of adults devoting at least two hours a day to caring for children, and the proportion of child families who do not pay for regular childcare. Setting the highest country value to 100, and expressing the remaining country values as percentages of the top, gives Italy a value of 90%, like Greece, Britain a value of 82%, and at the other extreme, France and Denmark values of less than 30%. On considering a wider package of care policies, in which they include elder care and childcare services, leave arrangements and financial provisions, Bettio and Plantenga again find that Mediterranean countries form a distinct cluster in which the management of care and income needs is largely delegated to the family.[4]

The gap in the italian provision of services for the under-threes and children aged three to six, as evident in Figure 3.4, reflects a delicate political compromise between the Catholic Church and left-wing parties. Universalisation of services for the under-threes was clearly in conflict with the Catholic view of the family (and within it, the mother) as the best locus of infant childcare, reinforced by the dominant pedagogical theories on the risks of child–mother separation. By contrast, expansion of childcare services for preschool children benefited from a shift from the contentious political debate over family and gender roles to the educational rationale on which consensus is easier to obtain (Della Sala, 2002; Naldini, 2003). Accordingly, 'scuole materne' became universal, but their weekly and annual opening times, like those of schools, were insensitive to the childcare needs of dual-earner families. Hence, grandparents were (and still are) used to provide substantial informal support also when children moved up to maternal and primary school (Plantenga and Remery, 2005).

The gap between services for the under-threes and for preschool children concerns not only the level of coverage but also costs and regional disparities. While preschool services, either public or private, have been heavily publicly subsidised, so that they are almost free for families, in the case of day nurseries for the under-threes, parents have often been required to pay income-related fees. The maximum amount of such fees set by municipalities is roughly equivalent to what some private nursery schools charge, and it amounts, in the early 2000s, to 400-600 euros per month (Plantenga and Remery, 2005, p 40). Moreover, regional differences are much more marked in the provision of day nurseries. At the beginning of the 1990s, attendance at nursery schools was around 95% in the North and 85% in Sicily and Sardinia. Instead, coverage rates in day nurseries ranged from a maximum of 19% in Emilia-Romagna, and 10% in Piemonte and Lombardia, to a minimum of about 3% in the Islands, and even less than 1% in Calabria and Campania (Saraceno, 2003a, table 4.1). Interestingly, and not surprisingly, geographical variation in day nurseries for the under-threes largely corresponds to variation in women's employment rates. This suggests that a perverse mechanism is in operation: *ceteribus paribus*, the lack of childcare services inhibits labour market participation by mothers, while the lack of a 'visible' demand legitimates a low service supply.

Unlike childcare services, since the 1970s, leave policies have been, in comparative terms, quite good in Italy. First, maternity leaves were first introduced in the 1950s and then improved, both in duration and in payment, by law 1204/1971. In more detail, compulsory maternity leave was set at five months, and it was compensated with 80% of the wage. In addition, employee mothers were entitled to a six-month period of optional leave until the child was one year old, with 30% of the wage. Mothers were also entitled to take unpaid leave if the child was ill until his/her third birthday. However, this strong protection applied only to mothers with employee contracts. Second, fathers had no independent right to childcare leave, so that traditional gender roles were assumed and reinforced (Ballestrero, 1993; Saraceno, 2003a). Only recently, with law 53/2000, has childcare been clearly defined as a parental, not just maternal, responsibility. Fathers have become entitled on their own account, irrespective of the wife's right. Moreover, they have been explicitly encouraged to take time off for childcare: if the father uses at least three months of the optional parental leave (recently extended from six to a total of 10 months) the couple gains an extra month of leave. The new law also acknowledges that couples differ in their preferences and working and family conditions, and that children need care not only when they are very small but also when they become older. Accordingly, the leave can be used by both parents continuously or intermittently, either on a full-time or part-time basis, and until the child is eight years old. Moreover, entitlement to take days off when the child is ill is extended until his/her third birthday. However, the law does not provide for paternity leave in this case (Gottardi, 2001; Lena, 2002; Saraceno, 2003a).

Although fathers are now individually entitled to parental leave, only 7% of them have taken it within the first two years of the child's life. Longer and unpaid leave is still a female option. Labour market sector and educational level differentiate the male take-up rate: most of the few men taking time off work are well educated, or they work as civil servants or in the public sector (Gavio and Lelleri, 2005; Plantenga and Remery, 2005). As discussed in Chapter Two, cross-country comparative research shows that the most decisive factor in the time-off-work behaviour of fathers is the level of replacement income, which is relatively low in Italy. However, cultural factors also seem to be influential. A European survey on men's attitudes to parental leave found that only 65% of the Italian men interviewed were aware of their rights, as against 72% in the UK and more than 90% in Sweden, Luxembourg and Denmark. Similar cross-country differences emerged in the intention to take parental leave to spend more time with children: 24% of Swedish men compared to 5% in the UK and 0% in Greece, Ireland, Italy and Spain. Moreover, in contrast to the EU15 average of 6% and 38%, in Italy 19% of respondents stated that another family member took care of their children, and only 24% that greater financial compensation would encourage them to take parental leave (EEIG, 2004).

Hence, apart from leave facilities, in Italy public support for the cost of children, in both cash and kind, is weak. As already noted, it is extended familialism that enables maternal employment, so that one might use the expression 'family dependency' for Italian families with children. This dependency, like any form of dependency, has a price. Even in a context of Catholic family values and a strong ethic of inter-generational mutual assistance, extended family dependency may hinder emancipation and require difficult negotiations. For those who receive help, it may favour labour market attachment and career but reduce privacy and autonomy. For those who give help, mainly grandmothers, it may mean less time for leisure and to acquire economic independence. In other words, while the kinship support network allows younger women to remain in full-time employment over the family formation phase, the women who provide this support, in the absence of employment opportunities and of flexible working-time arrangements in the regular economy, are confined to a mixture of domestic and informal work. Moreover, leaving the bulk of welfare provisions to the family, as the Italian and Mediterranean welfare regime does, means that inequalities are reproduced between those women who can count on generous cash and in-kind support and those who have access only to some or none of it (Bettio, 1988b; Sabbadini, 2002; Saraceno, 2003a).

Britain

At the end of the Second World War, Britain adopted a Keynesian economic policy and Beveridgean social policy, which located it between social democratic Sweden and the US with its voluntarism and reluctant collectivism. However, Thatcherism, which was characterised by a strong neoliberal ideology, moved the British welfare regime away from the European model towards the residual and deregulated model of the US (Ginsburg, 1992; Clarke et al, 2001). Under New Labour, new policies to 'make work pay' have been introduced, including a national minimum wage, generous wage subsidies in the form of tax credits, together with an effort to improve leave schemes and make collective provision for childcare. However, these policies have been pursued with persisting liberal features that do not greatly alter the British welfare regime. The neoliberal ideology has shaped both the income support and the caring support systems.

In the immediate post-war years, following the Beveridge Report (1942), the British state promoted the principles of collectivism and universalism by assuming increasing responsibility for individual welfare and for the production and reproduction of labour power. However, as stressed by feminist scholars, the Beveridgean concept and practice of citizenship was strongly gender biased. It rested on a male-breadwinner model of the family and society and on the presumption that a managed economy would deliver full (male) employment. Accordingly, wage (male) work was seen as the primary source of income, with the state offering a 'family wage' through the guarantee of the male's paid work and his income substitution in case of temporary unemployment or old age. Despite the growth of women's employment during the war, both in language and in actual policies women's waged work was conceived as a secondary or peripheral activity in transitional phases before marriage and children. Women were consequently structurally positioned in the benefit system as dependants (Millar, 1999; Clarke et al, 2001). The only independent source of income for women consisted of universal *Family Allowances*. As evidenced by Table A1 in the Appendix, these were introduced in 1948, paid to fathers from the second child onwards, and supplemented by tax exemptions for children. After a feminist campaign, in 1977 the Family Allowance and tax allowance system was abandoned in favour of a universal non-taxable *Child Benefit* to be paid to the mother for all children including the first. Moreover, in response to the increasing number and poverty risk of lone-parent households, also introduced was a supplement for lone parents. However, from the outset, the level of these family benefits fell far below the costs of child maintenance, and it was little improved during the 1960s and 1970s (Gauthier, 1996; Ringen, 1997; Clarke et al, 2001).

Also, in-kind support for childcare was limited in the construction and expansion of the British welfare state. Indeed, the provision of services for the under-threes increased greatly during the post-war period. However, because it assumed a stable male-breadwinner/female-carer type of family, it fell short of need, with the consequence that the family continued to be the main source of welfare services. The intention to support women's employment also played a marginal role in the policy for preschool children. Instead of this policy being targeted on children with social and economic problems, it was, as in Italy, driven by more universal educational and developmental concerns. Nevertheless, most of the expansion was in primary schools, in four-year-old or 'rising fives' classes, or in part-time state nurseries (Walker, 1988; Gauthier, 1996; Ringen, 1997). Moreover, it never came even close to universal coverage: in 1966, the proportion of two- to four-year-olds in state nursery education in England was less than 20%, while that of children aged three to four in school was around 15%.

Although unemployment, family breakdowns and out-of-wedlock births rose and gender roles changed after the 1970s, the post-war welfare state remained substantially intact until the advent of the Conservative government, which, with its driving (neo)liberal ideology, moved Britain definitively away from universalism towards targeted and limited support for select groups. The changes made to the income support system exemplify this trend. During the 1980s and until the mid-1990s, family allowances gradually declined in real value, proving inadequate either as support for maternal employment (for example to purchase care on the market) or as an anti-poverty measure. Rather, low-income families with children were compelled to rely on social assistance (Ringen, 1997; Maucher and Bahle, 2000). As is widely documented, the risk of poverty entrapment and a discouraged labour supply increased. Indeed, without a parallel improvement in reconciliation policies and job and wage opportunities, women with low earnings potential found that moving from *Income Support*, the general guaranteed minimum income scheme, to paid work supplemented by *Family Credit* often did not make economic sense.[5] Since the household income threshold and earnings disregard for the spouse were kept rather low, married mothers with low earning potential were discouraged from working. Indeed, dual-earner couples hardly ever received Family Credit and, in the early 1990s, constituted only 5% of the households receiving it (Scheiwe, 1994).[6]

A similar, even more serious, poverty trap existed, and still does, for single parents. Unlike couples with children, lone parents on social assistance during the 1980s and 1990s were not required to seek work until their youngest child was aged 16, or aged 18 if in full-time education. Moreover, by leaving Income Support a mother lost her entitlements to free school meals, milk for her child and full coverage of housing costs and interest on mortgage payments. Since the provision of subsidised childcare services was scarce, child benefits low and maintenance allowance from non-custodial parents often not paid, the mother had to find childcare arrangements and often to pay for them. In general, entering the labour market may not be advantageous for a low-educated lone parent. And, indeed, in the 1980s, British lone parents recorded one of the lowest labour market participation rates and one of the highest poverty rates in Europe. In order to encourage welfare-to-work transition, in the late 1980s and early 1990s the Conservative government changed the eligibility criteria for Family Credit by reducing the threshold to 16 hours per week and introducing a childcare disregard of £60 per week. Nevertheless, child family poverty and, in particular, lone-parent welfare dependency remained severe.

The residualist-neoliberal approach of the Conservative governments that shaped the restructuring of the income support system was also reflected in family policies. Many feminist scholars have described the British welfare state as strongly committed to the male-breadwinner family model (Sainsbury, 1994b, 1996; Lewis and Ostner, 1995; O'Connor et al, 1999). Given the high frequency of part time work among mothers, the expression 'modernised male-breadwinner model' has been coined (Pfau-Effinger, 1999). As we have seen, this model dates back to the Beveridge period, when the universal approach to social rights was restricted to the 'Fordist' male breadwinner. Although, given increasing women's paid work and 'alternative' family types, post-war assumptions on the family and the market no longer applied, few changes were made to family policies.[7] Indeed, the prevailing ideology of the privacy of the family, which was part of Beveridge's liberal collectivism, was further reinforced under Thatcherism, albeit with a different emphasis: Thatcher's neoliberalism tended to move beyond the preoccupation with the 'traditional' family model to a more consistent, presumably 'gender-blind', stress on individual autonomy (Randall, 2002). Accordingly, the right of women and mothers to work was acknowledged, but there was no development of 'active' gender equalisation and women's employment promotion policies. As Lewis (1992) maintains, it was still assumed that the family (women) would provide care, with the consequence that divisions between men and women, and among women, were reinforced.

These gender and liberal assumptions also marked leave and childcare policies. British maternity benefits are notorious for being among the lowest in Europe. As Table A2 in the Appendix shows, maternity rights legislation was first introduced at the beginning of the 1970s. It granted to insured employee and self-employed women 18 weeks of *Maternity Allowance*, the right to return to their jobs within 29 weeks of childbirth, and protection against unfair dismissal. Conservative governments during the 1980s restricted women's maternity rights, or made them more complex. The Maternity Grant of £25 was abolished and replaced by a means-tested grant of around £75 from the Social Fund. Moreover, a more generous benefit (*Statutory Maternity Pay*) was based on the requisite of continuous employment with the same employer, and it was paid for six weeks at 90% of the wage and for 12 weeks at a flat rate of £39.25 in 1990/91. The lower flat rate was available as a *Maternity Allowance* for 18 weeks to women with only six months of continuous employment provided they had paid contributions. Moreover, employers could choose to make maternity payments in addition to the Statutory Maternity Pay, or they could choose to make payments to women who did not fulfil the requirements. However, the amount and duration of this payment was discretionary (McRae, 1993; Burchell et al, 1997). In 1988, 60% of pregnant women qualified for Statutory Maternity Pay and the right to reinstatement, and only 14% of women, mainly in the public sector, received contractual maternity pay (McRae and Daniel, 1991).

During the 1980s, other rights linked to maternity were weakened: more written procedure was required to qualify for maternity leave, firms with six or more employees could offer women 'suitable alternative work' rather than the original job, while women employed in firms with fewer than six employees lost their right to reinstatement. Furthermore, the qualifying period for protection against unfair dismissal on grounds of pregnancy was extended from six months to two years if the woman was in full-time work, and to five years in the case of part-time employees (Ringen, 1997). Only in 1994, with 'compulsory' implementation of the EC Pregnant Workers Directive, were maternity rights improved in Britain, although they continued to be among the weakest in Europe. All employees qualified for a minimum of Maternity Pay regardless of length of service, and for protection against unfair dismissal. However, there were no statutory provisions on parental leave or leave for family reasons, notwithstanding broad consensus within the European Union and increasing support in Britain. Nor there was any statutory provision on paternity leave. As stressed by feminists scholars, the failure to extend leave to fathers was due not only to the liberal economic conviction that such provisions should be a private arrangement between employees and employers, but also to a persisting male-breadwinner assumption that childcare is essentially a 'female matter' (Kilkey, 2006).

The same economic and (more or less implicitly) moral arguments that shaped leave facilities spilled over to the provision of childcare services. Conservative governments insisted on the private nature of childcare arrangements, which were to be determined by the interplay between parental preferences, the market and the voluntary sector. They also changed the articulation and organisation of political interests around the childcare issue. Increasing centralisation weakened trade unions and local authority associations, both as actors in the policy process and as welfare providers. The result was that, from 1980 to 1991, local authority childcare places decreased, while the number of private nurseries and childminders increased more than threefold. Much of this policy continued under the Major government. However, growing pressure to improve nursery education, combined with increasing preoccupation with the welfare dependency problem, induced the Major government to introduce some changes: in 1994 a new *Child Care Allowance* for low-income working parents eligible for *Family Credit*, and in 1996, with four pilot projects, a *Nursery Voucher Scheme*. Although modest in terms of both the sums disbursed and the number of families affected,[8] these measures suggest that the intention of the Conservatives was to stimulate the demand for childcare rather than its supply (Randall, 2002).

The arrival of New Labour in power marked a change of approach and commitments. New Labour declared its intention to implement an explicit family policy with the twofold aim of helping parents to work or study and of offering children beneficial early education. This was part of a more general policy of promoting equal opportunities for all, tackling social exclusion and embracing an adult-worker model of the family. Ideologies on gender roles and motherhood, and in particular, assumptions on the marginal role of father-care and the 'goodness' of mother-care (at least of informal care), began to weaken. Women were involved in the building of a new type of 'active' welfare state, and men in the creation of a new balance between work and family life (Lewis, 2003). Accordingly, in 1998, New Labour launched the National Childcare Strategy, an initiative for the development, expansion, implementation and sustainability of early-childhood and childcare services in Britain. Moreover, it made improvements to the existing maternity leave and pay systems, introduced a new right to paternity and parental leave, and made it possible to request flexible working arrangements as well as to take time off in order to deal with family emergencies. Finally, New Labour broke with the long-established policy of supporting lone parents at home and explicitly switched to a policy of encouraging, if not obliging, lone mothers to work. This was the famous 'New Deal' for lone parents, which comprised various programmes aimed at easing the welfare-to-work transition (Conaghan, 2002; Lewis and Campbell, 2007).[9]

Under New Labour, both types of maternity leave have been extended, levels of payment have been increased, and parental and paternity leaves have been introduced. However, the former is unpaid, whereas the latter is paid at a flat rate and last only two weeks, as opposed to the 12 months potentially available to the mother. Moreover, both parental and paternity leaves are still based on length of service (Caracciolo di Torella, 2007). Data on take-up rates show that they are high for the paid part of the maternity leave, but relatively low for the additional unpaid period. Moreover, whereas the male take-up rate of paid paternity leave is almost universal, only 8% of eligible men make use of parental leave within 17 months of their child's birth, and three quarters for less than a week. Mothers do not make extensive use of parental leave either: in 2005, only 11% of them had taken it since the end of maternity leave, and two thirds for a week or less (Plantenga and Remery, 2005; Moss and O'Brien, 2006).

Nor have aspirations to universal childcare, as expressed in the National Childcare Strategy, been fulfilled under New Labour. Indeed, as with the Conservatives, the approach has consisted more in stimulating the demand for childcare rather than the supply. The main plank in New Labour's policy has been a system of tax credits aimed mainly at lower- and middle-income working families that makes assistance with the cost of childcare dependent on the parents' employment status. Moreover, on the supply side, the main commitment has been to preschool services rather than ones for 0- to three-year-olds, and still on a part-time basis (Lewis, 2003; Wincott, 2006). In addition, because public funding has been limited, parents pay 75-93% of the costs, which on average absorb around one quarter of a woman's earnings (Plantenga and Remery, 2005). The result has been that, in 2000, the provision of publicly funded childcare services for the under-threes still had only a 2% coverage rate, the same as it had been at the beginning of the 1990s, or 34% if private services are included, against a share of 77% in publicly financed care for children aged three to five. And out-of-school provision for school-age children is still very limited (Gornick and Meyers, 2003, table 7.2; Del Boca and Saraceno, 2005, table 5). Moreover, since New Labour has not shifted from its commitment to a mixed economy of care and a range of choices for parents, the overall system of childcare has remained rather heterogeneous and fragmented, with a complex pattern of finance, provisions and access.[10]

Contrary to the Conservatives' expectations, the market has not replaced the state in the provision of childcare. Although between 1980 and 1990, nurseries in the private and voluntary sector more than quadrupled, they catered for a tiny percentage of young children, mainly ones with high-earning parents. Moreover, relatively few nurseries were provided by employers: a 1988 survey of new babies conducted by McRae (1991) found that only 4% of women employed during pregnancy had access to workplace nurseries or received other help with childcare from their employers. As Table A4 in the Appendix shows, the share was higher at the beginning of the 2000s, but still low. Moreover, in the early 1990s, a full-year place cost around 16% of an average two-earner family income in the UK, a percentage not far from the 20% (or more) in Italy. Indeed, as Esping-Andersen (1999) argues, for both Britain and Italy one can speak of concomitant welfare state and market failures offset by kinship and inter-generational solidarity in Italy, and by part-time employment and, to a lesser extent, informal arrangements in Britain.[11] As the above-mentioned comparative study by Bettio and Plantenga (2004) reports, also in Britain informal arrangements are of crucial importance. In both 1983 and 1990, more than 90% of women in paid employment used a relative, the husband or a grandmother, or a friend or neighbour to look after their children for at least some hours a day (Burchell et al, 1997). However, the ways in which informal care is combined with formal care and the type of formal care used are class patterned. La Valle et al (2002) report that 42% of partnered mothers working full time use formal care, compared to roughly 20% of mothers working part time. In particular, the former tend to use private-sector day nurseries, especially if they are highly qualified and work long hours. The latter, especially those who work short part-time hours, use the cheapest form of childcare available: partners, kin and childminders.

Therefore, both in the Beveridgean post-war decades and under the Conservative and New Labour governments of the 1980s and 1990s, the amount of defamilialisation achieved by the British welfare state was limited. This has important implications for women's labour market patterns over the lifecourse and for inequalities among women. As illustrated earlier in this chapter, in Britain discontinuous employment around childbearing has always been the typical pattern: the introduction of maternity legislation in the mid-1970s and its subsequent improvement has indubitably contributed to an increase of stability in women's careers (McRae and Daniel, 1991; Duncan et al, 1998). However, because of the difficulties in sustaining childcare arrangements and benefiting from maternity provisions, many women did not manage, and are still unable, to continue working. This scant and uneven support for caring responsibilities has produced a marked polarisation among women. Indeed, it has had an unequal impact on mothers in low-paid jobs as opposed to those with better educations and higher incomes, who can afford to pay for private care (and thus not to exit the labour market), and on lone mothers as opposed to married mothers, given that the latter can at least rely on the income and time of a partner. Also, the reforms of the social security system during the 1980s and 1990s have increased inequalities. They have made low-educated lone parents (and, to some extent, married mothers) vulnerable to welfare dependency because working may not pay off. They have also made them vulnerable to entry and permanence in the secondary labour market, where they can find additional employment, such as home working or part-time work, compatible with their family responsibilities, but underpaid and underprotected (Walker, 1988).

Labour market regulation

Italy

International comparisons point to Italy as one of the most rigidly regulated labour markets in the 1980s and 1990s, especially in terms of hiring and firing rules and restrictions on the use of atypical contracts (Grubb and Wells, 1993; OECD, 1999). A major source of this longstanding labour market rigidity was the post-war construction of the welfare state based on the specific social, economic and demographic conditions that obtained in the 'Fordist era': full employment for male industrial workers, a lifelong secure career with increasing and relatively high wages and income insurance during the non-active stage of the life cycle, and a traditional stable family in which women had time for care. Social policies and industrial relations acted in tandem to guarantee this Fordist order. Unions campaigned for job security and full-time well-paid jobs, also on the belief that the entire family was dependent on the male's income and entitlements. At the same time, the assumption of a free female carer meant that scant attention was paid to the issue of conciliation between family and work. As Esping-Andersen (1996b) has argued, nowhere has the principle of the 'family wage' become as institutionalised as in Continental Europe, with its wage bargaining, employment protection and social benefits structure. In addition, as already noted, strong kinship and inter-generational solidarity was assumed and encouraged in the Mediterranean countries.

As discussed in Chapter Two, the conservative-corporative regime has responded weakly to the post-Fordist challenges. Rather than following the neoliberal deregulation approach of the English-speaking countries, or the public-employment-led strategy of the Nordic ones, Italy, and Continental Europe in general, has managed post-industrial labour market problems via supply reductions. In other words, conservative-corporatist countries have used public resources to support labour hoarding, mainly through early retirements and generous unemployment benefit for core, mostly male, workers. Social care services have remained underdeveloped. Moreover, as seen in the previous section, income supports for the active phases of the life cycle have remained scarce and uneven in the Mediterranean countries. Finally, at least until the late 1990s, the labour market has been strictly regulated, to the cost of new entrants and/or individuals seeking temporary or part-time employment.

As emphasised in Chapter Two, the regulation of atypical contracts has an important bearing on labour market participation by women and mothers. In Italy, part-time work was first introduced in 1984. However, the law did not include incentives: wages, social security and other working conditions were generally fixed pro rata to the equivalent full-time job. Further, part-time workers could not work overtime and, above all, could not switch directly to full-time work. The impact of the law was therefore limited. Employers preferred other means to achieve flexibility, mainly overtime and irregular labour. Although opportunities for part-time work were increased in the early 1990s,[12] the level of protection remained substantially the same as for full-timers. Hence, part-time work increased to only a minor extent, as shown by Table 3.2 (Addabbo, 1997; Samek Lodovici, 2000).

Since the early 1980s, the regulation of temporary work and working time has also been progressively relaxed. Post-war collective agreements set long and fixed working times, ranging from 40 hours per week distributed across five days (typically in the industrial sector) to 36 hours distributed across six days (in the public sector). Any deviation from these standard schedules was very difficult: employers could use atypical contracts and overtime only in a few well-defined circumstances; and employees had very little freedom in scheduling their working time. Only in the past two decades have collective agreements started to include or expand forms of flexibilisation such as shift work, multi-period scheduling and part-time work.

As Table 3.2 evidences, from 1995 to 2005, the share of part-time work and fixed-term contracts almost doubled. First, the '*legge Treu*' (L. 196/1997) and then the '*legge Biagi*' (L. 30, 2003) allowed for a variety of atypical contracts, such as fixed-term contracts, subcontracting and pseudo-self-employment, work on call, weekend work contracts and part-time work. However, as pointed out by numerous authors (Esping-Andersen and Regini, 2000, Micheli, 2006; Barbieri and Scherer, 2007), this deregulation was only 'partial and selective'. It amounted to no more than 20% of total employment; it made no change to the regulation of permanent jobs; and it was heavily concentrated among 'outsiders'. A large body of data shows, in fact, that young people have increasingly entered the labour market on atypical contracts, but with many fewer guarantees (in terms of wages, social protections, employment and occupational conditions) compared with previous cohorts, and with long and difficult transitions into the primary labour market. Entrapment in flexible and precarious employment varies according to cohort, area and education: the chances of moving into typical positions are higher for atypical workers in the North, with average education levels, and with only a short atypical work episode. Young people, women and the lowest or highest educated are those most likely to start their labour market careers in precarious employment, and to find themselves still in unstable jobs at the age of 35 (Barbieri and Scherer, 2008).

This entrapment in atypicality affects the process of family formation, which tends to be postponed or reduced (Schizzerotto and Lucchini, 2002; Bernardi and Nazio, 2005). It also affects women's movements in and out of paid work over family formation. Indeed, as discussed in the previous section, strong maternity and parental leave provisions only apply to employees in Italy. Self-employed women and those with pseudo-self-employment contracts are little protected, in terms of both duration and income replacement. Women with fixed-term contracts can, in theory, receive the same benefits as permanent employees. However, if they take long leave of absence, they risk non-renewal of their contracts by the employer. Moreover, they may be unable to negotiate a more equal sharing of family responsibilities within the couple: either because the partner is also precarious and without entitlement to leave or because, if he is an employee, he has the stable and often higher income (Saraceno, 2005).

As many authors have pointed out, the deregulatory reforms of the 1980s and 1990s did not greatly change either the performance or the distortions of the Italian labour market. They progressively eroded employment protection for new entrants, but the level of unemployment and of labour market segmentation was left virtually unaffected. (Esping-Andersen, 1996b; Samek Lodovici, 2000; Schizzerotto, 2002b). Wide labour force divides persisted between self-employment and employment, the public and private sector, big and small firms, the official and the informal sector. And gender and generational divides increased. Since men were the first and main targets of strong social and industrial protection in the post-war period, the lack thereafter of institutional reforms and long-term employment policies has particularly penalised women and the young, especially those resident in the South of Italy, for whom entry into paid work has been difficult, taken a long time and, as just noted, often consisted of precarious employment.

In the case of women, it is not just labour market entry or re-entry that has been difficult. With an official labour market characterised by long working hours and rigid working-time schedules outside the public sector, and scarce support for childcare costs (as described in the previous section) staying in the labour market may also prove problematic. In these circumstances, the work–family combination becomes strongly dependent on educational level, availability of informal help, type of contract and sector, and employment opportunities in the area where the woman lives. Some women have resorted to the strategy of anticipating the problem of motherhood by seeking to gain access to protected sectors with more family-friendly arrangements. This is particularly the case of the public sector and of highly educated women. Indeed, as discussed in Chapter Two, the public sector offers a package of working conditions that substantially reduces the monetary and non-monetary costs of reconciliation and is particularly attractive in a context of weak universal reconciliation policies and employment opportunities.[13] Other women are able to combine work and family responsibilities because of their positions as family helpers in small family firms or as homeworkers in industrial districts. Compared with self-employed professionals, private employees or atypical workers, these women work long hours but they enjoy greater flexibility in scheduling their working time over the day and the week (Bettio and Villa, 1996; Esping Andersen and Regini, 2000; Del Boca, 2002).

As in many European countries, the flexibilisation introduced in Italy has mainly catered to the needs of employers, without a parallel reform of social rights or the introduction of 'employee-friendly flexibility'. Only in 2000, with the same law that reformed parental leave schemes, did employee lifecourse needs begin to be addressed. By providing economic incentives, the law encouraged employers to implement family-friendly policies such as, for example, flexitime for working fathers and mothers, temporary part-time work and 'hours banks'. Moreover, in the same period, as we have seen, further laws expanded and improved the regulation of part-time work, permitting various forms of part-time work (vertical, horizontal, mixed) and granting greater flexibility for both employers (they were allowed to ask part-timers to work overtime and change their working time schedules) and for employees (they were able to shift between full-time and part-time work over the lifecourse) (Bettio and Villa, 1996; Saraceno, 2003a). As Table A4 in the Appendix illustrates, the result at the beginning of the 2000s was that Italian mothers and fathers were able to take leave or reduce their working hours for family reasons, enjoy a certain amount of freedom in scheduling their working time and receive extra-statutory maternity benefits from employers. However, to date, limited use has been made of these 'employee-friendly flexibility' measures; and the provision by firms of childcare, flexitime and voluntary part-time work has been low.

Britain

The neoliberal ideology that has shaped the British residualist welfare state has also given rise to a highly deregulated labour market. Compared to those of other European countries, the British labour market has always been relatively unregulated. For example, there have never been any general laws forbidding Sunday work, specifying annual holiday entitlement, or maximum daily work hours. Nor has part-time work ever been prohibited, either by statute law or by collective bargaining, so that it developed much earlier than in the rest of Europe. However, it was in the 1980s, when the Conservatives came to power, that the deregulation and deinstitutionalisation of the labour market was forcefully pursued. The purpose, the Conservatives argued, was to reduce unemployment and welfare dependency and increase productivity and growth. The process consisted in a shift from a collective bargaining system within the so-called 'voluntarist' framework to a strong legal framework, which restricted trades union action, individualised employment relations and, in turn, eroded employment rights and protections (Walker, 1988; Crouch, 1990; Dickens and Hall, 1995).[14]

This deregulation and liberalisation of the labour market has particularly concerned part-time work for fewer than 16 hours per week, casual work and temporary work, all of which was seen as a means to give employers the flexibility necessary to improve labour market performance. As already noted, part-time work in the UK was already relatively unregulated before the 1980s, and it was used as a flexible form of employment. However, the number of people working fewer than 16 hours with low protection and low pay greatly increased in the 1980s and 1990s. Since entitlement to most employment rights required part-time workers to work 20 hours per week and to have had at least two years of continuous employment, or 12 hours after five years, their precariousness increased. Also more precarious were the jobs of women working in small firms, who lost their right to reinstatement after maternity leave (Deakin and Wilkinson, 1991; Bruegel and Perrons, 1998).

Although employer-friendly flexibility increased during the 1980s and 1990s, employee-friendly flexibility remained meagre. The Conservatives viewed employment policies for families as imposing an unacceptable burden on employers, which were instead encouraged to reach private arrangements with workers with children. In turn, there was no statutory entitlement in Britain to flexible working hours or to a reduction in working hours for family reasons. Nor, until recently, were there provisions on leave for family reasons, such as a child's illness or problems with childcare arrangements. Although encouraged to do so, few employers did more than introduce part-time working arrangements. Other family-friendly practices (such as flexitime, annual hours, term-time working, jobsharing, childcare services and career break schemes) tended to be concentrated in certain industries, such as the public sector, where trades unions were relatively strong. They were also promoted in large private corporations, but only for a limited range of staff, typically for women in higher-level, white-collar and professional occupations (McRae, 1991; Ringen, 1997).

Since the advent of New Labour, some forms of family-friendly flexibility have been introduced. As summarised in Table A4 in the Appendix, both mothers and fathers are now entitled to take time off for emergency family reasons or to request flexible hours. As regards the latter right, this allows both parents of a child aged under six to request the employer, for example, for a switch to part-time work or to work from home for one or more days a week. The right has, however, two main shortcomings. First, it grants the employee the right to ask, but it does not imply an automatic right to obtain what is requested. The discretion left to employers reduces the potential for change: a sympathetic employer was previously likely to grant this right even before it was statutorily provided for, while an unsympathetic employer was encouraged but not forced to do so. Second, employers continue to assume that mothers, rather than fathers, have better grounds for requesting family-friendly working arrangements. Indeed, data show that more women than men take advantage of this new right (Palmer, 2004). Since the early 2000s, the work–family arrangements provided for by firms have also slightly increased. By contrast, normal working-time schedules are still long, reducing the time to care available to working parents. Britain, indeed, has negotiated an opt-out from the European Union Working Time Directive, which still allows British employees to work longer than a 48-hour week.

As many studies have shown (Deakin and Wilkinson, 1991; Barrell, 1994; Cousins, 1994; Bruegel and Perrons, 1998; Davies and Joshi, 2001, 2002), the outcomes of deregulation in the 1980s and 1990s have been unsatisfactory. While the Thatcher reforms succeeded in reducing union power and increasing the incentives to work, they did not improve – as was claimed would happen – the response of real wages to unemployment, nor did they significantly ease the transition out of unemployment, especially for men. In fact, those policies did not create jobs for the unemployed; rather, women married to men already in employment took up the vast majority of part-time jobs. The partners of the unemployed, or the unemployed themselves, were prevented from taking these low-paid jobs by loss of benefits (as discussed earlier). Moreover, the Thatcher reforms were accompanied by growing wage polarisation and, in turn, by an expansion in the numbers of the working poor. Since a large part of the secondary labour market in Britain relies on the exploitation of the woman's position in the family, by expanding the low-wage unregulated secondary sector, the Conservative governments penalised women especially. As discussed in Chapter Two, in the post-war decades, the British labour market was already segmented according to the gender division and the part-time/full-time divide. The Conservative's deregulatory shift to very short hours, reduced pay and security, and limited fringe benefits further reinforced the use of women as secondary workers. Together with their non-intervention in family and employment policies, the Conservatives also increased divisions among women: between full-time and part-time workers, between workers in union-regulated employment and those in unregulated employment, between highly and poorly educated women.[15]

Gender-role attitudes and the domestic division of labour

On considering young people and their parents or grandparents, it is indubitable that in all the advanced countries, attitudes to the family, gender roles and women's employment have markedly changed. Traditional sexual constraints and the associated moral norms on premarital sex, extra-marital sex and homosexuality have declined. Acceptance of family diversity and of women's labour force participation has instead increased. Yet support for women's employment is often still conditional on the stage in the family lifecourse, and it reflects concerns about the well-being of children and assumptions about the centrality of the maternal role. While acknowledging the right of women to paid work in general, many commentators still believe that the mothers of young children should reduce their labour force participation. Some believe that this reduction should also continue as the children grow older. These attitudes are stronger in some countries than in others, and in some segments of the population than in others. There are also differences within and across countries in the timing and degree of attitudinal change from the 1960s to the 1990s.

Comparative research based on the International Social Survey Programme shows that there is a greater similarity among countries on gender ideology statements than on those concerning maternal employment and its consequences for children. In 1994, nearly half of Italians and 60% of Britons rejected the traditional gendered division of labour. However, Italians, like Germans and Austrians, were much less likely (28%) to reject the statement that family life in general, and children in particular, suffer when women work, whereas the percentage for Britain was fully 50% and close to Sweden's (Scott et al, 1996). Also, the approval of maternal employment differs greatly between the two countries. As evidenced by Figure 3.5, there is a high level of agreement in Britain that married women without children or with grown-up children should work full time, but the level drops markedly when children are young. In Europe, Britain exhibits the widest gap in attitudes according to the age of the child. This gap parallels, on the one hand, the typical pattern of women's participation over family formation, and on the other, the scant public support given to preschool childcare and the wide availability of part-time work, which suggests, as discussed in Chapter Two, that attitudes, institutions and behaviours are closely intertwined. The gap also reflects norms on children's needs, on the goodness of the mother–child relationship, and on the quality of and trust in out-of-home care. Indeed, informal provisions are the most preferred type of childcare reported by British mothers and fathers (La Valle et al, 2002). As argued by Lewis (2003), these preferences have long been reinforced by psychosocial theories on the quality of the mother–child relationship and on the damaging effect of institutionalised childcare.

Figure 3.5: Attitudes towards women's employment in Italy, Britain and other selected European countries (early 1990s)

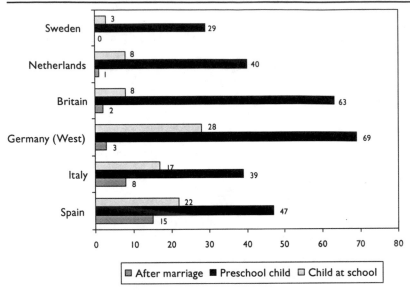

Notes: data refer to percentages in the population who agree that married women should stay at home in different situations ('after marriage, before having children'; 'when the child is 0-5', 'when child is in school age').
Source: Treas and Widmer (2000, table 1)

In Italy, by contrast, the approval of women's involvement in paid work when they have young children does not significantly differ from the approval when children are older. The gap is 22 absolute percentage points, which is similar to Spain and Sweden, whereas it is 55 percentage points in Britain and 41 in Germany. Compared to Britons, the finding that Italians express a more favourable attitude to maternal employment when children are young might come as a surprise. As was seen earlier in this chapter, most Italians believe that family care is the best solution for very young children, too. In addition, Italy has a much lower percentage of women in (official) employment and a higher percentage of people endorsing the view that maternal employment can be harmful for young children. A six-country study on attitudes towards the centrality of children found that Italians were the most likely to value children, while the Dutch were the least likely, with the British falling in between, like Germans and the Irish. This inter-country variation is not merely compositional. It also holds after controlling for gender, gender ideology, religion, socioeconomic status, employment status and family structure (Jones and Brayfield, 1997). The same non-compositional explanation applies to attitudes to women's labour force participation.

The reason for the greater approval expressed by Italians towards the employment of mothers with preschool children must be looked for elsewhere. As discussed in Chapter Two, preferences are endogenous to institutions. Hence, one possible explanation might be the different degrees of childcare support. A generous provision of leaves and nursery schools, coupled with the strong 'extended' family that compensates for institutional shortcomings, make conciliation between work and family responsibilities relatively easier. In turn, it mitigates the perception that the continuous employment of the mother may harm children, and it defines the mother's involvement in paid work as acceptable. Yet, at the aggregate level, many Italians approve of the employment of mothers with young children, but many of them think that the family and children suffer because of it. It is more likely that the reason lies in the fact that in Italy, unlike in Britain, the population is sharply divided. As Treas and Widmer (2000) show, this divide indeed exists and largely follows gender lines. Women everywhere tend to be more positive than men towards married women working. However, across Europe, it is only in Italy (and Ireland) that gender differences are so wide that one may speak of different 'attitudinal regimes'. Taking men and women together, Italy falls within the same cluster as Britain, Austria, Northern Ireland and West Germany. People in this cluster, labelled 'family accommodating', believe that mothers with small children should stay at home, while mothers of school-age children should only work part time. Yet if one considers only women's attitudes, Italy is more 'work oriented' and more similar to the Netherlands, Norway and Sweden. If only men's attitudes are considered, Italy belongs to the 'motherhood-centered' cluster, together with Spain. Interestingly, if Italian women's attitudes towards the employment of married women were as traditional as those of Italian men, Italy would also be 'motherhood centred', like the other Southern European countries.

This gender gap in attitudes seems to suggest that, in Italy, women's preferences have started to change despite a negative normative climate. However, accounting for this change requires one to also disaggregate within the male and female universe. As many studies show, in almost all countries, women's labour market experience, educational level and birth cohort are important predictors of their work attitudes: women who work (or husbands of working wives), highly educated people and young cohorts have more egalitarian gender attitudes (Alwin et al, 1992; Treas and Widmer, 2000). However, and not surprisingly, the effect of these factors varies across countries and between men and women. Italy is the only European country where both men and women's work attitudes are relatively stable over time. As Scott (1999a) shows, once education and women's labour force involvement are controlled for, in Italy more recent cohorts do not show a significantly higher propensity to endorse work by mothers. In Britain, the cohort influence persists for both men and women in attitudes towards the employment of mothers with preschool children, but it disappears for mothers with a school-age child. In Italy, gender-role attitudes in general also seem to have changed little across cohorts. On comparing the mean scores of the two age groups 16-45 and 46-98 across five ISSP items, Künzler (2002) shows that Italy has one of the narrowest gaps (2.78), together with Belgium and Luxembourg, whereas Britain has one of the widest (3.31).

Hence, attitudinal change has been almost entirely 'compositional' in Italy. The change has come about through increasing investment in education and labour market careers by younger women. Yet this has not given rise to a general attitudinal shift. That is to say, approval of work by married women has increased because more women and men have the individual characteristics that have always implied less traditional attitudes. Interestingly, for Italian women, education is the strongest predictor of both attitudes and actual labour market supply.

As Figure 3.6 illustrates, Italy is relatively traditional not only in attitudes but also in its gendered division of domestic labour. Italian men, like Spanish men, are those who spend least time on unpaid work; Swedish men are the most cooperative, while British, French and German men lie in the middle. Italy also has the highest ratio between women and men in the absolute time devoted to domestic work (Künzler, 2002). Moreover, from the 1960s to the 1990s, Italy exhibited one of the smallest changes in the gendered division of unpaid work (Bimbi, 1995; Künzler, 2002). Also in Britain women have always done the great majority of domestic and childcare work. In the mid-1990s, in those (few) households where men and women were employed for roughly the same number of hours, women on average worked in the house nine hours per week more than men (Gershuny, 1997). Yet,

Figure 3.6: Gender division of labour: time spent on paid and unpaid work for working men and women aged 20-74 in Italy, Britain and other selected European countries (late 1990s)

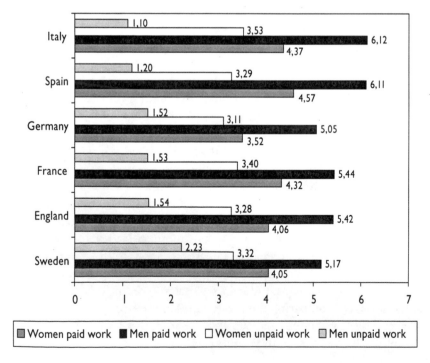

Notes: Median durations in hours and minutes; data for time on paid work also include time on education. For Britain only data for England are available.
Source: Romano and Sabbadini (2007, table 5 and 6)

unlike in Italy, in the same period, men's contribution to unpaid domestic and care work increased (Künzler, 2002), although to a much lesser extent compared to attitudes. As Scott (1999a, 1999b) suggests, this discrepancy between practice and ideology reflects an age of 'political correctness' where men's opposition to gender egalitarianism can be more easily expressed in terms of worries about children than in those of the needs of husbands and the duties of women. Moreover, this discrepancy is paralleled in the widespread divergence between wives' and husbands' statements: women tend to report that their husbands spend less time in the house than husbands say that they do.

Conclusion

Italy and Britain differ greatly in their economic, normative and institutional systems and in how they have changed since the 1950s until the 2000s. In Italy, where both industrialisation and tertiarisation occurred late and with great regional variation, labour demand began to shift in favour of women only in the early 1970s, but it did not expand sufficiently to absorb the increasing supply, especially in the South. By contrast, Britain experienced a much earlier and more intense trend towards a service economy and, in particular, towards part-time service jobs for women. Indeed, part-time work – never prohibited and restricted by statute law and collective bargaining – has been increasing since the 1940s and 1950s, and it has represented the main channel for women's integration into the labour market. Britain also experienced a much earlier and more intense family and gender change. Here, rates of cohabitation, divorce and procreation outside marriage have risen significantly, and approval of married women's employment has generally increased across cohorts. Also on the increase is the time devoted by men to domestic and care work, although not to the level of Scandinavian men. By contrast, in Italy, where attitudinal change is almost entirely compositional – being driven by expansion in education – men's share of unpaid work remains among the lowest in Europe, and the standard nuclear family, with its distinctive mode of extended functioning through inter-generational and kin solidarity, is still predominant and is still a central and relatively stable institution.

Britain has moved away from a relatively regulated, unionised labour market and pro-universal Beveridge welfare state, based on the assumptions of a 'stable male-breadwinner/female-carer' family model and of full (male) employment, to being a 'liberal' country with a presumably gender-neutral emphasis on individual and family autonomy and on market efficiency. That is to say, it has developed a residualist welfare state both in income support and services and a strong deregulated economy. In particular, the Conservative policies of the 1980s and 1990s removed institutional support for the wage floor and weakened employment and social security protections (including maternity leaves) for short part-timers and non-continuous employees, without improving in parallel the poor provision of childcare services typical of the post-war Beveridgean decades. In so doing, the Conservatives transferred to private arrangements, and ultimately to women, full responsibility for childcare, and they stimulated the growth of the low-wage unregulated secondary labour market, which relies largely on married women and mothers. The well-known outcome has been increasing polarisation: between dual-earner and one-earner families, between highly and low-educated workers, and between full-time and part-time women. With the decline of the 'traditional male breadwinner/female carer' into 'a male breadwinner/female part-time earner', rather than a 'dual-earner/state or marketised care' or a 'dual-earner/dual carer' society, gender inequities also remain high. The reforms introduced under New Labour – in order to promote an adult-worker family model, which includes expansion of leaves and of employee-friendly flexibility, support to childcare costs, and incentives for the welfare-to-work transition – have overall contributed to reducing poverty traps, welfare dependency and women's exits from paid work. Yet, because these reforms have focused on stimulating demand rather than supply, on promoting childcare in disadvantaged areas, and on assisting the cost of childcare on the basis of parents' income and employment status, they have not greatly reduced divisions between better-off highly educated mothers and poor ones. Moreover, the refusal to reduce normal working hours schedules, as the European Working Time Directive prescribed, has made it difficult for both mothers and fathers to find time for care.

In Italy, by contrast, the institutional context of the 1980s and 1990s changed little from the post-war Fordist arrangements. It still comprised a highly regulated labour market aimed at protecting core (mainly male) breadwinners via strong employment protection and relatively generous social insurance schemes (including maternity and parental leaves) in big firms and the public sector, and de facto flexibility achieved through small firms, self-employed people and the informal economy. Here women have been integrated into the labour market through full-time employment, part-time de facto in the public sector, and informal employment – this last being the functional equivalent of legalised deregulated part-time work in Britain. The 'partial and selective' deregulation pursued since the end of the 1990s has been to the detriment of 'outsiders', namely young people and women, for whom entry and permanence in the labour market has increasingly occurred with atypical unprotected jobs. At the beginning of the 2000s, leave facilities, in terms of duration, flexibility and fathers' individual rights, were improved and some measures of 'employee- and parent-friendly flexibility' were promoted. Overall, these reforms have expanded women's opportunities to work over family formation. Yet the low level of income replacement and the still prevailing traditional gender and childcare norms have dampened their effect. Moreover, the other pillars of a good reconciliation package as discussed in Chapter Two – namely income and services – have remained poor. As a result, in the 1980s and 1990s Italy still had a familistic welfare state with scant provision of both care services and income support for child families and low-wage or unemployed workers. The assumption and the practice was, and still is, that kinship and inter-generational solidarity will compensate for disparities between 'protected' and 'unprotected' segments of the labour market, and for the inadequacies of social services. Amid a persisting traditional gender order, where norms and policies give little support for work–family conciliation and a 'dual-earner/dual-carer model', this caring role, which ultimately falls on women, has hindered the labour supply of young wives or of their mothers. It has also hindered the demand for female labour because it inhibits the 'externalisation' of female-intensive goods and services.

What, one may ask, is the impact of these contextual features on the lifetime employment patterns of women who have entered the labour market and built their families in different decades? What are the differences between Italy and Britain? The next chapter, after a description of data, method and variables, links the theoretical debate on the effects on women's employment patterns outlined in Chapter Two with the description given in this chapter of the features of the British and Italian economic, institutional and normative contexts. This will enable the formulation of hypotheses on the impact of these contextual features on changes across cohorts in the incidence, timing and correlates of women's labour market transitions.

Notes

[1] Note that here and in the following pages I shall use 'the UK' instead of 'Britain' because, unlike in all other tables and figures in the book, Figures 3.1, 3.2 and 3.3 and Tables 3.1, 3.2 and 3.3 are drawn from Eurostat or OECD databases where the reference is to the UK as a whole.

[2] In October 1992, ISTAT, the Italian National Statistics Office, which furnishes data to the Organisation for Economic Co-operation and Development (OECD), changed the definition of unemployment to meet the standard international criteria. While previously defined as 'unemployed' was a person who had been actively searching for a job in the previous six months, in 1992 the limit for 'active search' was reduced to 30 days. As Bettio and Villa (1996) note, this statistical redefinition has penalised the records of the most vulnerable segments of the labour force: first jobseekers, women, and the unemployed in the South of Italy. Owing to their (perceived) difficulty in finding jobs, these types of workers may suffer most from discouragement, consequently reducing or giving up their 'active' job search.

[3] Capturing informal employment is difficult, and this may hinder the fully reliable measurement of the total female employment rate. As Bettio (1988a, 1988b) emphasises, in Italy the degree of underestimation of women's total involvement in the labour market has probably remained largely constant over the decades, because the weight of the informal economy has not changed substantially over time. In fact, the decline in agriculture and other traditional family-based activities, where women's work was largely unrecorded, has been offset by the post-war development of a modern informal sector comprising, for example, industry-related home work and work in specialised craft-based family enterprises, or seasonal work in tourism.

[4] The other four clusters they find are these: the Scandinavian countries, with high levels of provisions in terms of services, time and income both for children and older people; the UK and the Netherlands, where care is largely privatised for children but not for older people; Austria and Germany, with large reliance on informal care but with generous financial support; finally, Belgium and France, where formal care and financial transfers are well developed for both children and older people, but less so are time-off arrangements.

[5] Family Credit is the means-tested benefit for 'working poor' families with children introduced in 1977 to replace Family Income Supplement with a reduction of the minimum number of working hours required to gain access to it (both couples and single parents had to work at least 24 hours per week, instead of the previous threshold of 30 for couple parents). The aim was to subsidise low-wage sectors of the economy without broader intervention on wage settings, as liberal policies prescribe, and to maintain work incentives for families with children.

[6] Also, unemployed women or wives of unemployed men risked poverty traps. Because the eligibility criteria for Unemployment Benefit were very strict, the benefit was paid at a flat rate, and its duration was no more than 52 weeks, many families ended up on Income Support, whose amount and income threshold were low and for which a second earning was discouraged.

[7] Although policy in support of maternal employment was not improved during the 1980s and 1990s, taxation policy did move in a pro-employment direction for women. In 1988, the government introduced the separate taxation of husband and wife within a system of non-transferable personal exemptions that penalised single-earner couples. It also eliminated other tax penalties associated with marriage, the possibility for unmarried couples to claim two additional personal allowances, whereas the additional transferable exemption for married couples could be claimed only once (see Table A3 in the Appendix).

[8] The results of the four pilot projects on nursery vouchers were widely criticised, and the policy was soon abandoned.

[9] More specifically, *One Parent Benefit* and the *Lone-Parent Income Support Premium* were abolished in 1999. Instead, the government introduced a general *National Minimum Wage* for the first time in Britain, and a *Working Families' Tax Credit* to replace Family Credit. Compared to Family Credit, the rates of payment were increased and, in order to reduce the 'poverty trap', the withdrawal rate against new income was reduced from 70% to 55%, and the youngest-child age limit was lowered to eight years old. Child Maintenance Payments were now ignored in the income test, and *Childcare Tax Credit* was altered so as to also assist working families with moderate incomes. Moreover, the Child Benefit level for those on social assistance was raised, and leave and childcare policies were generally improved (Kamerman and Kahn, 2001; Marsh, 2001).

[10] The British childcare system comprises a wide range of services. For children aged 0 to four, there are local authority day nurseries, with income-related fees and priority to poor children; private or voluntary day nurseries; and childminders (registered or unregistered). For children aged three to four, there are local authority nursery schools and classes, free but open for only two to three hours during term-time; and playgroups run by parents and voluntary groups, which are low-cost but open only a few hours for two to three days per week. Finally, for four-year old children, there are reception classes within primary school, from 9am to 3 30pm (Kilkey, 2000; Maucher and Bahle, 2000; Lewis, 2003).

[11] There is a large share among British women of not only part-time jobs but also jobs entailing evening and night work when children can be left with their fathers.

[12] In 1988, authorisation was given for the recruitment of part-time workers in public sector services and agencies; a law of 1991 introduced phased retirement with transition from full-time to part-time work before full retirement, with the pension still based on full-time pay; in 1994, and again in 1997, incentives for employers were introduced in the form of a reduction in social security contributions.

[13] This package includes access to jobs through educational credentials and seniority as the main criteria for career and wage progression; shorter and more flexibly scheduled hours of work; and more generous maternity and parental leaves without the penalties on re-entry relatively widespread in the private sector. In fact, some studies report that in the private sector, and especially in the North, employers often ask women about their childbearing intentions during the hiring procedure, and sometimes force them to sign an undated resignation letter for use when they fall pregnant or return from maternity leave (ISTAT, 2000; Ministero del Lavoro e della Previdenza Sociale, 2000).

[14] For example, the 1980 Employment Act further reduced protection against unfair dismissal by introducing a trial period of two years for workers in small firms. Compulsory trades union consultation on redundancy was abolished and tribunal proceedings were made more difficult. The 1993 Trade Union Reform and Employment Rights Act slightly improved pregnancy and maternity rights, in compliance with the requirements of EC law, but in areas not covered by EC requirements, deregulation and deinstitutionalisation were further reinforced. For example, wage councils, which regulated wages in many low-paid industries, were abolished and wage bargaining was decentralised to the company level. The enforcement of minimum wages and of health and safety legislation was also reduced.

[15] During the post-war decades, it was mainly in the public sector, where union organisation was quite active, where women enjoyed better terms and conditions in service and manual occupations. However, in the late 1980s, following the Conservatives' trades union legislation and policy of privatising public sector services, the distinction between the public and private sector started to diminish.

FOUR

Method, data and hypotheses

Introduction

As mentioned earlier, in this book I use two longitudinal datasets and event-history methods in order to capture and explain changes across cohorts in Italian and British women's lifetime employment patterns. The analysis is conducted within an institutional rational-action framework, which recognises different forms of rationality, the role and heterogeneity of both preferences and constraints, and their complex interrelations. This chapter provides a description of the methods, datasets, variables and techniques used for the empirical analyses described and discussed in the rest of the book. More precisely, it starts, in the next section, by illustrating the nature and advantages of a lifecourse perspective and of longitudinal data compared to cross-sectional data. The section also briefly describes the different longitudinal designs in order to show when and why an event-oriented observation design is more suitable. The following section focuses on the specific method used in my empirical analyses, namely discrete-time logit models. It then addresses the problems of sample selection and unobserved heterogeneity and discusses how they are dealt with in my models. The next section then describes the two datasets, the sample of women used and the variables chosen. The final section links the previous two chapters with the current chapter and the following two by formulating hypotheses on what has changed across cohorts in the types and correlates of women's work histories in Italy and Britain.

The role of time: longitudinal versus cross-sectional analyses

The lifecourse perspective

At a very intuitive level, the concept of change comprises a temporal dimension. Thus, any data that track the same subjects over time and measure the relevant micro and macro variables at different time points should 'by definition' afford better understanding of social change than cross-sectional data. As has been well conceptualised by Elder (1975, 1985), a pioneer of lifecourse theory and research, individual biographies and social phenomena are time dependent in different ways. First, they develop across a person's lifetime, that is, through the chronological process of growing up and ageing. Second, they take shape within a specific generation and a specific historical period, with its cultural, economic and institutional arrangements. Third, they are influenced by normative definitions of the 'proper' timing, sequence and interrelating of the various experiences that mark the lifecourse. Indeed, as noted by Neugarten (1968), 'natural' periods of life, such as childhood, adolescence and old age, are socially constructed. They influence positions, role and rights in society and are based on culturally shared age definitions. As Giele and Elder put it (1998, p 22), the lifecourse is 'a sequence of socially defined events and roles that the individual enacts over time'. A lifecourse perspective therefore directs attention to the connection between individual lives and the socioeconomic and cultural contexts in which those lives unfold. In other words, it connects the micro with the macro: an individual's own developmental path is embedded in and transformed by conditions and events occurring during the historical period and the geographical location in which that person lives. As has been well argued by German scholars (Mayer and Schöpflin, 1989; Mayer, 2009), and as discussed in Chapters One and Two, the welfare state plays a crucial role in structuring individual lifecourses, defining entry and exit doors, delivering resources, establishing the degree and type of decommodification and defamilialisation and, in turn, shaping (gender, class, cohort) inequalities.

The issue of stratification is central to lifecourse theory and research. Drawing on the sociology of age stratification (Riley et al, 1972) and integrating it with the 'classical' literature on social stratification (Erikson and Goldthorpe, 1992, Blossfeld and Shavit, 1993), many lifecourse scholars have overcome the fallacy of cohort centrism and addressed heterogeneity and diversity in structures and processes. Although generations and cohorts have shared histories, they are not homogenous collections of people: they differ in such influential dimensions as gender, social class, race, family structure and so on. In so far as they have access to and command different (private and public) resources, they also differ in how they adapt to lifecourse developments or period changes.

Elder (1985, 1998) defined the lifecourse as a bundle of short-term transitions nested in long-term trajectories giving each transition and each trajectory its shape and meaning. Since then, the issues of multiplicity and interdependence have become central to the lifecourse perspective. Lives are interdependent and reciprocally connected on several levels. First, the various dimensions of a person's life are intertwined – the employment career with the educational career, the marital and fertility career, or the geographical career. Second, 'own' lives are linked with the lives of 'others', those with whom we interact everyday, *in primis* partner, parents or relatives. Societal and individual experiences are linked through the family and its network of shared relations. Third, subjective and objective dimensions interact to define the timing, sequences and outcomes of individual transitions and trajectories. According to lifecourse scholars, individuals are active agents who not only mediate the effect of social structure but also make decisions and set goals that shape that social structure. As actors build their lifecourses, they also construct their identities and moral careers (Olagnero and Saraceno, 1993). In rational choice terms, as outlined in Chapter Two, individuals construct their lifecourses through the choices and actions that they undertake on the basis of their orientations and definitions, and within the opportunities and constraints of history and social circumstances.

Therefore, as Kohli (2001) and Saraceno (2001) emphasise, because the lifecourse approach focuses on processes and dynamics that develop over time, on the micro–macro link and on the interplay between objective and subjective dimensions, it enables the integration of three lines of inquiry, which have traditionally been pursued separately: one that examines behaviours and life events; one that analyses institutional and cultural models; and one that focuses on how individuals define reality and themselves and build their identities. In methodological terms, it invites the integration of qualitative and quantitative research instruments, or at least, of the literature deriving from both. In what follows, only quantitative longitudinal data will be used. Yet, as also evident in the theoretical chapter, narratives on changing transitions and trajectories will be drawn from both qualitative and quantitative studies.

Time and causality

As many authors have argued, longitudinal data, and more precisely quantitative longitudinal data, are particularly suited to furnishing causal explanations because of the central role that time performs in structuring them. It is widely accepted that three criteria are necessary (if not sufficient) to establish a causal connection. First, the variables in questions must co-vary. Second, the relation must not be spurious but must persist even when other variables are controlled. Third, there must be a temporal order between the cause and the effect (Menard, 1991; Corbetta, 1999). By recording all the changes in the dependent and independent variables and their timing, longitudinal models allow the testing not only of covariance and spuriousness, but also of a time order and interval between the supposed cause and effect. They also make it possible to determine whether and how the causal connection changes over time as the process develops (Blossfeld and Rower, 1995). On modelling variables as dynamic processes over the lifecourse, therefore, longitudinal data offer a statistical representation closer to the reality than that yielded by ordinary regression models.

Not only is it impossible to use cross-sectional data to measure the timing of the supposed cause and effect and to distinguish between cohort, age and period effects, such data are less suited to drawing causal inferences because they do not usually provide information on either the previous history of the units of analysis or the time that units spend in different states. This means that they do not permit proper control for selectivity and duration dependency (Blossfeld and Rower, 1995). As Mayer (1991) argues, the lifecourses of individuals involve complex and cumulative time-related layers of selectivity. That is to say, there is a strong likelihood that only individuals with specific histories have entered a specific state. These histories in different domains of life cannot be captured by static measures. Furthermore, compared to longitudinal studies, cross-sectional analyses are less powerful in the estimation of biases from missing data and in the tools for correcting them. Indeed, when data from previous points in time are available, it is possible to make a better assessment of the characteristics of non-respondents or lost units (Blossfeld and Rower, 1995).

Although the criterion of time order and interval is necessary to establish causality, it raises some problems. As Marini and Singer (1988, p 377) write:

> Because human beings can anticipate and plan the future, much human behaviour follows from goals, intentions, and motives; i.e, it is teleologically determined. As a result, causal priority is established in the mind in a way that is not reflected in the temporal sequence of behaviour or even in the temporal sequence of the formation of behavioural intentions.

For example, in a study on the effect of first pregnancy/first childbirth on the rate of entry into first marriage for couples living in consensual unions in Germany, Blossfeld et al (1993) find that as soon as women get pregnant, the rate of entry into marriage increases strongly. But it could be that the causation is the other way around; that is, it could be that a woman decides to marry and, on the basis of that decision, gets pregnant and finally marries as planned. The event 'pregnancy' occurs before the event 'marriage' but is not its cause. Yet, as argued by Blossfeld et al (1999), this possibility does not alter the role of time order in causal reasoning. Rather, it underlines the importance of the type of data used to test causality. These data should also include information on attitudes, preferences, intentions and expectations.

According to many authors, in particular those who endorse the view of causality as an actor-centred generative process and not as robust statistical dependence, or as the effect of consequential manipulation (Goldthorpe, 2000, 2001; Barbera, 2004), the time criterion is not in itself a test of causality. For causality is a property of the theory, not of the data: it cannot simply and directly be inferred by empirical analyses, regardless of whether or not they are based on randomised experiments, from complex research designs, or from advanced statistical models. To be sure, longitudinal data and, in particular, as we will see below, retrospective event-oriented data, yield richer time-related information and provide more appropriate techniques with which to make causal inferences. Yet, like any empirical source, they require theories for their interpretation.

The different longitudinal designs: virtues and vices of event-history data

'Longitudinal' is a very broad term that includes several types of methodologies and analytical techniques for the collection and analysis of data based on repeated measurements: retrospective event-oriented designs, repeated cross-sectional studies, prospective studies, and data from any combination of these (Menard, 1991; Ruspini, 2008). Among them, event-history data are often the most appropriate for describing patterns of change and drawing causal inferences. In fact, since the same units are measured neither repeatedly nor for multiple periods, repeated cross-sectional analyses can only show net changes, not the flow of individuals or any other units of analysis (Firebaugh, 1997; Ruspini, 2008). In prospective panels, the same subjects or units are observed at a series of discrete points in time, so that it is possible to investigate how particular outcomes are related to the earlier circumstances of the same individuals, to the changing set of opportunities and constraints, and to the generation they pertain to. However, prospective panels suffer from the problem of panel attrition and panel conditioning. Moreover, since information is gathered at predetermined survey discrete points, what has happened between the discrete points in time remains unknown. As a result, important events may be missed, so that partial or even misleading conclusions are drawn (Magnusson et al, 1991; Blossfeld and Rower, 1995; Ruspini, 2008).

These problems do not arise with retrospective panels. First, these are not sensitive to the length of the time between waves relative to the speed of the process (Coleman, 1981). Moreover, because they report the entire history, they can be used to capture the threefold role of time in causal explanation: that is, the time order between events, their temporal interval, and the temporal shape of the causal relation (Blossfeld and Rower, 1995). Event-history data also allow for the inclusion of information about past history, so that better control can be made for unobserved heterogeneity, duration dependency and sample selection.

Obviously, retrospective data also suffer from drawbacks. First, they are based only on survivors. If those who have not survived have systematic characteristics relative to the process under study, biases will arise. Second, there is a limit to the respondents' tolerance of the amount of data that can be collected at one time, and there may be distortions due to memory errors or to ex-post rationalisations. The likelihood of giving a wrong date (what, in technical terms, is called the 'telescoping effect') or of forgetting an event ('recall decay effect') is greater, the longer the time that has elapsed since that event, the less important the event for the respondent, and the shorter its duration.[1] Finally, as mentioned earlier, retrospective questions on motivations, attitudes and, generally, cognitive and affective dimensions are highly problematic. Respondents find it difficult to accurately recall the timing of changes in these states and their profiles, and they often engage in ex-post rationalisation: that is, they revise past events on the basis of their current attitudes, beliefs and situation. A desirable design would therefore be one that combines panel observations of beliefs, preferences and intentions with retrospective information on behavioural events since the last wave (Ruspini, 2008).

In order to combine the virtues of prospective panels with the strengths of event-history-oriented data, a mixed design employing a follow-up and a follow-back strategy is usually applied in modern panels – for example, the BHPS, the ILFI, the German Socio-Economic Panel and the Panel Study of Income Dynamics – where event histories are gathered retrospectively for the period before the panel started and between the successive panel waves. However information on attitudes and beliefs is either missing, as in the ILFI, or collected only at certain points in time, as in the BHPS. It is therefore not included in my models. In its absence, conclusions based on analyses that only rely on behavioural observations should be drawn with caution. Yet, as noted at the end of Chapter Two, the use of a lifecourse approach with a comparative design and within an institutional rational-action paradigm is my 'insurance' policy for the causal narratives proposed.

Method

Discrete-time event-history models

Event-history analysis is concerned with the patterns, timing and correlates of the occurrence of events and with the duration of episodes before such occurrence (Yamaguchi, 1991; Blossfeld and Rower, 1995). In particular, in order to describe the development of the process at any point in time, it models transition rates.[2] In technical terms, transition rates express the likelihood of the event occurring at time t, given that it did not occur before time t. There is a broad range of transition rate models, which differ in how they measure time (as discrete or continuous) and in their assumptions about the form of the time dependence of the process.

Here I shall use *discrete-time methods*. These are non-parametric models where the dependent variable is the conditional probability of the event in each discrete-time interval and where duration in the origin state can be introduced as a normal time-varying covariate and thus modelled in different ways (linearly, non-monotonically with a linear and quadratic term, or categorically through different dummies corresponding to various time lengths). The conditional probability as a function of time and a set of covariates can then be analysed using standard binary regression models, such as logistic or complementary log-log regressions. Discrete-time methods are appropriate when, as in my case, the concern is more with the effects of covariates than with the shape of the transition rate. Moreover, they are necessary when the measurement unit of time is relatively crude, such as a year, an individual's age, or a decade, but they are also attractive when the time unit is smaller, such as a month. There are various reasons for this 'attractiveness'. First, numerous events occur at discrete intervals. This is the case, for example, with regard to labour market changes in most countries: typically, people leave jobs at the end of the month and start new ones at the beginning of the month. Second, when dates are all measured in relatively small time units such as months, discrete-time models are good approximations of continuous-time models. In practice, time is always observed in discrete units, however small. When these discrete units are very small, relative to the rate of event occurrence, it is acceptable to treat time as if it were measured continuously. When the time units are larger, this treatment becomes problematic. However, a monthly time interval is so small relative to average durations that the conditional probability of making the transition is also very small. Although there is some loss of information because the exact time of the event is not known, this loss will usually make little difference in the estimated standard errors. Thus, the choice between discrete- and continuous-time methods should be decided on grounds of convenience. Discrete-time models are convenient because they allow the straightforward introduction of time-dependent covariates and they can be run using standard statistical packages. When the explanatory variables are all categorical (or can be treated as such), discrete-time models can be estimated with log-linear methods for the study of contingency tables. This, as is well known, allows the analysis of large samples at a very low cost. When explanatory variables are not all categorical, a logit model can be easily applied: that is, each individual event history is broken up in a set of month-observations in which the event either did or did not occur (and the various covariates either changed or did not). Then, all month-observations over all individuals are pooled and maximum-likelihood estimators for binary regression models can be calculated. In the case of repeated events, a multinomial logit can be used. The resulting estimators are true maximum-likelihood estimators of models that are exact analogues of those for continuous-time data (Allison, 1982, 1984; Yamaguchi, 1991).

Although quite flexible and easy to use, discrete-time methods have two major drawbacks. First, unlike in continuous-time models, the values of the coefficients depend on the length of the time. Thus, when comparing models across countries or cohorts it is important to make sure that the same time unit is adopted. Second, the assumption of independent observations behind maximum-likelihood estimates can be problematic in case of person-month files. In fact, when the variables included in the model do not exhaust all the sources of individual variation in the transition rate, as typically happens, it is assumed that the disturbance term ε_{it} and the vector of covariates X_{it} are independent for all i and t. But, for a given individual, ε_t will be almost certainly correlated with $\varepsilon_{t+1}, \varepsilon_{t+2}$ and so on. In other words, the unobserved heterogeneity will have some stability over time. As in ordinary least-square regression, dependence among observations leads to inefficient estimates. However, as noted by Allison (1982), continuous-time models also present the same problem, although it is somewhat less conspicuous. The problem therefore concerns more model specification than the type of method used. I shall return to this issue in the next section.

In this study I use *discrete-time transition rate models with the logistic link function*. The concept and measure of the transition rate is strictly connected to those of risk set and of *risk period*. When conceptualising the period of occurrence or non-occurrence of the event under investigation, one must decide and state 'when the clock starts'. As said in the introduction, previous research has been mainly cross-sectional; or if it has been longitudinal, it has looked at labour force transitions around childbirth, or it has restricted its analyses to single cohorts. By contrast, analysed here are women's employment dynamics over a long historical period, and for an important part of their working and reproductive lives. In more detail, *my clock starts when a woman has her first job experience, and it finishes at age 40, or at the time of the interviews with the youngest cohort.* The widening of the individual observational window makes it possible to depict overall work histories and also to capture exits and re-entries occurring at later ages. It also allows the study of repeated events and determination of whether the factors affecting women's first exit and re-entry are the same as those for the second exit and re-entry. In fact, a woman may enter and exit employment more than once in her adult lifecourse. However, as evident from Table 4.1 later in this chapter, in Italy a very small percentage of women experience more than one housework break. Thus, for comparative reasons, I shall not use multiple transition rate models.

So as to fit discrete-time logistic regressions, I have transformed the original data from the BHPS and ILFI into a *'person-month file'*,, where for each person there are as many observations as the number of months elapsing from first job until age 40 for the first three cohorts, and until age 30-40 for the last cohort. Consequently, the unit of analysis is the woman-month, and the *dependent variable* is the log-odds of the monthly conditional probability of making the transition over the observed lifecourse. More precisely, when the transition out of employment is studied, the dependent variable will be the conditional probability of leaving employment within a particular month, given that the woman has worked until the month before. For the opposite transition, the dependent variable will be the conditional probability of re-entering paid work, given that the woman has been a housewife until that time. In the case of Italy, since many women never start a labour market career, first entry into paid work is also modelled. However, because my interest is in participation decisions rather than in the duration of job search, the analysis is cross-sectional. More precisely, I investigate the probability of entering employment by using cross-sectional logit models and by distinguishing between women who have never worked and those who experience at least one job episode by age 35. The regressors comprise variables that are either time-constant (like cohort and characteristics of the father) or vary with time, in which case they are measured on completion of full-time education (level of education and region of residence).

For theoretical reasons, I do not use multistate or competing risk models, so that the occurrence of other events such as unemployment or return into full-time education is treated as censored observation. The focus, in fact, is the issue of work–family reconciliation. Moreover, as some preliminary checks have shown, women's unemployment spells before or after a withdrawal appear to be too rare (or at least too underreported) to allow meaningful analysis of the role of unemployment as a step out of or back into paid work. Its role is, instead, partly explored through covariates that capture labour market experience. This applies to the part-time/full-time distinction. As seen in the previous chapter, this distinction is important for the British labour market but less so for the Italian one. Furthermore, the BHPS records changes in time commitment only when they involve a change of employer. I have therefore preferred to consider the distinction between part-time and full-time jobs through a covariate rather than through analysis of separate or competing transitions.

Dealing with sample selection and unobserved heterogeneity

As just said, in this work I focus on a relatively long span of adult women's lifecourses, and on the behaviour of four different cohorts of women, who have entered the labour market and formed their families and careers in different decades. This has important advantages. First, the use of longitudinal data and the comparison across time and space allow better examination of the 'compositional versus non-compositional' nature of changes. In particular, it sheds light on how different normative and institutional contexts shape women's work choices and outcomes in the labour market. Second, the relatively long observational window chosen also has the advantage of capturing not only single transitions but also entire trajectories. However, two problems arise when the observational window is widened to this extent. First, comparison across cohorts is limited by the shorter time of observation for the last cohort. Indeed, given the date of the last interview (2005), the youngest birth cohort (1956-74) can be observed at most until age 40-30, while the first and second cohort can both be observed until age 40. This means that, in the case of the youngest cohort, exits and re-entries into paid work are not observed simply because they happen later. While in the regression analysis this problem of the shortest time of observation for the last cohort is overcome by controlling for age and duration in current labour market status, it persists in the descriptive figures on the career as a whole. For this reason, in Chapters Five and Six I look at types of individual work history only until age 35, and I exclude, from the last cohort, women born after 1970.

The widening of the observational window also allows for better inclusion of information about past history. This is very important for dealing with the problem of mis-specification that occurs if the initial conditions on entry into the episode are not taken into account; or in other words, in dealing with the problem of highly sample-selective processes. As suggested by Heckman and Borjas (1980), it is important to take account of different types of history dependency: duration dependency, that is, the time spent in the current origin state; lagged duration dependency, that is, lengths of time previously spent in the same state; and occurrence dependency, that is, number of times previously spent in same state. One may also look at the length of time elapsing between the last two events, or specify more complex kinds of dependency, although, as Allison (1982, 1984) maintains, in most cases relatively simple models should suffice.

However, even when appropriate information on previous history is controlled for, and many important women's individual and family characteristics are measured, there is no guarantee that relevant heterogeneity has not been left out. An additional strategy with which to tackle the problem of sample selection and unobserved heterogeneity is to control for it statistically through the joint estimation of two equations: the usual regression equation on the probability of the outcome $Y=1$ under study, and a selection equation on the probability of observing Y at all. As is well known, this strategy was first introduced by Heckman (1976, 1979) in the context of ordinary least squares (OLS) and probit regressions and was then extended to the analysis of dynamic data (Flinn and Heckman 1982a, 1982b).[3] A common solution is to use instrumental variables: that is, to find variables that strongly affect the chance for observation (women's decision to work) but not the outcome under study (their wage). If good instruments cannot be found, the solution is the joint estimation of two equations (selection and regression) and the modelling of their correlation. In fact, allowing the error terms of the two equations to be correlated means assuming that there are unobserved factors affecting both the probability of observing the outcome (women's choice to work) and the level of the outcome (wages). The importance and direction of these potential unobserved effects are captured by means of a parameter (Rho). If Rho is not significantly different from 0, this means that the coefficients obtained with the Heckman selection model are the same as those that would derive from the estimation of separate models. If Rho is instead significantly different from 0, the implication is that sample selection is not well captured in the specification of the regression equation and, if not controlled for, will lead to biased estimates.

The Heckman selection model can be easily reformulated for binary outcomes with the application of maximum-likelihood probit estimation with sample selection. Much more complicated is its reformulation and application for transition rate models. As is well known, failure to correct for unobserved heterogeneity in hazard models may give rise not only to biases in the estimates of the included covariates but also to estimated hazard that declines more steeply (or rises more slowly) than the true hazard.[4] However, modelling unobserved heterogeneity is a very difficult and 'slippery' task. Together with Flinn, and in line with most studies at that time, Heckman initially proposed a parametric approach, which assumed that frailty was distributed over individuals as a normal curve (Flinn and Heckman, 1982a, 1982b). Yet, in a work with Singer, he showed that, for a given parametric representation of the baseline hazard, the results may be very sensitive to the choice of the parametric form of the distribution function for heterogeneity, even when a flexible form is chosen (such as normal, log normal or gamma). Hence, Heckman and Singer proposed a non-parametric strategy for handling unmeasured heterogeneity in continuous-time hazard models (Heckman and Singer, 1982a, 1982b). Moreover, they extended previous work by allowing unobserved components to be correlated across spells: that is, to differ not only among individuals but also over time for the same individual. With this extension and this non-parametric description of the frailty distribution, they used Monte Carlo experiments to show that coefficients for the included covariates can be estimated with great precision. However, a non-parametric approach also encounters crucial problems, because in order to achieve a non-parametric representation of the distribution of heterogeneity, it is necessary to impose a parametric form on the hazard function. And, as argued by Trussell and Richard (1985, p 273):

> The investigator who wishes to avoid model misspecification by correcting for unobserved heterogeneity is treading on dangerous

ground … results can be extremely sensitive to the choice of parametric form for the distribution of heterogeneity. Even with a non-parametric representation of heterogeneity, results can be sensitive to choice of hazard.

This does not necessarily mean that models that ignore unobserved heterogeneity are preferable to models that try to control for it. Rather, it implies that caution is required, and that robustness should be checked by comparing results across different models. Moreover, I would add, it highlights the role of theory. It is theory, in fact, that should guide not only the choice of hazard but also the choice of corrections for unobserved heterogeneity. The researcher should first think about what relevant sources of heterogeneity may cause a correlation in the error terms between the selection and regression equation (or more generally between X and Y) and then consider whether some of the measures that they have included may not in fact have dealt with them, or only partially. If they have not, controlling for unobservable heterogeneity becomes highly desirable.

Besides the problem of sample selection, there is that of endogeneity. The two are similar; the problem of endogeneity is in many respects a problem of unobserved heterogeneity. This means that, whereas it is thought that X causes Y, there are in fact some factors that determine both X and Y and are not measured. Obviously, many variables in my data cannot be considered as truly exogenous – particularly education and children. Economists typically raise this issue and control for it either via instrumental variables or via a joint modelling approach of participation and fertility. However, most of their studies are based on cross-sectional data (Di Tommaso, 1999; Bratti, 2003) or they focus on mothers' transitions around childbirth (Dex et al, 1998; Elliott, 2002). Here I instead use longitudinal data, which, as discussed earlier, are always better than cross-sectional data when dealing with causal connections and, hence, also with endogeneity. Moreover, I consider the entire adult lifecourse, and a large set of time-constant and time-varying covariates.

As said repeatedly, the main shortcoming of my data (like most retrospective data) is that they lack information on beliefs, expectations and attitudes (the last, as we shall see, being weakly proxied only by a variable on the mother's work experience). In the absence of such longitudinal measures, the problem of endogeneity and of progressive sample selection in second-order transitions cannot be considered as satisfactorily solved, However, as argued earlier, modelling unobserved heterogeneity in event-history models is a very difficult undertaking. It is even more difficult in my case because, unlike Heckman and Singer, I use discrete-time methods, and because both my selection and regression equations are hazard rate models. Consider, for example, the case of the first transition back into paid work. Clearly, only women who have previously interrupted employment enter the risk set. That is to say, selection for the later transition is a function of the hazard rate model for the earlier transition. Consequently, for the second transition (from housework back into employment) one should model a hazard rate that, compared to the usual one, has an extra condition: namely that the starting time of the risk set (say t) must be greater than the time spent in employment before exiting it (say τ_1). The hazard for the first transition (from employment to housework) is instead the usual one. Since the time to the first transition τ_1 appears in both equations, these have to be estimated jointly. Yet this proves to be very difficult for two reasons. First, the condition involving τ_1 in the second transition is '1- the survivor function', that is, the cumulative hazard rate of the first transition, which also depends on the βetas and will prove to be very difficult if there are time-varying covariates. Moreover, even without time-varying covariates, it would be very difficult with a discrete time approach. Second, even if discrete-time models and time-varying covariates are not used, it is still necessary to be able to estimate a bivariate function of the hazard rate of the second transition and the survivorship function of the first, which is also going to be very difficult.

Since I adopt a discrete-time approach, a cruder method to use would be *Heckman's bivariate probit model with selection*, where the regression equation is the usual discrete-time model for, say, the transition back into paid work, whereas the selection equation predicts not whether a woman makes the transition out of paid work in any given month but whether or not, in each month, she is out of paid work. Then, as for any bivariate probit model with selection that follows Heckman's procedure, one gets the estimate of the coefficients for the two equations (the Xs and the Zs) and of a parameter called 'Rho'. If Rho is significant, one should look at how the coefficients for the Xs differ from the hazard rate model that does not correct for sample selection and speculate on the likely sources of such biases.

This cruder method is clearly not the best way to tackle the problem of sample selection in transition rate models, because it does not treat the selection equation as a transition rate model as it is in reality. Nevertheless, I maintain that it has the advantage of being simple to apply and to interpret, and that it gives a reliable first idea about the existence or otherwise of a significant problem of sample selection. Thus, in chapters Five and Six I shall check for the presence of sample selection by running a Heckman's bivariate probit model for the transition back into paid work. In fact, in both Italy and Britain, only a subset of women exit employment and are consequently at risk of making the transition back into it. For Italy, where not all women start labour market careers, the transition out of employment will also be checked for sample selection. In the empirical chapters I shall report logit estimates without correction, but I shall comment on whether and how Rho is significant and Probit estimates with correction differ. Moreover, given the person-month file structure, where observations are not independent, in order to obtain more efficient estimates I shall run logit regressions with the option 'cluster (Pid)' (personal identification number).

Data and variables

The empirical analyses in this book draw on the British Household Panel Survey (BHPS) and on the Italian Household Longitudinal Survey (ILFI). The BHPS started in 1991, and since then it has been carried out every year on a nationally representative sample of over 5,000 households across England, Wales and Scotland South of the Caledonian Canal. The ILFI (*Indagine Longitudinale sulle Famiglie Italiane*) was first carried out in 1997 by the University of Trento, Istituto Trentino di Cultura and ISTAT (Italian Office of National Statistics) on a national representative sample of 9,770 individuals belonging to 4,714 households throughout Italy. Since then, four other waves have been conducted, in 1999, 2001, 2003 and 2005. Both surveys combine a retrospective with a prospective panel design and use standardised interviews including questions on the lifecourses of respondents in a number of different areas (such as education, family events, work and job history).

Here I use the entire history of the ILFI as updated in 2005, and I employ retrospective and prospective information from the BHPS until the 15th wave, also dated 2005. More precisely, for Britain I draw on the data concerning the employment and occupational histories constructed by David Mare at the Institute for Social and Economic Research at the University of Essex.[5] These data combine the retrospective labour market histories collected in waves 1992 and 1993 with information on employment and occupational status collected in the following waves. I also use the retrospective lifetime information on marital and fertility status collected in 1992, which has been recently updated to 2005 by Chiara Pronzato.[6] Moreover, because I am interested in women's labour force movements over the entire adult lifecourse, my British sample is composed only of those women whose full life histories were available: that is, those women who were interviewed in 1992 and 1993, when the retrospective employment, occupational and family questions in the BHPS were asked; but also in wave 1, when information on the mother's work experience was gathered. Women entering the survey later were excluded. Overall, and in regard only to women born between 1935 and 1974, the samples that I use are composed of 2,614 women in Britain and 3,731 women in Italy. These are further reduced when the focus is only on women who have started a labour market career. More precisely, in Italy, where the share of women who never officially start to work is much higher, the sample decreases in number to 2,976. On moving to later transitions, the sample of women obviously gets smaller. Table 4.1 shows the absolute number of women, by transition and cohort, on which the event-history models in subsequent chapters are based.

On the basis of what the BHPS and ILFI both include, I have operationalised relevant concepts deriving from different theoretical approaches on the determinants of women's employment transitions over the lifecourse. *The dependent variable* derives from the variable 'employment status' aggregated in three categories: 'employment', 'housework' and 'other'. More precisely, a woman is defined as employed when she is working, when she is on maternity leave or on other forms

Table 4.1: Sample sizes by birth cohort, transition and country

	Italy				Britain			
	1935-44	1945-54	1955-64	1965-74	1935-44	1945-54	1955-64	1965-74
All women	751	953	958	1,069	557	795	792	470
Women who have started to work	561	760	804	851	553	792	783	456
1st transition out by age 40	224	261	238	156	433	595	491	205
1st transition back by age 40	66	95	83	58	351	491	432	195
2nd transition out by age 40	24	25	20	21	123	187	239	119
2nd transition back by age 40	11	9	6	11	105	160	204	91

Source: BHPS (2005); ILFI (2005)

of paid or unpaid leave, and, for Italy, when she is on '*cassa integrazione guadagni ordinaria*'. A woman is defined a 'housewife' (ILFI) or, more appropriately, a 'family carer' (BHPS) when she has no links with the labour market and is dedicated full time to unpaid domestic and care work. 'Other' comprises the following statuses: unemployed (for Italy including women on '*cassa inregrazione guadagni straordinaria*' and on 'mobility lists'), retired, full-time student, unable to work. As mentioned earlier, I am not interested in transitions from employment to 'other' or the reverse, so that months spent in these statuses are censored.

As *explanatory variables* I have included measures of women's human capital, labour market position and family situation. Because most of these factors change over a person's lifecourse, they are introduced as time-varying covariates.

Human capital and labour market position are captured by measures of education, labour market experience, type of job (full-time versus part-time) and occupational class. More precisely, *education* is measured in four categories: no qualification, lower-secondary qualification, upper-secondary qualification and higher education.[7] However, except in the cross-sectional logistic regressions on women's probabilities of starting work, I have treated education dichotomously in two levels: low-educated (level 1 and 2) versus high-educated (level 3 and 4). In Italy, education has a very strong effect on women's chances of starting and having continuous careers, so that very few women graduates experience the first transition out of employment to be then at risk in making the transition back. Moreover, in both Italy and Britain, a very small number of women in younger cohorts have a primary level of education. In keeping with the arguments of many sociologists, and with the theoretical framework chosen, I regard education as capturing both instrumental and cognitive rationality. Indeed, education may also yield non-monetary advantages because it offers women new forms of identity, social legitimation and autonomy, and because the opportunity to earn an independent wage gives women greater bargaining power within the family. Type of time commitment in the labour market is measured by distinguishing between *full-time and part-time jobs*. While in the ILFI all types of workers are asked about their time commitment, in the BHPS the distinction between part-time and full-time is made only for employees. Consequently, for Britain I decided to code self-employed women as full-time workers. Moreover, in the retrospective part of the BHPS, job changes are recorded only when they imply a change of employer. Thus, changes from part-time to full-time jobs, as well as between different occupational positions (such those following a promotion), are underestimated.

Labour market experience is measured by distinguishing between duration dependency and lagged duration dependency (Heckman and Borjas, 1980). Duration dependency is the *time spent in current status*. It is measured monthly as a continuous variable and it refers to the time spent in employment since first job for the first transition out, and to the time spent in housework since withdrawing from the labour market for the first transition back. Lagged duration dependency is instead a time-constant variable. More precisely, it refers to the *duration of previous labour market experience* when women have their first housework spell: that is, when they are at risk of making the first transition back into employment. I have also checked the role of unemployment history. However, I have not shown it in the tables because it was only slightly significant in some cohorts.

In addition to the full-time/part-time distinction, I have captured labour market position and social stratification through a variable on *class*. This is coded with a collapsed five-category version of the Erikson–Goldthorpe classification in order to reduce the number of parameters to estimate and to avoid single categories into which few women fall. The five categories chosen are: service class together with petty bourgeoisie, farmers and smallholders[8]; routine qualified non-manual employees; skilled manual workers; unskilled non-manual workers; and unskilled manual workers. Class is updated monthly in the study on transitions out of paid work; although for Britain, as mentioned earlier, it captures only job changes corresponding to a change of employer. In the study of the transitions back into paid work, class is a time-constant variable that refers to the last job held before interrupting. Moreover, when analysis is made of different employment trajectories for low- and high-educated women, or for women with high- and low-status husbands, class (both 'his' and 'her') is collapsed into three categories.

As much research shows, women's risks of withdrawing from the labour market also depend on other job characteristics. It is important, for example, whether the job is in the public or private sector, in a small or big firm, with a permanent or fixed-term contract, or takes the form of self-employment in the free professions or in small shops. However, in the BHPS, this information is available in the panel part of the survey, but not in the retrospective life-history part. It is fully available in the Italian survey, but for comparative reasons it is not used. Unfortunately, neither the BHPS nor the ILFI furnish retrospective information on earnings and income. As argued by Goldthorpe and McKnight (2003) and Bernardi and Nazio (2005), in the absence of proper measures, occupational class, properly ordered, can be taken as a proxy for earnings.[9] In particular, in my analysis social class is meant to also capture earnings differences in conjunction with labour market experience and part-time work. Moreover, since information on the characteristics of the partner will be included only later (see the third section of Chapter Six), in most of my models I do not control for income effect. As a consequence, to some extent, women's own social class or Rho (unobserved heterogeneity) may indirectly also capture the effect of the partner's social class through patterns of homogamy.

It is well known that women's labour market choices are strongly influenced by the family life cycle and the family's circumstances. Changes in marital status, in the number and age of children and in the situation of the partner, alter the demand for time and financial resources. In order to account for these family life influences, I use the following variables in my analysis. First, a set of time-varying dummy variables on the *age of the youngest child* that should account for differences in the time-demand of care. The distinction is among four states: not having children, being pregnant (with the first, second, third and so on child), having the youngest child aged 0-3, or older. When sample sizes become smaller, as in the transitions back or in the analyses separated by education, being pregnant is combined with having a child aged under three. Obviously, the birth of each subsequent child sets the age of the youngest child back to zero. Second, my models include, in a continuous form, *number of children*, which should account for the greater demand of time but also for the greater financial needs of families with several children. Finally, changes in *family status*, particularly *in partnership*, are captured by a dummy equal to 1 in the months when the woman has been part of a couple (either cohabiting or married) or otherwise (single or divorced, separated or widowed). In both datasets this time-varying variable registers all changes occurring de facto regardless of the legal status of the woman.

As emphasised by lifecourse scholars, lives are interdependent, and especially those linked together in everyday situations. As discussed in Chapter Two, the family is a crucial locus for the production and redistribution of income and care. It is where consumption but also labour supply and fertility decisions are taken, and where gender and intergenerational models are defined and practised. Within the couple, individual choices are negotiated with those of the partner, with crucial outcomes in terms of actual but also future living conditions. At the same time, such choices also derive from the previous education and occupational histories of each partner. Therefore, in Chapter Six I shall also introduce measures of the partner's resources into my event-history models. More specifically, I shall open the observational window one year before marriage, as is usually done (Blossfeld and Drobnic, 2001), and I shall analyse how a partner's level of education and occupational class influence a woman's risk of moving in and out of paid work. Education will be measured on two levels (high versus low) and class on three (high, middle and low). Since data on attitudes, on intentions but also on incomes are not available, it will not be possible to disentangle the monetary or non-monetary dimensions of the effect of 'his', as it was of 'her', class and education. However, as discussed, the reference to previous qualitative and quantitative literature, and the use of a lifecourse approach with a comparative design and within an institutional rational-action paradigm, give 'legitimacy' for advancing narratives around possible mechanisms behind observed associations.

There are two reasons why I shall introduce this information on the partner's educational and occupational profile only at a later stage. First, a focus from the beginning only on married women would have impeded me from looking at the entire life trajectory since leaving full-time education, and from capturing the effect of marriage. In particular, I would not have been able to determine to what extent and for whom the timing of interruptions has been postponed from the period around marriage to the period around childbirth. Nor, as noted, would I have been able to avoid the problematic sample selection inherent in research that focuses on specific groups of women, such as that which analyses only transitions around childbirth. Second, restriction to married women implies a sample size reduction and thus requires the introduction of fewer variables or rougher specifications of them (such as class in two or three categories rather than five).

Another important time-varying variable typically included in women's labour supply models is *age*, which is mainly used as an indicator of family responsibilities. However, I do not include age in my models because I directly measure marital and childbearing history and also employment and occupational history, and compare across cohorts.

Neither the BHPS nor the ILFI contain attitudinal questions. Nevertheless, a proxy for gender identity, or at least for work attitudes, can be drawn from the variable on the *work experience of a woman's mother*. This is a time-constant variable defined differently in the two datasets. In Italy, it is coded 1 if the woman's mother has ever been employed, 0 otherwise. In Britain, instead it is coded 1 if the woman's mother was not employed when the woman was 14 years old. At first sight this distinction seems important. Yet it becomes less of a problem if one considers the different patterns of labour market participation by Italian and British women, also in the cohorts of the mothers of my women subjects.[10] This variable makes it possible to identify women who have grown up in a family with a traditional division of gender roles and to see whether this has in some way been transmitted to the daughter. However, it could be argued that having a working mother does necessarily mean being exposed to a positive evaluation of female work. The employment of the wife may be contested by the husband and thus generate conflicts within the family, especially when conciliation is very difficult. Or employment may be chosen by women out of necessity and be a source of frustration. But one can counterargue that, in a context where the normative model was the stay-at-home housewife – like Britain and Italy in the 1950s and 1960s (although with different degrees and emphases) – women who anyway decide to enter employment or remain in it while building a family should be highly motivated. And in fact previous studies using this variable have found that it has a positive significant effect in Italy (Bernardi, 1999; Bratti, 2003). A recent paper by Van Putten et al (2008) further corroborates the role of intergenerational reproduction and transmission. In the Netherlands, where the part-time divide is very strong, daughters of working mothers tend to work more hours than daughters of homemaking mothers. But even if a variable on the labour market behaviour of the mother yields meaningful results, one should be cautious about treating it as a general proxy for attitudes on the gender division of labour. As discussed in Chapter Two, attitudes are the outcome of a complex process of primary and secondary socialisation, and they may not only lag but also lead changes in women's behaviour. Moreover, they are structured not only by cultural models but also by existing options. Hence, in my models some heterogeneity in 'tastes' is certainly unobserved.

In order to account for temporal variation in the demand for labour, I also introduce the *yearly unemployment rate* into the transition rate models. Ideally, account should also be taken of levels of gender segregation and the impact of local labour market conditions, because the total unemployment rate is too crude a measure of the demand for female labour. However, total levels of unemployment rates do not represent demand effects alone. The perception of a negative economic climate may in itself discourage women from entering or re-entering the labour market. It may also discourage women from exiting if they want to do so. Given the wide gap in unemployment rates between the South and the Centre-North of Italy, I use not national but regional yearly unemployment rates for Italy.[11] Yet the South of Italy differs from the Centre-North not only in total demand for labour, but also in the types of jobs available, in the way the labour market functions and in the availability of out-of-home care services. It differs in cultural models as well. The same applies, although with much less marked divisions, to England as compared with Scotland or Wales. I therefore introduce a three-category *region variable* distinguishing between North, Centre and the South in Italy, and between England, Wales and Scotland in Britain.

When studying women's first entry into the labour market in Italy, I also use an indicator of the *father's occupational position*, namely the de Lillo-Schizzerotto occupational score (de Lillo and Schizzerotto, 1985). This is intended to capture the possible existence of a family income or social capital effect net of women's education. That is to say, it is used to determine whether a woman's family background directly influences her determination to start a labour market career and her chances of doing so, regardless of its well-known indirect effect through educational attainment.

Table 4.2 gives descriptive statistics of the various variables used in my analyses, by cohort and country.

Hypotheses: what has changed across generations in women's employment over the lifecourse in Italy and Britain?

In a rational-action framework, women's employment behaviour reflects a complex choice process whereby women actively mediate their preferences with those of their 'significant others', *in primis* the partner, and with the existing set of opportunities and constraints. As outlined in Chapter Two, this set comprises various macro factors that range from cultural norms to the functioning of the family, the welfare state and the labour market. They also include micro-situational constraints, such as family situation, level of education and position in the labour market. Hence, in order to account for changes across generations and differences between countries, attention must be paid to all these various elements, and their concrete features in different times and spaces must be verified. As we saw in the previous chapter, Italy and Britain differ greatly in their cultural, institutional and economic arrangements, and in how these have changed from the 1950s to the 1990s. What do I expect to be the outcomes in terms of women's employment patterns over the lifecourse? Summarising and linking together what has been described throughout Chapters Two and Three, and referring only to the effects I can measure as described earlier in this chapter, here I shall advance causal narratives on what I expect to have changed in the types and correlates of women's employment histories in Italy and Britain. Like the research question, the hypotheses must combine various levels and dimensions: comparison across time and space and attention to several micro and macro 'Xs' and 'Ys'. In order to disentangle this complex set of features, I shall divide the hypotheses into three subsections.

In the first subsection I shall compare Italy and Britain and look at the 'quantity' and 'type' of overall change. Have women's employment patterns over the lifecourse changed more in Britain or in Italy? At what stage: on first entry into paid work; on transition out, having entered; or on transition back ,having interrupted? In what period? For all women, or only for those with high educations and low family burdens? In other words, to what extent has growth in women's labour market participation since the Second World War been due to a 'compositional' effect?[12] As discussed in the introduction to this chapter, the 'compositional issue' is important because it signals different degrees and types of 'universalisation' of women's and mother's involvement in paid work. It signals, on the one hand, whether women's employment has become a norm, so that nearly all women start a labour market career, and on the other, whether this norm also applies to mothers with young children, and likewise to mothers differently educated or differently geographically located. It thus involves changing cultural models or institutional and economic opportunities that make work–family combination more or less feasible and desirable, and women more or less able to act upon preferences.

In the second subsection I shall discuss in more detail the effect of specific changes in cultural norms, institutions and labour demand on the various micro correlates of women's transitions between employment and housework. In other words, what do I expect to have changed across cohorts in the influence of education, class and family responsibilities? Has polarisation between highly educated and poorly educated women or between women married to high- or low-class husbands diminished or increased over time? Why?

The last subsection is more explicitly comparative, in that it resumes and qualifies hypotheses on differences between Italy and Britain in the incidence, timing and correlates of women's transitions in and out of paid work.

Table 4.2: Descriptive statistics for the independent variables, by birth cohort and country (women who have started to work by age 40)

	1935-44	1945-54	1955-64	1965-74
Britain				
Median age first job	15.3	16.1	16.7	17.3
Educational level at first job (%)				
primary	47.5	30.6	15.8	7.0
lower-secondary	27.1	35.6	43.2	48.2
upper-secondary	4.7	6.3	10.1	17.5
tertiary	20.6	27.4	30.9	27.2
Class at first job(%)				
service class and petty bourgeoisie	12.1	14.6	19.6	15.9
routine non-manual workers	41.7	44.7	36.7	28.7
skilled manual workers	10.8	11.0	9.6	6.6
unskilled manual workers	21.5	12.8	17.6	19.4
unskilled non-manual workers	13.7	16.7	16.3	29.2
Working time first job (%)				
part-time	1.1	2.0	6.4	15.3
Mother's work experience (%):				
Not working	61.4	48.3	39.3	36.9
Geographical region at first job (%)				
England	73.7	76.5	76.6	77.6
Wales	18.1	14.5	12.7	11.4
Scotland	8.1	8.9	10.6	10.9
Median duration in months of employment when exiting to housework	83	83	88	68
Median age when exiting to housework	22.8	23.8	24.7	23.2
Median duration in months of housework when re-entering employment	72	63	42.5	25
Median age when re-entering employment	29.5	29.3	29.4	26.4
Marital status by age 35(%):				
never married	6.6	6.6	10.9	19.6

continued

Table 4.2: continued

	1935-44	1945-54	1955-64	1965-74
Italy				
Median age first Job	17.9	18.1	19.4	20.6
Educational level at first job (%)				
primary	53.9	31.6	10.2	3.8
lower-secondary	22.1	27.6	32.5	30.3
upper-secondary	17.3	27.7	42.9	46.4
tertiary	6.6	13.1	14.3	19.4
Class at first job(%)				
service class and petty bourgeoisie	39.3	36.7	44.0	37.2
routine non-manual workers	6.4	10.1	10.9	12.8
skilled manual workers	2.6	4.7	4.9	5.7
unskilled manual workers	38.3	30.1	26.7	21.9
unskilled non-manual workers	13.2	18.2	13.3	22.2
Working time first job (%)				
part-time	4.8	6.5	11.3	15.8
Mother's work experience (%):				
never worked	57.1	55.6	53.2	38.7
Geographical region first job (%)				
North	56.9	53.8	48.3	51.7
Centre	19.4	20.5	22.8	19.3
South	23.6	26.5	28.8	28.9
Median duration in months of employment when exiting to housework	94	81	79	71.5
Median age when exiting to housework	25.3	23.7	24.9	25.9
Median duration in months of housework when re-entering employment	62.5	60	57	25.5
Median age when re-entering employment	30.4	29.3	30.7	28.4
Marital status by age 35(%):				
never married	11.3	10.2	13.7	32.9
Number of children by age 35 (%)				
none	17.6	15.5	23.2	44.7
1	23.4	28.2	28.6	27.3
2+	59.0	56.2	48.2	27.9

Overall, how much and what has changed?

In both Italy and Britain, the behaviour of the first cohort was regulated by specific 'Fordist' social norms and conditions. These supported the 'male-breadwinner' model on explicit moral grounds. Women's employment was seen as detrimental to the family and as secondary to their caring and domestic work. Although its realisation differed across social classes, the approval of a traditional gender division of labour between paid and unpaid work cut across gender and classes. This normative model was paralleled by a women-unfriendly welfare state and labour market regulation. Indeed, as we have seen, in the development of the British and Italian post-war welfare states, the issue of conciliation between work and family responsibilities was ignored even when women's labour market participation began to increase.

We saw in Chapter Two that women's attachment to paid work is best supported by a coordinated package of policies revolving around three pillars (income, time and services) providing universal and generous benefits (in terms of both levels of coverage and levels of wage replaced or integrated), and promoting the father's involvement in childcare. The first forms of support for maternal employment were introduced during the 1970s: in Britain with the introduction of maternity leave in the late 1970s; in Italy with the implementation of maternity/parental leave and universal preschool services in the early 1970s, and individual taxation in the late 1970s. In Italy these changes occurred when the first cohort was between 30 and 40 years old and was therefore still building families and careers. However, women in the second cohort, who were in their twenties at the beginning of the 1970s, could fully benefit from the changes. Instead, in Britain, only younger women in the second birth cohort and all of them in the third cohort started to benefit from the new maternity legislation. Thereafter, in both countries until 1997, neither leave schemes nor the provision of childcare services for the under-threes, nor income support to families with children and family-friendly flexibility, significantly improved. The assumption that reconciliation is a 'mothers' issue' remained strong in both countries. Only in the early 2000s did reforms of leave provisions explicitly give rights to fathers, although the low level of income replacement, in addition to persisting traditional gender models, prevented them from taking time off. In the early 2000s, some new forms of flexibility for employees with family responsibilities were also introduced in both countries. Britain promoted a system of tax reductions for childcare costs as well. However, as discussed in Chapter Three, to date the pro-women effect of these measures has been limited.

Furthermore, in Italy, the approval of maternal employment, the value attached to the family and the definition of children's needs have remained relatively constant. Or rather, the change has been almost entirely compositional, and it has been mainly brought about by women. Moreover, tertiarisation arrived later in Italy, and has never become as widespread as in other countries. The post-1997 deregulation was selectively concentrated on new entrants, without reducing the overall level of unemployment, and it exacerbated labour market segmentation. Britain, by contrast, experienced a much earlier and more intense trend towards a service economy, and a stronger growth of part-time jobs after the 1950s. Thus, when my first cohort entered the labour market and the family formation phase, the demand for female labour was already relatively high. Deregulation by the Conservative governments of the 1980s and 1990s did not greatly change the level of overall demand, but it stimulated the growth of the secondary segment and increased polarisation.

To summarise in a stylised form, in Britain both women's preferences and societal gender norms have changed, while 'women-friendly' institutional arrangements and the overall demand for labour have altered little. Since women in younger cohorts have become less oriented towards a 'marriage career', *it is likely that they have generally reduced their exits, increased their re-entries, and shortened their breaks out of the labour market regardless of their family and personal characteristics.* With the relaxing of the traditional male-breadwinner norm, *women's career paths have become more heterogeneous.* Yet, as has emerged in the debate on gendering welfare states (see Chapter Two), since the state still does not adequately alleviate the conflict between family and work, the strategy used to resolve it will depend on differences in education, social class and income, as well as on differences in preferences. Thus, women's work histories have also *become more polarised.* This should be observed in the women of the third and fourth cohorts, who were building their families during the 1980s and 1990s, when the Conservative policies were implemented. *In particular, I expect these two cohorts to exhibit an increasing incidence of fragmentised careers, and an increasing differentiating effect of education and class.*

By contrast, as already argued by Schizzerotto et al (1995), *in Italy a much stronger 'compositional effect' is likely to emerge.* Indeed, women's preferences have changed in Italy, but in a context of relatively stable gender and childcare norms, institutional arrangements and labour market demand. As in the past, the strategies used to resolve the conflict between family and work will depend on differences in education, in the access to 'women-friendly' jobs such as those in the public sector, in the availability of informal family help, as well as differences in preferences. In technical terms, I expect to find that the effect of marriage, children, education and class on movements between employment and housework has not, *ceteris paribus,* significantly changed across cohorts. *Education should prove to be, in both old and young cohorts, the strongest determinant of women's work histories.* Moreover, compared to Britain, the lower demand for labour in Italy, especially in the South, and greater labour market rigidity should, together with a persisting traditional gender order, produce *an overall lower level of female employment* due to the *many women who never start working, or if they start work and interrupt, never return to it.* Because of a 'partial and selective' flexibilisation concentrated on the early careers of young cohorts since the late 1990s, likely to be observed is, *in the fourth cohort, an increase in the rate of interruptions around childbirths but also of re-entries later on.*

Within a micro–macro model, it is also plausible to hypothesise that *in Britain differences emerge in the work paths during family formation, whereas in Italy they count more in the early labour market career*, and in fertility decisions. This is closely linked with the type of welfare regime. A liberal welfare state, with its relatively high tertiarisation and labour market deregulation, and with its traditionally high level of (unmarried) female employment, gives women more chances to start a labour market career but also more options to move during the lifecourse. It therefore allows gender-role preferences and work orientations to differentiate to a greater extent. Obviously, since policies in support of work–family combination have been poor, the option taken between these various alternatives may not correspond to the one most preferred. Instead, in Italy, where employment opportunities are low (in the South), where the rigid official labour market reduces the variety of working arrangements and renders exits relatively costly, and where the informal childcare offered by the family is quite widespread, values have less impact on work histories over the family course. They have more effect on decisions regarding education, perseverance in the job search (especially in the South), and the type of entry sector (public/private; employee or self-employed; formal or informal).

How has the effect of education, class, motherhood and partner changed?

As emphasised in the literature, during the immediate post-war period in Britain, the norm was to stop working at the time of marriage and to re-enter when children were grown up. However, only the wives of the middle-high class typically followed the actual practice of this traditional male-breadwinner norm. Wives in the working classes could not afford to stay for long out of the labour market. Since the late 1950s, the employment of married women has become more 'respectable' and acceptable, partly because of the further growth of types of jobs more compatible with family responsibilities. As the model of stay-at-home housewife has declined, women have grown much less dependent on the occupational position of their husbands, and much more on their own education and class. Although the relaxing of the male breadwinner norm has helped 'universalise' women's involvement in paid work, the persistence of poor defamilialising policies and of strong labour market inequalities has polarised their permanence over family formation. Consequently, *I expect the effect of a partner to decline over time* and *polarisation in women's behaviour to become based more on their profile than on their partners. I also expect that education and labour market experience and position will differentiate between women more in younger than in older cohorts.* Moreover, such differentiation should emerge at different stages of women's lifecourses. Since the desire of women to invest (in both economic and identity terms) in the out-of-home sphere has increased, and has been accompanied by a general acceptance of the new roles and experiences of women, *I expect to find that the crucial decision has moved from whether and when to re-enter paid work to whether and when to interrupt it in the first place.* Furthermore, *if women interrupt, they tend to do so later, around childbirth and not around marriage.* In any case, in a liberal welfare regime like that of Britain, the proportion of interruptions remains high. Put in more technical terms, *the effect of motherhood on women's transitions in and out of paid work remains relatively strong*. In line with the cross-sectional figures shown in Chapter Three, and with previous longitudinal studies, in Britain women's labour supply was and still is more sensitive to age than to the number of children.

In Italy too, during the late 1950s and early 1960s, when Italians were enjoying the post-war economic boom, the normative model of the stay-at-home housewife became widespread. However, it could not be adopted by large sectors of the population. Women in working-class families in the Centre-North and in many families living in the South often had to supplement the low earnings of their husbands. In the late 1960s, the male-breadwinner norm began to decline as more and more women entered paid work. However, because gender norms and women-friendly institutional arrangements had not significantly improved, employment patterns over the lifecourse did not change greatly across cohorts. Consequently, *I expect to find an increasing incidence of women who officially start working, but little change in the incidence of continuous and discontinuous work histories*. In terms of factors, it is likely that *in younger cohorts, women's first entry into the labour market has become less differentiated by education and family background, especially in the North*, where the demand for labour has been higher and gender-role norms have changed to a greater extent. Instead, *the effect of education and class but also of children on subsequent transitions out of and back into the labour market should remain constant across cohorts*. In general in Italy, where the extended family largely compensates for the lack of public childcare services and where education strongly mediates gender-role attitudes and facilitates access to family-friendly jobs such as those in the public sector, *women's labour supply responds more to education than to motherhood*.

As evident from overall rates, therefore, in Italy – and especially in the South of Italy, women's entry into paid work has not become 'universal' as it has done elsewhere. *This means that a woman's labour supply may still depend not only on her attitudes and resources but also on her partner's*. The wives of low-educated, low-class men may still be discouraged from working by socially negotiated views on the 'goodness' of full-time maternal care, unless an extra income is necessary. In a context where education is a *passepartout* for acceptance of a modern role of women, only the high education of women may counteract such discouragement, because these women have more pro-work orientations, because they have more bargaining power or because they have partners who share different moral rationalities.

How do Italy and Britain differ in the incidence, timing and correlates of women's labour market transitions? A summary

In light of the different institutional and cultural contexts and the findings of previous longitudinal studies, I expect to find the following differences between Italy and Britain in women's labour market transitions:

- *In all cohorts, a larger proportion of Italian women never start a labour market career compared to British women.* Indeed, in Britain, where there is a longer history of industrialisation and of the employment of urban married women, where a service economy has developed much earlier and to a greater extent, where the greater availability of part-time jobs and easier re-entries make it possible to conciliate family with paid work, or to move back, and hence where people are more supportive of married women's employment, very few women have never worked over their lifecourses.

- *British women experience a higher number of transitions over their lifecourses.* The British labour market is much more flexible than the Italian one, and this flexibility has increased over the past few decades. This, as just said, makes entry and re-entry into the labour market, as well as shifts from full-time to part-time work, easier in Britain than in Italy. Moreover, because childcare support measures are scarce, many women are unable to maintain their attachment to paid work when they become mothers.

- I expect not only the incidence but also the timing of transitions out of and into the labour market to be different in the two countries. Although women who have stopped working in Italy can re-enter earlier and rely on the help of the extended family to solve their childcare needs, they are inhibited from doing so by difficulties in finding new jobs. Furthermore, precisely because of these well-known difficulties, women who anyway decide to interrupt are a very selective group: typically with low educations, mainly working in the informal sector or in low-grade regular employment, and/or with a preference for the 'marriage career'. This makes them *more likely never to re-enter, or to re-enter later than British women when children are grown up or when the family income is too low.*

- As regards factors affecting the various labour market transitions, I *expect stratification factors, and particularly social class, to be more influential in Britain than in Italy.* There is evidence that in both countries working on a service versus a labour contract or in the public versus private sector differentiates women's propensity to have a continuous, curtailed or discontinuous labour market career. However, in Britain, a highly deregulated labour market, which has allowed for a wide spread of earnings, along with a residualist welfare state, tend to produce low levels of both decommodification and defamilialisation. This, as underlined by many welfare state scholars, reinforces class inequalities. By contrast, in Italy, wage dispersion in the official labour market has been low. Moreover, although the provision of childcare services for the under-threes is as scarce in Italy as it is in Britain, and the opening-time schedules of preschool and school services are generally not favourable for working parents, the extended family still provides important compensation. This help works in the form of monetary transfers, but especially in the form of childcare services, which are not class related.

- Instead, I hypothesise that *in Italy it is education that has the stronger impact and that such impact is not fully mediated by class.* As discussed in Chapter Two, the effect of education and class is institutionally and culturally embedded. Compared to Britain, I expect to find that in Italy high investments in education matter more, not only because, as in Britain, they are crucial for securing access to and advancement in good occupations, but also because, to the extent that traditional gender-role norms are still influential, they pay off with greater legitimation for women's work, even when the wage returns are relatively small. Moreover, to the extent that the official Italian labour market is still rigid, highly educated women are less disposed to run the risk of being unable to re-enter the official labour market. They therefore tend to keep attached to their jobs even when they are not in 'good' ones. In liberal Britain, by contrast, highly educated women without access to the primary labour market may have to interrupt around childbirth, although they *may try to reduce the cost of such interruptions by re-entering earlier than low-educated women*.

- In Britain, maternity and parental leaves are very short and strictly controlled, and childcare services are very scarce. Moreover, compared to Italy, 'family compensation' is weaker, while the risk of permanent exclusion from the labour market once it has been exited is lower (even though it is risky in terms of downward mobility and poverty entrapment). Consequently, *in Britain the effect of children on the risk of exiting the labour market will be higher*.

Notes

[1] It seems that family-related events such as marriages, childbirths and divorces are rarely reported wrongly, whereas recall errors are more frequent in labour market histories – especially those that are rather fragmented, with many different spells, which are not typical among Italian women and are in the minority among British women. Moreover, omissions of short spells occur more often than omissions of longer ones, as family-care spells usually are (Eisenhower et al, 1991; Holt et al, 1991; Bound et al, 2001). Sometimes, omissions reflect the priorities and definitions of the researcher, and the consequent lesser attention paid by interviewers to certain spheres and events. This, for example, is the case of Italian women's spells of maternity leave and of 'jobseeking' after some time spent out of the labour market, both of which are too low in the ILFI to be considered reliable.

[2] Transition rate analyses have been conducted in a variety of disciplines. Consequently, the 'transition rate', a term mainly used in sociology, can also be called the *hazard rate, intensity rate, failure rate, transition intensity, risk function or mortality rate*. Here, as most sociologists do, I use the term 'transition rate'.

[3] The example typically given is that of women's wages. Studying the determinants of women's wages entails focusing only on women who have started a labour market career. In more technical terms, this means that whether one observes the dependent variable 'level of wage' depends on women's decision whether or not to work. If women made this decision randomly, one could easily ignore the fact that wages are observed only for a subgroup of women and use ordinary regression to estimate a wage model. But this is obviously not the case: those women most likely not to participate in the labour market

are those who are poorly educated and with low earnings potential, so that the sample of observed wages is biased upward.

[4] Actually, the shape of the estimated hazard may be distorted also when the omitted variables are uncorrelated with the included variables. Take, for example, a population divided equally into two groups, one with a high risk and one with a low risk. If the researcher estimates a single hazard for the whole population then the estimated hazard will not be a simple average of the constant hazards of the two groups but will decrease over time. Indeed, as time passes, more individuals from the high-risk group will have made the transition of interest, so that the population is increasingly composed of low-risk individuals. In other words, estimated hazard functions exhibit negative duration dependency.

[5] For a detailed description of how the dataset has been constructed, see Maré (2006).

[6] See www.data-archive.ac.uk/findingData/snDescription.asp?sn=5629&print=1

[7] For Britain, lower-secondary qualifications correspond to GCSE/O level plus CSE grade 2-5 and apprenticeship; upper-secondary qualifications to GCE A levels; while higher education corresponds to any further level of education, such as nursing or teaching diplomas, first or higher degrees. For Italy, the basic qualification corresponds to '*scuola elementare*', lower-secondary qualification to '*scuola media*', upper-secondary to '*diploma*' and higher education to '*laurea*' or above. Moreover, while in Italy education is a time-varying variable, in Britain it is cross-sectional and corresponds to the level of education at wave b or c, when retrospective work and family careers were collected. Indeed, unlike the ILFI, the BHPS contains no information on educational careers. However, using for Britain level of education at the interview seems not to be a problem since a very tiny percentage of women in my four cohorts return to full-time education after having started to work.

[8] Petty bourgeoisie is combined with the service class because a minuscule number of women in Britain, even in the oldest cohort, belong to it: 0.3 against 16.4 in Italy.

[9] However, it should be borne in mind that occupational class is only a rough proxy because it does not capture earnings differentials within the same class and jointly captures other interrelated dimensions that may keep women attached to their jobs regardless of strict income considerations (such as the level of qualifications, responsibilities and social prestige).

[10] In fact, women have participated in the labour market since the immediate post-war years in Britain. The differences among them have been more in terms of conciliation between family and work responsibilities: that is, in terms of whether or not they have interrupted paid work and for how long. In Italy, instead, the main divide has been whether women have entered the labour market or not at all. It is therefore reasonable to assume that an

Italian woman with weak work orientations, whom Hakim would term 'home centred', will never start working (provided that she can afford not to have earnings), whereas an equivalent British woman will enter employment but interrupt it without returning, or only do so when all children are grownup. In other words, I maintain that the variable 'mother's work experience' is comparable between the two countries.

[11] For Britain, data on yearly unemployment rates are taken, for the period 1930 to 1970, from Mitchell (1975); and from www.statistics.gov.uk/statbase/TSDtables1.asp for the period 1971 to 2005. For Italy, data derive from ISTAT Labour Force Surveys and they have been built into a consistent long-term series by Paola Casavola. For the period 1954 to 1998, a description of the series can be found in Casavola (1994). For the subsequent period, Casavola has again drawn on ISTAT but has considered changes in official definitions and made them as comparable as possible with past definitions. I would like to thank her for the data she has kindly made available to me and for the time she spent in explaining to me how the updating was done.

[12] As in social mobility and discrimination studies, I use the term 'compositional' in a purely descriptive and technical sense. Consequently, those changes that refer to the marginal distribution of the variables are labelled as 'compositional', while 'non-compositional' changes are those that refer to the parameters, in other words, to the relations between variables. In terms of women's labour market behaviour, there is a non-compositional effect when the influence of education, marriage, children and so on significantly changes across cohorts. There is a compositional effect when those characteristics that have always been associated with higher levels of participation, such as childlessness, increase their share within the female population while having a constant impact on female labour supply.

FIVE

Who leaves the labour market and who returns? The changing effect of marriage and children

Introduction

The growth in female labour market participation in the post-war decades has raised important questions concerning changes in the factors fostering or inhibiting women's labour supply over the lifecourse. Has the share of women pursuing a continuous or discontinuous career changed? Who, once they have started to work, tend more to exit from and return to paid work? Have these risks changed across generations, and if so, how? In particular, has the trade-off between work and family changed? How and for whom?

In this chapter I first look at the entire observed work trajectory from first job up until the age of 35 in order to furnish a descriptive picture of how many and which women, in each cohort, have entered employment and experienced none, one or several family-care breaks. I shall then focus on specific transitions within the entire trajectory and, using the technique of event history analysis, examine their changing correlates. In other words, as described in Chapter Four, I shall study transitions between employment and housework and the changing effects of a woman's education, labour market experience, occupational class, type of job (full time or part time), marital and childrearing histories, her mother's work experience and the yearly unemployment rate of the region in which she lives. By running first a single additive model for all the four birth cohorts, and then separate models by cohort, I shall also indirectly address the 'compositional' issue of the post-war increase in women's employment. The last section summarises and discusses the main findings.

Cohorts, motherhood and types of work history: descriptive evidence

There are various ways to define and identify types of work histories. One of them is to 'let the data speak' by detecting typical career pathways using the sequence analysis method (Abbott and Hrycak, 1995; Chan, 1995; Halpin and Chan, 1998; Han and Moen, 2001). Another way is to define significant types of career path a priori by referring to theory and previous empirical findings. Given that here the main concern is to analyse the correlates of different transitions rather than entire trajectories, I shall use the latter method. More precisely, I shall define types of work history on the basis of the number of family-care breaks experienced by a woman over her adult lifecourse. Accordingly, my definition of discontinuity does not include episodes of maternity (or other) leave, unemployment or education. Rather, maternity leaves and certain types of unemployment spells, such as Italian '*cassa integrazione guadagni ordinaria*' (a wages guarantee fund, which preserves the employment status of workers during periods of temporary lay-off) are considered as 'employment'. Further, my identification of types of work history considers neither the timing nor the duration of diverse events, as sequence analysis would do, nor whether a woman has prevalently worked part time or full time and the type of job at re-entry after a break. This distinction would be relevant to Britain, but not to Italy, where re-entry rates are low and official part-time work is rare. Thus, for comparative reasons, it has been neglected.

With these definitions in mind, I have developed a summary work-history variable that distinguishes between five career patterns from end of full-time education up to age 35:

- 'never worked' for those women who have never recorded a job episode;
- 'continuous participation' when a woman has never experienced a housework episode by age 35 or the maximum age observable, although she may have stopped working for different reasons (unemployment, return to full-time student);
- 'one break, no return' or 'curtailed' when a woman withdraws from employment and does not return;
- 'one break, with return' when a woman re-enters the labour market and does not interrupt again;
- 'two or more breaks' for those women who experience several transitions between employment and housework over their lifecourses.

As discussed in the previous chapter, comparison across cohorts up to age 40 is limited by the shortest time of observation for the youngest cohort. Indeed, since the data stop in 2005, women born after 1965 cannot be followed up until their 40th birthday. While in event-history models this problem is overcome by measuring a woman's age and duration on a monthly basis, it persists in the descriptive figures. For this reason, in the latter case I have decided to look at types of work history up to age 35 and to consider, within the fourth cohort, only women born between 1965 and 1970.

Figure 5.1 shows how the distribution of types of work histories has changed across cohorts in Italy and Britain. Continuous careers have clearly increased in both countries. However, in Britain the increases have been sharper and they have been mainly due to a decline in the 'one break, with return' type of work history, but also, at the same time, to a growth in the 'two or more breaks' type of career. In accordance with the findings of other studies (Joshi and Hinde, 1993; Joshi et al, 1996), and with one of my hypotheses, this suggests that in the past the norm was to interrupt work when getting married or having children and to return when all the children were grown up. Women in younger cohorts have reduced their interruptions, or the time spent out of paid work once it has been interrupted, by re-entering more often between births and more quickly after

Figure 5.1: Incidence of different types of work history up to age 35 in Italy and Britain, by birth cohort (all women, women who become mothers or not, who have 1 or 2+ children by age 35)

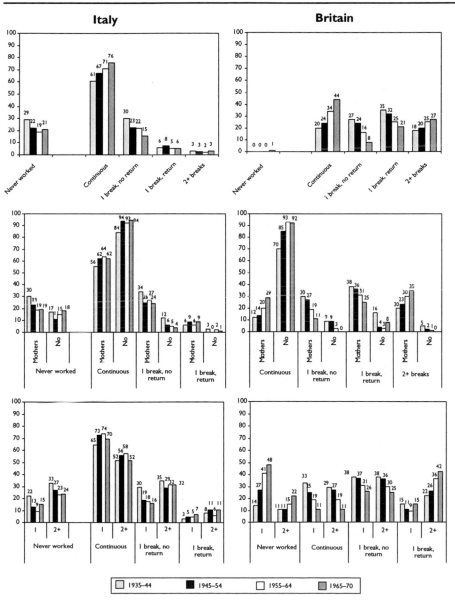

Source: ILFI, 2005; BHPS, 2005

childbearing. However, women's careers have also become more fragmented, especially in the third and fourth cohort.

By contrast, in Italy, women in younger cohorts have increased their continuity to a lesser extent (an increase of 24% compared to 120% in Britain), and this increase has mainly derived from a decline in the proportion of women who have never started work over their lifecourses. As expected, the biggest change has occurred with the second cohort, that is, with women who began their families and careers in the 1970s when labour demand and family policies became more women friendly and when women's investments in education increased. But, as in the past, once women have started to work, they differ little in their employment patterns: either they never stop working or, if they do stop, they never restart. Continuous participation has always been by far the most typical pattern. Further, in a context of few part-time job opportunities, the great majority of women from all cohorts have never worked part time. Compared to British women, not only do Italian women experience fewer movements out of and back into paid work over their adult lifecourses, they also more rarely change jobs or contracts or fall into unemployment (Solera, 2005). Indeed, since the post-war decades Italian workers have always exhibited, by international standards, quite stable and rigid careers (Breen, 2004). In addition to labour market constraints – that is, in addition to the higher risk of not being able to re-enter the labour market having exited – stronger inter-generational and kinship solidarity contributes to making female work histories more stable in Italy than in Britain. Italy, indeed, can be described as having an 'opt in/opt out' participation pattern.

Differences across cohorts in the incidence of continuous and discontinuous careers may be due to compositional differences in the 'tempo' and 'quantum' of fertility. Consequently, Figure 5.1 shows the distribution of types of work histories by cohort and motherhood, and number of children. As expected, motherhood appears to have a stronger effect on British women's work histories than on Italian ones, with a percentage reduction of continuous careers of around 50% in Italy against 68-82% in Britain. It also emerges that fewer changes are apparent across cohorts in Italy than in Britain. In Italy, continuity is the most typical pattern among both mothers and non-mothers, the gap being around 30 percentage absolute points in all cohorts and with only, as expected, a slight increase in the last cohort. If one focuses only on mothers and distinguishes between those who, by age 35, have had only one child and those who have had two or more children, one again finds that in Italy having more children has had relatively little impact on women's chances of pursuing a continuous career. This impact was slightly lower in the oldest cohort, when those fewer working women were evidently a quite selective group in terms of human capital, job conditions and work orientations. Similar findings emerge from the ISTAT survey on the mothers of children born in 2001/02, a category which largely corresponds to my fourth birth cohort: 16% of these new mothers have never worked, 21% have interrupted before pregnancy, 12% during pregnancy or around childbirth, while 47% have remained continuously employed (ISTAT, 2006, figure 4.1).

In Britain, by contrast, in all cohorts a lower share of mothers pursue continuous careers, although this proportion has increased across cohorts, and its gap with respect to non-mothers has diminished. Discontinuous careers are particularly widespread among mothers with more than one child, whose gap with respect to one-child mothers has increased across cohorts. Indeed, as pointed out earlier, in the youngest cohorts mothers have increased their labour market attachment, either by never interrupting at first child (one out of two one-child mothers has a continuous career in the 1965-70 birth cohort) or by re-entering more rapidly. Indeed (nearly one out of four two-children women experiences a continuous career while one out of two experiences two or more breaks). As Joshi and Hinde (1993) argue, it is changes in the behaviour of mothers that have driven female employment growth since the Second World War, at least until the 1980s. Drawing on the National Survey of Health and Development, Joshi and Hinde find that, among women who bore their first child in 1946, only around one in 20 had re-entered the labour market before the first child was one year old. In regard to their daughters, those who were born in 1946 and mostly had children in the 1970s, the proportion was around one in five (Joshi and Hinde, 1993). During the 1980s, too, maternal employment increased: the rate of British mothers of children under five rose from less than one third at the start of the 1980s to over one half in the mid-1990s. Yet as Chapter Six shows in more detail, the increase was concentrated among better-educated women, whose gap with respect to the least-educated widened (Davies and Joshi, 2002). Moreover, despite this increase, Britain still exhibits one of the strongest 'child effects' on women's labour supply and social position in Europe. Using the ECHP, Spiess et al (2004) find that reductions in working hours and in earning potential after first motherhood are highest in Britain and Germany, and lowest in Belgium, Denmark and France, while they are relatively low in Italy and Portugal. This was also evident from cross-country comparative figures set out in Chapter Three.

If the Italian figures are broken down by geographical area, the differences between Italy and Britain appear less marked, and especially among the most recent cohorts. Only 8% of women born since 1955 have never started an employment career in the Centre-North of Italy, as opposed to 35% in the South. The gap was also high in the post-war decades, when nearly one out of two women in the South was excluded lifelong from paid work, against one out of five in the North. But once women had started to work, continuity was the most typical pattern in both areas of Italy. However, while for oldest cohorts continuous participation was more common in the South, for the youngest cohorts it became more frequent in the North. Moreover, more recently, in the North, continuity has increased among both mothers and non-mothers, with a constant gap of about 30 absolute percentage points. By contrast, in the South, continuous participation has diminished for women who have had children by age 35, while it has slightly grown for those remaining childless. In other words, the 'motherhood effect' has increased over time in the South, rising from a difference of 10 absolute percentage points in the first cohort to 38 in the last cohort (Figure 5.2).

Figure 5.2: Incidence of different types of work history up to age 35 in Centre-North and South of Italy, by birth cohort (all women and women who become mothers or not by age 35)

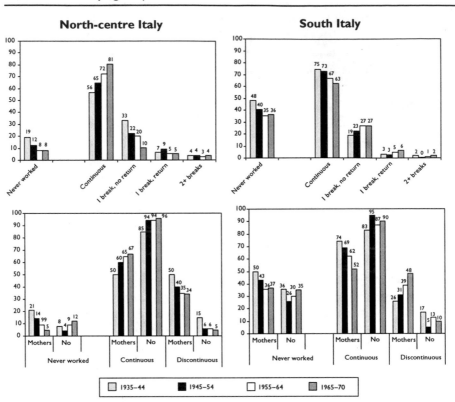

Source: ILFI, 2005

These geographical differences in types of work history may be largely due to compositional differences in the types of jobs that women hold. Indeed, in the post-war decades, public employment in the South was the main channel of women's integration into the official labour market, especially for the highly educated. This means that fewer women (officially) worked in the South, but those who did work were a selective 'privileged' group, being typically more motivated, more highly educated and more frequently employed in well-protected sectors where the risk of leaving the labour market was lower. As feminist critiques of standard labour market segmentation theory have pointed out, women are discouraged from working by the interplay between cultural and structural barriers. Since the 1980s, a severe economic recession and strong restrictions on public sector expansion in the South have reduced women's employment opportunities, so that unemployment has formed the largest component of the rise in female labour market participation (Bettio and Villa, 2000; Battistoni, 2003, 2005). In the South, not only are employment prospects (at least in the formal market) much worse than in the North, but also traditional gender roles are more widespread and legitimated (Brown and Scott, 1998). Hence, women are discouraged from seeking a job, from continuing to look for one after unsuccessful searches, or from re-seeking employment after an interruption. Bettio and Villa have proposed that this hidden discouraged labour supply should be treated by supplementing the official measures of unemployment with women who have looked for a job but not enough to be included in official statistics, or those who have not looked for a job but declare themselves willing to work on certain conditions. Bettio and Villa show that, at the beginning of the 1990s, the gap between the standard and the corrected unemployment rates was larger for women than for men, and particularly high for women in the South. Indeed, whereas for Southern women aged 15-70 the rate rose from 27% to 49%, for women in the North it did so from 10% to 20%, and for those in the Central part of Italy from 14% to 28% (Bettio and Villa, 1996, table 20). Moreover, as underlined by studies concerned with the role of income and economic necessity in shaping women and household employment patterns (see Chapter Two), in poor economic contexts such as the South of Italy, large sectors of the population are, out of necessity, engaged in a mix of domestic work, informal economy and subsistence production. Thus, although difficult to capture in the survey data,[1] one should bear in mind that the assumption that women not (statistically) employed act as full-time carers may not hold. The incorrectness of this assumption has 'computational' consequences because, as explained in note 2 of Chapter Three, female actual rates of employment and continuity over the lifecourse may be underestimated. It also has material and symbolic sides. As argued by feminists in polemic with standard human capital theory, investments in education and labour market careers respond to both monetary and non-monetary rationales. However, paid work may have a non-monetary value for low-educated women as well. Indeed, although their decision to work has historically been mainly driven by income needs, the opportunity to earn an independent wage has also offered these women new forms of identity, as well as greater bargaining power within the family, thereby contributing to the diffusion over time of different gender normality models (Bimbi, 1992; Saraceno, 1992; Groppi, 1996).

Figure 5.3 focuses only on women who have experienced discontinuous careers by age 35. It shows the percentage of those interrupting at different stages of the family lifecourse: before marriage, after marriage, or after the first or second child.

In both countries, the timing of interruptions has been progressively postponed, moving from the period around marriage to the period around childbirth. However, in Italy, the fewer women who interrupt tend to do so earlier than their British counterparts: in the oldest cohort, 53% withdrew from paid work around marriage, as against 28% in Britain; in the youngest cohort, the figures were still 44% in Italy against only 9% in Britain. Moreover, an increasing proportion of women in Britain seem to remain attached to paid work as long as possible, exiting at second child, not the first. Indeed, as shown elsewhere, Italy and Britain differ markedly in the time spent out of the labour market. In Italy, episodes of

Figure 5.3: Incidence of different timings of interruptions (among women who interrupt by age 35) in Italy and Britain, by birth cohort

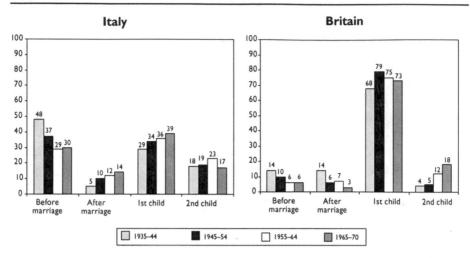

Notes: interruptions at 1st child and 2nd child include also the pregnancy period, that is, they may have occurred during the 9 months before the birth of the 1st or 2nd child or any time after.
Source: ILFI, 2005; BHPS, 2005

housework generally last much longer: for the oldest cohort, the median duration is 14 years in Italy as opposed to five years in Britain, and for the third cohort eight years against two years (Solera, 2005, table 5.3). This is the result of differences in behaviour between the two countries: in Italy, fewer women stop working once they have started; but many of these women do so before marriage, many never re-enter the labour market – or, if they re-enter, they do so later compared with British women, or at least British women from the second cohort onwards.

Has the trade-off between employment and family responsibilities changed? Evidence on women's transitions in and out of paid work

The first entry into paid work

As seen in the previous section, women's work patterns have changed little across cohorts in Italy. Continuous participation has always been by far the typical work path of women entering the Italian labour market. What has instead changed greatly over time is the proportion of women who start labour market careers. Gaining better understanding of the Italian case thus requires closer examination of the first entry into the labour market. What influences a woman's choice in regard to getting a job? Have these influences changed across cohorts? Or is it the same type of women who start a labour market career? An affirmative answer would provide evidence of the compositional nature of the post-war increase in women's employment, as hypothesised.

Table 5.1 reports the results of logit models used to estimate the probability of women having experienced at least one job episode by age 35. Since the dependent variable is the entire trajectory, and not specific transitions within it, and since the interest is in participation decisions rather than in the duration of job search, in these regression models I do not use event-history or other time-related methods. However, I could have benefited from the availability of longitudinal information by also introducing time into the covariates. For example, I could have used variables measured at different points in time (such as family or labour market situation at different ages) or which summarise the prevalent situation over the entire observational period. But these models would have raised serious problems of endogeneity. Hence, I decided to use only variables that are time-constant (such as cohort and family background) or, if time-varying, those that refer to the situation at first job. Although neither of these factors can be considered as fully exogenous to subsequent labour market choices and outcomes (particularly, as discussed in the previous chapter, in the case of educational attainment, where women's attitudes, plans and expectations vis-à-vis paid work may play an important role), they are at least measured prior to observed employment paths. Furthermore, as with the descriptive figures set out in the previous section, the observational window is closed at age 35.

Table 5.1: Logistic regression of women's first entry into the labour market by age 35 in Italy, by birth cohort

	All	1935-44	1945-54	1955-64	1965-74
Birth cohort: 1935-1944					
1945-1954	0.05				
1955-1964	0.24*				
1965-1974	−0.01				
Mother has never worked					
Mother has worked	0.33***	0.46**	0.64***	0.26*	**0.10**
Father's occupational score	−0.005*	−0.000	**−0.01***	0.005	**−0.01*****
Region: North					
Centre	−0.66***	−0.47*	−0.97***	−0.66**	−0.68***
South	−1.64***	−1.29***	**−1.87***	−1.83***	−1.79***
Education: Primary					
Lower Secondary	0.56***	0.59**	0.46**	0.17	0.80**
Upper Secondary	0.83***	0.60**	0.96***	0.95***	0.58*
Tertiary	1.15***	1.85***	2.37***	**0.69***	**0.76***
Constant	1.56***	1.16***	1.87***	1.74***	2.15***
Log-likelihood	−1593.1	−359.6	−389.1	−370.7	−448.3
Number of women	3,523	692	900	918	1013

Notes: ^ Robust Standard Errors; * p<.10; ** p<.05; ***p<.01; in **bold** = coefficients of second, third and fourth cohort that are different from the first cohort at least at .10 probability level.
Source: ILFI, 2005

Women's propensity to start a labour market career is significantly linked to education level, region and family background. As shown by Figure 5.2, compared to the Centre–North, in the South more women have never had a job episode up to age 35. As just said, this is the combined effect of social norms and scarce job opportunities, which discourage women's employment.

The importance of gender models also emerges in the effect of the mother's work experience. As other studies have found (Bernardi, 2001; Bratti, 2003), women who grew up within a dual-earner family are more likely to participate in the labour market, and they are also more likely to find a job. Evidently, women from families with less traditional gender roles – or at least families where the mother being at work was part of everyday 'normal' life – assimilate positive attitudes towards women's paid work, which make them more determined to start a labour market career. By contrast, once educational attainment is controlled for, the occupational score of the father matters little.[2] This suggests that, although the position of the father may influence his daughter's educational attainment, it has neither an independent influence on her attitude nor an independent 'social capital' effect that may help her find a job. If occupational score is used as a proxy for earnings capacity – that is, for the largest component of family income – my results indicate that non-own family income does not have an independent, significant influence on a woman's decision to first enter work, nor on the employment sector at first entry (Solera and Bettio, 2007). This echoes one of the most common findings in the female labour supply literature, namely that non-own income tends to have less of an impact than own wage or education on a woman's choices concerning work (for example, Di Tommaso, 1999; Bratti, 2003). The next chapter will show whether this also applies to the partner's resources, and whether and how this feature has changed over time.

As expected, the rise in women's labour market supply in Italy seems mainly a compositional effect. Indeed, when a single model is run for all cohorts, and controlling for educational level, social origin and region, the cohort coefficients on the probability of having never started to work are insignificant. Instead, region is the main effect that significantly changes across cohorts. More precisely, the North–South divide has widened over time: Southern women in the younger cohorts exhibit a lower probability of entering employment compared with those in the North, and with previous cohorts.

Also, the effect of education on the probability of entering paid work slightly changes across cohorts. Indeed, the odds of starting a labour market career for a woman with a tertiary degree are six times those of a woman with a basic education in the oldest cohort, and twice those of a woman in the youngest cohorts. That is to say, the gap between highly and poorly educated women has diminished over time, and entry for women into paid work has become, as expected, more 'universal'. Yet, as Bison et al (1996) report, this may hide a difference in behaviour between women in the South and North of Italy. Indeed, at least until the early 1990s, the labour supply increased for the middle educated (those with lower-secondary and upper-secondary qualifications) in the Centre–North of Italy, while it remained constant for the least and highest educated. In the South of Italy, by contrast, the labour supply changed only for the lowest educated: that is, it declined, probably as a result of diminished demand for labour in the agricultural sector without a parallel increase in other sectors.

Albeit with geographical differences, education in Italy is indubitably a powerful driving force behind women's labour market supply. In particular, education strongly affects not only whether or not a woman enters the labour market, but also the type of career that she will have once she has entered – as we shall see in the next section and, in more detail, in the next chapter.

Table 5.2: Estimated rates of women's first transition from employment to housework in Italy, by birth cohort (discrete time hazard rate models)

	All	1935-44	1945-54	1955-64	1965-74
Birth cohort: 1935-1944					
1945-1954	−0.13				
1955-1964	−0.09				
1965-1974	−0.19*				
Duration in employment	−0.001*	0.001	0.000	−0.001	−0.001
Education: up to lower-secondary					
upper-secondary or tertiary	−0.78***	−0.45**	−0.70***	−0.74***	**−0.94***
Class: service-petty bourgeo.					
routine non-manual workers	0.36**	0.80***	**0.05**	**0.20**	0.35
skilled manual workers	0.51***	0.70**	0.52*	0.35	0.25
unskilled non-manual workers	0.83***	0.80***	0.70***	0.90***	0.93***
unskilled manual workers	0.67***	0.80***	0.67***	0.52**	0.64**
Working time: full-time					
part-time	−0.24*	−1.19**	−0.14	0.34	**0.11**
Region: North					
Centre	0.03	0.005	0.10	−0.002	0.27
South	0.07	−0.05	**0.59***	**0.69***	**1.29***
Mother did not work					
mother worked	−0.03	0.09	−0.04	−0.10	−0.11
Yearly Unemployment rate	0.02	−0.18**	−0.17***	**−0.03**	**−0.03**
Marital status: not in couple					
married/cohabiting	−0.10	−1.18***	**−0.27**	0.15	0.86***
Child status: no children					
pregnant	1.97***	2.51***	2.13***	**1.63***	**1.65***
youngest child aged 0-3	1.01***	1.62***	**0.76**	**0.79**	**0.59*
youngest child aged 3+	0.10	0.24	0.15	0.11	−0.10
Number of children	−0.23***	−0.20*	−0.18	−0.07	−0.01
Constant	−6.60***	−5.77***	−5.97***	−6.42***	−7.04***
Log-likelihood	−5847.8	−1422.5	−1714.6	−1630.7	−1007.7
Number of months-persons	438,654	90,973	130,896	128,091	88,694
Number of women	2,886	541	733	783	830
Number of transitions	879	224	261	238	156

Notes: estimates using option « cluster » * p<.10; ** p< .05 ***p< .01; in **bold** = coefficients of second, third and fourth cohort that are different from the first cohort at least at .10 probability level.
Source: ILFI (2005)

Table 5.3: Estimated rates of women's first transition from employment to housework in Britain, by birth cohort (discrete time hazard rate models)

	All	1935-44	1945-54	1955-64	1965-74
Birth cohort: 1935-1944					
1945-1954	−0.18**				
1955-1964	−0.38***				
1965-1974	−0.62***				
Duration in employment	−0.003***	0.000	−0.002*	−0.005***	−0.004**
Education: up to lower-secondary					
upper-secondary or tertiary	−0.16**	−0.06	−0.10	−0.13	−0.36**
Class: service-petty bourgeo.					
routine non-manual workers	0.52***	0.26*	0.48***	**0.64***	0.36*
skilled manual workers	0.67***	0.43*	0.50***	**0.81***	**0.92***
unskilled non-manual workers	0.64***	0.35*	0.57***	**0.78***	**0.86***
unskilled manual workers	0.68***	0.32*	0.60***	**0.98***	**0.90***
Working time: full-time					
part-time	−0.20**	−0.70***	**−0.10**	**−0.30***	**0.05**
Region: England					
Wales	0.05	-0.10	**0.15**	0.06	**0.24**
Scotland	0.02	0.54***	**0.03**	**−0.22**	**−0.39**
Mother did not work					
mother worked	−0.12**	−0.21**	**0.02**	−0.11	−0.21
Yearly unemployment rate	−0.005	−0.12**	**−0.02**	**−0.001**	**0.06**
Marital status: not in couple					
married/cohabiting	0.68***	0.84***	0.80***	0.71***	**0.37***
Child status: no children					
pregnant	4.18***	3.77***	**4.28***	**4.40***	**4.63***
youngest child aged 0-3	3.15***	2.79***	2.96***	3.30***	**3.91***
youngest child aged 3+	1.68***	0.42	**1.92***	**2.54***	**1.48**
Number of children	−0.88***	−1.45***	−1.40***	**−0.57***	**−0.21*
Constant	−6.80***	−6.31***	−7.13***	−7.53***	−8.34***
Log-likelihood	−7262.5	−1785.2	−2293.2	−2104.3	−946.2
Number of months-persons	313,069	64,116	95,789	100,707	52,457
Number of women	2,514	538	765	761	450
Number of transitions	1,724	433	595	491	205

Notes: estimates using option «cluster» * p<.10; ** p<.05; ***p< .01; in **bold** = coefficients of second, third and fourth cohort that are different from the first cohort at least at .10 probability level.
Source: BHPS (2005)

The first transition out from paid work

Table 5.2 shows the results of models on Italian women's transition rates from employment to housework for all cohorts together, and then cohort by cohort. Highlighted in bold are the effects for the second, third and fourth cohorts, which differ significantly from the effects for the first cohort. Table 5.3 does the same for Britain.

As Bison et al (1996) and Bernardi (1999) also demonstrate, and in line with both human capital and social stratification theories, education and class importantly distinguish between women who leave the labour market and those who have continuous careers. The higher the level of a woman's education, the less likely she is to interrupt employment. Moreover, if she works in the service class, her risk of interrupting is lower than that of working women in the other classes, although the difference with respect to routine non-manual workers and skilled manual workers disappears in the youngest cohorts. In the last cohort, however, the gap between high- and low-educated women slightly increases. As noted in Chapter Two, institutional and cultural arrangements mediate the effect of individual-level characteristics such as education and class. Given an unfriendly set of opportunities and constraints, which, as seen in Chapter Three, has improved little since the 1970s reforms, it seems that Italian women have had to acquire the characteristics that have always fostered their labour market attachment in order to work and improve their careers, *in primis* investments in education. Education becomes particularly important for the fourth cohort, as women have had to undertake the Italian route to flexibilisation, which, as seen, has consisted in 'selective and partial' deregulation targeting only the early careers of young cohorts and offering very few guarantees in terms of income, stability, professional development and social protection. Education mitigates such lack of guarantees. In fact, although some studies show that entrapment in atypical jobs is lower for the middle educated than for the lowest and highest educated, and, in general, for those who have had only one, and a short, episode of atypicity (Barbieri and Scherer, 2008), others maintain that the highly educated are better equipped to cope with uncertainty. Indeed, they usually have higher earnings and savings and are better able to build 'good' social capital, that is, informal professional communities that exchange information and trust, useful for manoeuvering in a flexible labour market. In a familistic welfare regime, where coping with the risks associated with the new individualised employment relationship is left to private resources, highly educated people are also more protected by their 'richer' families (Bertolini and Rizza, 2005).[3]

Over time, the gap between southern and central-northern Italian women has widened as well (Villa, 2004). However, this regional effect disappears in all cohorts when controlling for sample selection, which suggests that there are unmeasured factors affecting both first job entry and first exit, and that such unmeasured factors have different 'weights' in the two regions. As stated in the previous chapter, in my analyses I do not measure micro preferences (only partly captured by the 'mother's work experience' but here used as a selection variable) and macro constraints in terms of work–family reconciliation supports and gender-childcare norms. Moreover, information on the partner is, for the moment, missing. Since Rho is positive (but significant only for the fourth cohort), it is unlikely that Rho captures preferences, or policies and norms: these, in fact, should work in the opposite direction, encouraging entries and discouraging exits, or vice versa. More plausibly, the positive sign of Rho reflects a mix of demand factors and family pressures. As suggested by attitudinal studies, women have become more work oriented over time; but because of the stagnant economic situation and the consequent worsening of employment opportunities during the 1980s and 1990s, especially in the South, women have also encountered more difficulties in finding good jobs and in keeping them. Faced with this negative economic situation, many southern women have probably been induced to work more out of necessity than out of strong preferences – that is, in response to low or unsure family incomes – or they have entered less well-paid or less fulfilling jobs. These women are thus also ready to leave their jobs when income needs become less urgent or domestic and care work more demanding.[4]

Not only the effect of education and class but also the effect of family responsibilities has changed little in Italy, at least compared to Britain (Table 5.3). Indeed, in both countries, pregnancy and the presence of a young child increase the risk of leaving the labour market. However, as was also evident from the cross-sectional comparative figures in Chapter Three, they have a weaker effect in Italy than in Britain. Moreover, in Britain the marriage effect grows weaker across cohorts, and the typical timing of exiting shifts from marriage to childbirth. At the same time, the proportion of continuous careers among married women increases. In Italy, by contrast, the marriage effect was negative in the oldest cohort, suggesting that those women who started to work (70% by age 35, see Figure 5.1) and those few who interrupted once started (40% by age 35) tended to interrupt before getting married, probably in view of marriage. Then the effect of marriage disappears in the second and third cohorts, to become positive in the last cohort, when polarisation generally increases. Finally, compared to Britain, in Italy not only does the age of the youngest child matter less but also the number of children. In fact, as described in Chapter Three, women in Italy enjoy much better protection during pregnancy and after childbirth (if they are in the formal economy and employees) and can more frequently rely on the help of the 'extended family' to resolve their childcare needs.

The work experience of the mother was and still is irrelevant in shaping women's movements out of paid work once it has been entered, whereas, as seen in Table 5.1, it has always mattered in inducing women to enter paid work. If the work experience of the mother is taken as a proxy for her daughter's work attitudes, this deposes in favour of one of my hypotheses. That is to say, in Italy, women's values and work orientations have little impact on work histories over the lifecourse. Rather, they matter earlier: when women decide how much to invest in education, whether or not to enter the labour market, in which type of sector, and how many children to have.[5]

Inspection of the first column of Table 5.2, where the cohort coefficients are insignificant once important individual characteristics are controlled for, but also of the few coefficients in bold in the following four columns, shows that the factors that keep women in the labour market are fairly constant across cohorts. Only in the last cohorts has the gap between highly educated and poorly educated women and between southern and northern women widened, while responsiveness to the age of children has diminished. Furthermore, as seen, the type of women starting labour market careers has remained quite constant, at least until the third cohort – that is, until the 1990s. Thus, in Italy the post-war growth in women's employment seems to have been mainly the result of a 'compositional' change: that is, women's involvement in paid work has not become 'universal', cutting across regions, levels of education and social classes. Rather, polarisation has assumed new forms: geographical disparities have increased in the first entry into paid work, while disparities between highly educated and poorly educated women have diminished. Moreover, both geographical and educational gaps have widened in the permanence over family formation.

We have seen that in Britain women from younger cohorts, and particularly from the last cohort, are less likely to leave the labour market. But if they do leave, they are more likely to return. These changes across cohorts in exit and re-entry rates seem not to be explainable by changes in the composition of the female population alone: in fact, in Britain the cohort coefficients are significant after controlling for important individual characteristics (Table 5.3, first column).

The main change has been brought about by married women and mothers. Indeed, the effect of marriage on exits from the labour market has grown weaker, while the effect of children, and particularly of pregnancy, has strengthened. Thus, the timing of employment interruptions has changed: while women from the older cohort typically stopped working when they got married, in the younger cohorts women tend to withdraw later, when they have their first child. In line with the attitudinal data shown in Chapter Three, this suggests that norms have changed over time. In the past only the work of single women without children was accepted and supported. Women with household and childcare responsibilities typically interrupted employment, and fewer of them restarted work. As a consequence of changes in women's orientations and behaviours, but also in social policies and labour market opportunities, more recently the employment of married women and mothers has become more feasible and desirable. Women in younger cohorts tend to work regardless of their family status, and when they have children, they tend to exit less or later, or to return to paid work more rapidly and on a larger scale. The changing effect of the number of children further confirms this: while in the oldest cohorts having more children was a strong disincentive to exit if the woman had not exited earlier, in the youngest cohorts this 'income needs inhibition' diminishes. This signals, on the one hand, a relaxation of income pressures, and on the other, an increase in women's labour market attachment: women try to stay in paid work as long as possible, some of them exiting not at the first child but at the second, when caring needs and work–family reconciliation probably become too onerous.

Although paid work has become central in female normality, participation by the younger cohorts is still strongly affected by the family life cycle. Whether this is due more to preferences or to constraints is not directly testable from the data available. However, as discussed in previous chapters, in a context where women, and not men, are still seen as mainly responsible for family care, where statutory maternity payments and support to childcare have remained poor and uneven, many women are still not protected and/or expected to leave paid work around childbirth. Many authors argue that the introduction of maternity legislation in 1976 has contributed to the greater stability of women's careers: their return to work after childbirth has increased and has become more rapid (McRae and Daniel, 1991; Duncan et al, 1998). However, gains from maternity leave and other family-friendly policies have been far from uniform. Because of the difficulties in sustaining childcare arrangements, and because of strict requirements for the right to maternity payments and to reinstatement, many women in the 1980s and 1990s still did not manage to remain in work, especially those with short-term jobs in the secondary labour market (McRae, 1991, 1993; McRae and Daniel, 1991; Joshi et al, 1996). Improvements in the early 2000s under New Labour were too timid and too recent to be captured in my data.[6]

As evident from the descriptive figures above, and as hypothesised, over time British women have become more attached to paid work but also more heterogeneous in the incidence and timing of their exits and re-entries. Indeed, for the older cohort, housework interruption was mainly driven by family-related factors. Education, labour market experience and position mattered little. Only women working part time, and women from the service class and petty bourgeoisie showed a significantly lower propensity to exit. As described by McCulloch and Dex (2001), and as we shall see in the next chapter, in the post-war decades women's exits and re-entries responded more to their partner's than to their own education and occupation. In the absence of general support for maternal employment, women in the past were also more affected by the gender and family model in which they had grown up. Indeed, women whose mothers worked were less likely to exit from employment and more likely to return to it if they did exit.

Subsequently, as the employment of married women and mothers became more accepted, individual characteristics began to differentiate to a greater extent: in younger cohorts the time spent in employment and the social class also started to play a role, while whether or not the woman had grown up with a working mother decreased in importance. As expected, class differences became more accentuated with the last cohort, which formed its families and careers under the Conservatives' deregulation of the 1980s and 1990s. Instead, in contrast to human capital predictions, women with different educational levels do not show significant differences in their job-leaving rates, except in the youngest cohort. Only if one omits class from the model does education become significant. Evidently, in a liberal regime, with a residualist social policy and high wage dispersion, class is more important than education. Education itself does not guarantee employment continuity. Rather, British women who, to use Hakim's (2000) terms, are not 'home centred' but in more structural terms are anyway constrained by the context, need to have spent a long time in the labour market and to have reached relatively good positions if they are to enjoy some maternity protection and/or sufficient incomes to purchase care.

Unlike in Britain, in Italy the differences in exit rates between highly educated and poorly educated women are greater and still persist when controlling for class. In 'deregulated' Britain, women can obtain a new job relatively easily; in 'rigid' Italy, women's future work careers and their possibilities of combining them with children depend strongly on initial conditions, and particularly on the education that they receive and the type of job with which they begin. In fact, unlike in Britain where career mobility is high (Heath and Cheung, 1998; Breen, 2004), in Italy mobility chances are low and education exerts a strong and direct influence on first occupational attainment (Schizzerotto and Cobalti, 1998; Pisati and Schizzerotto, 1999, 2003). Moreover, in a context of relatively poor job opportunities and reconciliation policies, education offers extra competitive advantages. Not only does it ease the access, as elsewhere, to many good occupations and to the career ladder; it also eases entry into family-convenient jobs such as those in the public sector, which, in the Italian type of welfare regime, have represented the main public 'resource' for the combination of family and work responsibilities. In Italy, indeed, wage, employment and career protection policies have been used as surrogates for a wider and a more universal package of reconciliation provisions, offering very attractive conditions in some sectors while further segmenting the labour force.[7] Finally, education in Italy has a strong effect, beyond class and wages, on women's entry and permanence in the labour market because, more than elsewhere, education also differentiates approval of women's new roles. As outlined in Chapter Two, there is evidence that where a general cultural shift has not occurred, the non-monetary side of investments in education tends to be stronger. Education may indeed convey higher legitimation to work from self and others.

In Britain, only in the last cohort do highly educated women exhibit a stronger attachment to paid work regardless of their occupational class. Since their chances of reconciliation when they have low-paid jobs are not particularly dissimilar from those of low-educated women, this can be read as an 'attitude effect'.[8] That is to say, it can be interpreted as being more an agency than a coping strategy. Evidently, for either instrumental or cognitive-identity reasons, these women are less ready to give up their investments in education and in the labour market, and they remain attached to paid work even when the income, the conditions and presumably the satisfaction of their jobs are not as good as expected.

Interestingly, while in Italy education and class influence women's likelihood of stopping work, the time spent in employment does not matter. This further reinforces the role of education and class. A woman who is not self-employed or in the service class risks, in relative terms, exiting from the labour market regardless of how long she has been employed. This is again different from what happens in Britain, where labour market experience does matter for the second cohort onwards.

The first transition back into paid work

Contrary to the case of the first transition out of paid work, in Italy changes across cohorts in re-entry rates are not entirely compositional (Table 5.4, first column). However, if separate models by cohorts are run (second to fifth column), one finds that, in all cohorts, very few factors drive women back into paid work, and that, over time, only the effects of southern mothers' work experience and number of children have significantly changed. Without controlling for sample selection, women from the South have a higher propensity to exit and a lower propensity to re-enter the labour market compared with those living in the Centre-North

Table 5.4: Estimated rates of women's first transition from housework to employment in Italy, by birth cohort (discrete time hazard rate models)

	All	1935-44	1945-54	1955-64	1965-74
Birth cohort: 1935-1944					
1945-1954	0.35**				
1955-1964	0.50***				
1965-1974	1.20***				
Duration in housework	−0.007***	−0.008***	−0.01***	−0.005*	−0.003
Previous labour market experience	−0.002**	−0.003	−0.002	−0.002	−0.001
Education: up to lower-secondary					
upper-secondary or tertiary	−0.24	−0.36	0.01	−0.21	−0.16
Class: service-petty bourgeo.					
routine non-manual workers	−0.44*	−1.25*	−0.51	−0.51	−0.31
skilled manual workers	−0.75**	0.13	**−1.50****	—	0.65
unskilled non-manual workers	−0.22	0.05	**−0.87*****	−0.08	0.01
unskilled manual workers	−0.35**	−0.26	−0.19	−0.45	−0.70*
Working time last job: full-time					
part-time	0.04	0.08	0.52	−0.24	0.14
Region: North					
Centre	−0.09	0.44*	**−0.30**	0.20	**−1.11****
South	−0.62**	0.80	**−1.53****	0.000	**−1.78***
Mother did not work					
mother worked	0.14*	−0.21	−0.22	**0.56****	**1.05*****
Yearly unemployment rate	−0.05*	−0.33*	−0.10*	**−0.06**	**0.02**
Marital status: not in couple					
married/cohabiting	−0.87***	−1.10**	−1.64***	−0.49	−0.78*
Child status: no children					
pregnant or youngest child aged 0-3	−0.28	−0.43	0.47	−1.34***	0.43
youngest child aged 3+	0.37*	0.30	1.17*	−0.29	0.69
Number of children	0.18***	0.50***	0.38***	**0.07**	**−0.34***
Constant	−4.32***	−3.49***	−3.69***	−3.78***	−4.05***
Log-likelihood	−1944.2	−427.8	−598.1	−532.9	−330.9
Number of months-persons	106721	29425	34345	29365	12164
Number of women	912	220	263	251	167
Number of transitions	302	66	95	83	58

Notes: estimates using option « cluster » *p< .10; **p< .05; ***p< .01; in **bold** = coefficients of second, third and fourth cohort that are different from the first cohort at least at .10 probability level.
Source: ILFI (2005)

part of Italy. Controlling for sample selection, women from the South have the same propensity to exit but still a lower propensity to re-enter.[9] Indeed, as already noted, in the South of Italy employment prospects are much worse and gender norms more traditional, so that women are discouraged from working. It might also be that, in view of these constraints, southern women who start to work and anyway decide to interrupt are a very selective group. They are probably women who have mainly entered paid work out of necessity, who work in the informal sector or low-grade regular employment, and who are oriented towards a 'marriage career'. Therefore, these types of women do not intend to re-enter the labour market or may accept the risk of permanent exclusion from it if they later desire or need to re-enter.

Furthermore, Italian women in younger cohorts seem more affected by the behaviours of their mothers. This suggests that in more recent times preferences (at least those captured by mothers' work experience) have started to differentiate work histories later, also during family formation. They do not count only at the very beginning in the decision on how much to invest in education and on whether to start to work in the first place, as was the case for the oldest cohorts. They also matter later, in the decision on whether to return after having interrupted. Finally, in younger cohorts, the income pressure to re-enter in response to an increasing number of children seems to diminish.

While both family and social stratification factors affect a woman's exit from the labour market, her re-entry is independent of the social class of her last job and of her level of education. It is also independent of the working time of the previous job and of the overall time previously spent in employment. Yet, as in Britain, and as in the case of any 'second' transition, this may be partly a sample selection effect, which has reduced the variability of these factors. In Italy, however, the selection is stronger because, given difficult re-entry opportunities, women who anyway decide to interrupt are a very selective group, as just noted. After these women have interrupted, only few circumstances seem to encourage or inhibit their return to paid work. In addition to the already-mentioned number of children and region, the breakdown of a partnership seems to matter, pushing women back into paid work. This is indubitably due to the fact that, until recently, in Italy separation and divorce have been middle- and upper-class phenomena: that is, they have concerned women who are relatively well educated and with high earnings potential, whose intentions and actual chances of finding another job are higher (Barbagli and Saraceno, 1998; Todesco, 2008). However, a welfare mechanism may also be at work. Indeed, apart from a general family allowance when the woman is an employee and has a low income, Italy does not provide any specific income support for single mothers. Nor does it have any general national minimum income scheme. Thus, without a husband's support, and with weak public support, separated or divorced women may actually have to work.

In Britain, by contrast, divorce does not seem to drive women back to work. Rather, in younger cohorts, it prevents them from re-entering (Table 5.5). The different welfare systems certainly play a role in this difference. British single

Table 5.5: Estimated rates of women's first transition from housework to employment in Britain, by birth cohort (discrete time hazard rate models)

	All	1935-44	1945-54	1955-64	1965-74
Birth cohort: 1935-1944					
1945-1954	0.22**				
1955-1964	0.55***				
1965-1974	1.03***				
Duration in housework	−0.003***	0.000	**−0.003**	**−0.004**	**−0.004***
Previous labour market experience	0.002**	0.001	**−0.000**	0.002**	0.002
Education: up to lower-secondary					
upper-secondary or tertiary	0.05	0.09	0.03	0.16	−0.06
Class: service-petty bourgeo.					
routine non-manual workers	−0.22**	−0.31*	−0.26	−0.01	−0.69***
skilled manual workers	−0.45***	−0.70**	−0.46**	**0.13**	−1.17***
unskilled non-manual workers	−0.25**	−0.38*	−0.27*	**0.15**	−0.80***
unskilled manual workers	−0.35***	−0.23	−0.38**	−0.33*	−0.62**
Working time last job: full-time					
part-time	−0.02	−0.00	0.22	−0.06	−0.02
Region: England					
Wales	−0.13*	−0.44***	**−0.10**	**−0.12**	**0.61***
Scotland	0.03	−0.11	0.18	−0.12	0.23
Mother did not work					
mother worked	0.13**	0.27**	0.06	0.04	0.29*
Yearly unemployment rate	−0.03**	−0.09*	**−0.01**	**−0.01**	−0.04
Marital status: not in couple					
married/cohabiting	0.34***	0.16	0.20	0.28*	0.45*
Child status: no children					
pregnant or youngest child aged 0-3	−0.76***	−0.87***	−0.64**	−0.63**	−1.01**
youngest child aged 3+	0.07	−0.04	0.34	0.17	−0.35
Number of children	0.08**	0.04	0.02	0.12*	0.13
Constant	−4.47***	−4.14***	−4.04***	−4.32***	−2.92***
Log-likelihood	−7636.7	−1932.4	−2623.1	−2175.1	−897.9
Number of months-persons	133,975	41,128	49,141	33,461	102,45
Number of women	1,779	434	583	518	244
Number of transitions	1,469	351	491	432	195

Notes: estimates using option « cluster » *p<.10; **p<.05; ***p<.01*; in **bold** = coefficients of second, third and fourth cohort that are different from the first cohort at least at .10 probability level.
Source: BHPS (2005)

mothers who do not work can rely, like any other person without earnings, on means–tested benefits. By leaving income support, a mother loses entitlement to free school meals and milk for her child, and to the full coverage of housing costs and interest on mortgage payments. In addition, if she has a young child, she needs to find childcare arrangements and to pay for them. Although social assistance is relatively ungenerous, for a woman who has interrupted her labour market participation and experienced human capital depreciation entering paid work may not pay off, or at least it was not so until the early 2000s when New Labour launched the New Deal for Lone Parents (Solera, 2001).

Contrary to the case of the first transition out of paid work, in Britain the factors affecting transitions back into the labour market have changed little across cohorts. Re-entries into the labour market by the oldest cohort were affected by childbearing responsibilities, region, social class and work attitudes. Education, time spent out of paid work and previous labour market experience seemed not to matter. Most of these effects do not change in subsequent cohorts.[10] Thus, the probability of re-entering still does not differ significantly by number of children, level of education and type of job, although this, again, may be partly due to a sample selection effect.[11] Yet, unlike in the oldest cohorts, regional differences in re-entry rates disappear in the second and third cohorts, to appear again in the youngest cohort (but with an opposite sign – that is, with a greater tendency to re-enter in Wales than in England and Scotland).

In youngest cohorts class also starts to weigh more, and previous labour market experience starts to matter. As seen, the decision whether or not to interrupt has also become, in youngest cohorts, more responsive to duration in employment and to occupational class. In other words, polarisation has increased. This is consistent with institutional theories and, in particular, with the earlier-discussed expectations concerning the consequences of the Conservatives' policies of the 1980s and 1990s. It also supports criticisms against individuation theories: women now appear more heterogeneous and less constrained by rigid normative prescripts on motherhood, lifecourse sequences and gender roles, but they are also now more differentiated by social class. As institutional-oriented scholars and feminists have pointed out, class shapes, at the micro level, both attitudes and behaviours, and both material and symbolic resources. Class is also institutionally and culturally embedded. In a liberal welfare regime like that of Britain, women with low educations and low-paid jobs may not be able to afford to purchase private care and stay attached to the labour market. At the same time, they may have different work orientations, being *à la* Hakim (Hakim, 2000) more 'family centred' or building, *à la* 'doing gender' theory, different moral rationalities and moral careers. Again, the data available do not allow direct tests to be made of Hakim's claims, or more generally, of the weight of individual intentions versus social structure. However, contrary to individuation claims, the data show that class is not 'dead' in either British or Italian society.

Conclusion

In the post-war period, women's employment increased markedly in all the advanced countries. Indeed, not only did women begin to enter the labour market on a more massive scale, but they also reduced their exit rates or they shortened their family-care breaks. Yet, countries differed greatly in the incidence of continuous or discontinuous careers, in the profile of those who left the labour market and those who returned, and in how this changed across cohorts.

Taking a long break during the childrearing years was the distinctive pattern in Britain during the post-war decades. Since the mid-1960s, an increasing percentage of women have never left the labour market and, if they have done so, more of them have returned, and more rapidly. Among those who have returned, a higher proportion have subsequently stopped working again. Consistent with previous findings, this suggests that women in younger cohorts are less ready to remain out of the labour market during the entire family formation phase until all the children have grown up. Rather, they return into employment more often between births and more rapidly after childbearing. Yet their tendency to re-enter with part-time jobs, and not to shift to full-time ones later, or to interrupt again, has remained high. In other words, as expected, British women have indubitably become more attached to the labour market, but they have also become more polarised.

Also in Italy women's attachment to the labour market has increased across cohorts. However, this has occurred through a reduction not in the share of discontinuous careers or in the duration of employment breaks, as in Britain, but in the proportion of women who have never started a labour market career. Indeed, in Italy during the 1950s and 1960s about one in five women in the Centre-North and one in two women in the South never experienced an episode of paid work. Later, when labour demand and policies became more women friendly, women increasingly entered the labour market and sought to do so even when job opportunities were scarce, as in the South. In the Centre-North, where demand for labour, childcare services and norms are less penalising, they have also increasingly pursued continuous careers. But, as in the past, once they have started to work, women in younger generations differ little in terms of their employment paths: either they never stop working or, if they stop to take care of their families, they never restart. In Italy, continuous participation has been by far the most typical pattern. Moreover, although in both countries the timing of interruptions has been progressively postponed, in Italy the fewer women who interrupt tend to do so earlier than their British counterparts and to re-enter less and later. Thus, overall, Italy can be described as displaying an 'opt-in/opt-out' participation pattern.

Italy and Britain differ not only in the incidence and timing of continuous, discontinuous or curtailed careers but also in the profile of those who follow these types of careers. In Britain, the increasing attachment of women to paid work seems not to be entirely 'compositional'. Indeed, many of the factors affecting women's exits from and re-entries into paid work have changed across cohorts. The employment of married women and mothers has become more acceptable. In the past, women typically left the labour market at the time of marriage, regardless of their level of education, their occupational class and their labour market experience. Only women from the petty bourgeoisie or service class or those who had grown up within a dual-earner family had a significant lower propensity to interrupt. In the oldest cohort, women differed much more in their return to paid work. As the norm of the stay-at-home mother declined, and the institutional support for work–family reconciliation improved, maternal employment became more widely accepted while women's preferences grew more heterogeneous and influential at an earlier stage of their lifecourses. In other words, the crucial decision shifted from whether and when to re-enter employment to whether and when to leave it in the first place. Consequently, in more recent times, women have begun to reduce exits, or to postpone them from the time of marriage to the time of childbirth. Their decisions have also become less influenced by the number of children and more responsive to social class and labour market experience.

The biggest change in women' employment behaviour has occurred with the third and fourth cohort: that is, among women who built their families and careers in the 1980s and 1990s. These women were the first full beneficiaries of statutory maternity provisions. But they were also those who were fully exposed to the liberal policies of the Conservative governments, under which the experience of employment in connection to motherhood polarised. As expected, polarisation has been essentially based on human capital and class position: the longer women have been working and the higher their occupational position, the less they stop working. Indeed, labour market experience and entry into high-grade jobs not only enable women to benefit from new maternity schemes; when public childcare services are scarce, they also enable women to purchase private childcare. Because the Conservatives' deregulation widened class as well as part-time/full-time differences, since then a division has emerged in the younger cohorts between highly educated and poorly educated women. The next chapter will explore this changing role of education more thoroughly.

Unlike in Britain, in Italy changes since the Second World War in women's lifetime employment patterns have been mainly driven by changes in the composition of the female population. Indeed, the effects of education, social class and children on the risk of exiting from and returning to paid work have remained quite constant across cohorts. Only in the last cohort, and in contrast with my hypotheses, has the gap between highly educated and poorly educated women widened, while exits around childbirth have diminished. In recent decades, also the divide between the South and the Centre-North of Italy has widened, especially in the first entry into paid work, with 36% of southern women never starting a labour market career against only 8% in the Centre-North. Moreover, in the last cohorts, re-entries have become more closely affected by the gender models within which women have grown up, and less by increasing numbers of children. Overall, these findings suggest that, in more recent times, preferences have started to differentiate work histories later, and also during family formation. They not only count at the very beginning in the decision on how much to invest in education and on whether to start working in the first place, as it used to be for the oldest cohorts, but they also matter later in the decision on whether to interrupt or to return after having interrupted. These findings are also consistent with accounts of the effect of post-1997 Italian deregulation policies. In the face of 'partial and selective' deregulation targeted on new entrants, offering few social protections and not accompanied by general welfare reforms, highly educated women have more individual and familial resources on which they can draw to cope with uncertainty.

Despite these changes, Italy exhibits a much higher stability over time compared with Britain. Indeed, changes have concerned entries and re-entries much more than exits, and they have mainly appeared with the last cohort – that is, since the mid-1990s. For many decades, in Italy the profile of those able to pursue a continuous career remained the same. In particular, education was (and still is) the main discriminating factor. This suggests, as hypothesised, that in Italy it is more a 'compositional effect' than a 'gender inequality effect', which explains the growth of women's employment from the 1960s to the 1990s. In a study on gender differences in the chances of participating and remaining continuously in the labour market, Schizzerotto et al (1995) also show that in Italy, by controlling for education, family burdens and type of occupation, inequalities between men and women have not diminished across cohorts. Nor have disparities among women diminished: being highly educated, unmarried and childless increases a woman's chances of starting to work and having a long full-time career to the same extent in old and young cohorts. Using cross-sectional data on changes in activity rates by levels of education, Reyneri (2002) calculates that about two thirds of the increase in the female labour supply during the 1970s and 1980s was due to the increase in education. Overall, these findings suggest that, in order to increase their labour market participation and to improve the length and the quality of their careers, women have had to become well educated. But not only this. Without a general cultural shift in support for the new roles of women, and without significant improvements in defamilialisation policies, in parent-friendly flexibilisation, and in employment and occupational prospects, if women have wanted to keep attached to the labour market they have also had to reduce their family responsibilities – as cross-country comparative figures on marriage and fertility rates reveal. Thus, behind the apparent compositional change observed in Italy, there is women's agency. That is, there are important changes in women's attitudes, expectations and strategies. As the literature on women's identities has pointed out (Bimbi, 1992; Saraceno, 1992; Mapelli, 2005; Piccone Stella and Salmieri, 2007), the meanings women in younger cohorts give to paid work, as well as to marriage and motherhood, are different from those given by their mothers and grandmothers. Together with institutional and demand-side changes, this has induced women to adopt different choices: women have intentionally increased their – material and symbolic – investments in education and in the labour market in order to assure themselves 'room' outside the domestic sphere. As we shall see in the next chapter, education seems to have helped women also to increase their bargaining power and become more individualised within their partnerships. This appears in the declining importance of the partner's education and occupation together with the increasing importance of the woman's own education and occupation in affecting her entry and permanence in the labour force.

As expected, in Italy, differences between highly educated and poorly educated women are greater than in Britain, and they are still observable after controlling for class. Moreover, in Italy, women's movements in and out of paid work are less affected by age and number of children. As many welfare state scholars point out, the different institutional and structural settings of the two countries certainly play a role. In Britain, where a highly deregulated labour market has generated a wide spread of earnings and where a residualist welfare state has induced women to rely on private resources (market and family) while still defining them as mainly responsible for family work, educated mothers must also have long work experience or high-ranking jobs in order to enjoy some maternity protection, or sufficient income to purchase care. In Italy, by contrast, well-educated women tend to remain in employment even when they do not have access to the primary labour market because, like the low educated, they can rely on informal childcare from extended family more often than their British counterparts. Italian educated women may also be prevented from exiting by the higher 'rigidity' of the labour market and the 'partial and selective' deregulation of recent decades. The opportunity cost of not being able to re-enter, in fact, is too high for women who have invested in human capital and who have not built their moral careers only within the domestic sphere. Moreover, in a context such as Italy where traditional gender and childcare norms are still quite widespread, education may pay off with higher legitimation (from self and others) to work. Differences across countries in the impact of motherhood are also, partly, a selection effect. Compared to Britain, more women never start a labour market career in Italy; but those who do so – despite continuing cultural and structural barriers – are generally 'privileged', being typically more motivated, better educated and more frequently employed in well-protected sectors, especially in the South.

How, therefore, have the employment trajectories around marriage and children of highly educated and poorly educated women changed across generations? And how have they differed in time between women married to high- or low-class men? By running separate analyses by women's education, and then by adding information on the education and the social class of their partners, the next chapter will add further insights into changing forms of polarisation in Italian and British women's work–family combinations.

Notes

[1] This difficulty applies to any quantitative survey, including the ILFI. More precisely, the ILFI, unlike national statistical sources such as ISTAT, records as irregular employment only 'black' employment, that is, jobs without any form of contract or protection. Moreover, the ILFI collects data only for persons aged over 18 resident in Italy: hence, unlike ISTAT, it excludes irregular jobs held by the under-18s and by non-resident immigrants. As a result, in 1997 the proportion of non-regular employees was estimated at 12% by Istat, but at 5% by the ILFI (Schizzerotto, 2002a, table 6.2).

[2] The same result is obtained when using the father's social class instead of his occupational score.

[3] Another possible explanation for the increasing effect of education on women's risk of exiting paid work may be 'compositional': that is, it is due to different rates and types of entry and permanence in atypical positions of highly educated and poorly educated women. Yet the increase in the last cohort is still observable when, in addition to class and part-time work, one controls for type of contract, private/public sector and firm size (these variables are available in the ILFI but not in the BHPS, and are consequently not used in the comparative analyses). Thus, a more plausible explanation is that women with the same types of contract, firm and occupational class, but with different educational profiles, occupy more fulfilling and qualified jobs and/or have more resources with which to survive when the atypical contract expires, and to shorten the duration of unemployment, finding new job opportunities more rapidly.

[4] In the case of Italy, control for sample selection (using the selection variable 'mother's work experience', a variable that affects the chances of entering employment in the first place but not of interrupting later, once started) is significant only in the last cohort. In the fourth cohort, Rho is equivalent to 0.30 (p 0.005) against 0.01 ($p = 0.33$) in the third cohort, and 0.07 ($p = 0.60$) and 0.24 ($p = 0.20$) in the first two cohorts. In fact, since many women in the youngest cohort can be observed only up to 30-35 years old instead of 40 as in previous cohorts, estimates for the last cohort capture only certain types of women. Throughout the last decades, when entry into stable jobs has been difficult and lengthy, and when motherhood has been postponed, those few women entering paid work and motherhood relatively early, around their thirties, probably exhibit specific profiles: they are more 'family centred' and/or they have more unstable or less fulfilling jobs. They therefore tend to enter paid work more frequently and more rapidly, but also to exit from it.

[5] More precisely, in Italy, in the last cohort, having had a working mother or otherwise seems no longer to make any difference to the chances of starting a labour market career (Table 5.1). This, together with the declining effect of education, is a further signal of the 'universalisation' or 'diffusion' of women's entry into paid work.

[6] Indeed, the majority of women in the youngest cohorts tended to become mothers before the implementation of New Labour reforms. Median age at first birth is equal to 23.9 and 27.2 for low-educated and high-educated women born between 1955 and 1964. For those born between 1965 and 1970, the numbers are 23.2 and 27.5 respectively.

[7] In particular, jobs in the public sector have traditionally offered: shorter hours; lower pressure to work long hours and more flexible schedules; greater tolerance of absenteeism and better opportunities to take unpaid or paid leave without penalties on re-entry; access to jobs through educational credentials and wage and career advancements through seniority; until the late 1990s, generous early retirement schemes.

[8] In a liberal welfare regime like that of Britain, the chances of work–family combination depend strongly on the overall resources to which women have access, and therefore also

on the partner's resources. Given the high level of homogamy in mate selection, it is likely that highly educated women are married to highly educated men, even those who do not reach good job positions. Thus, the increasing polarisation in employment transitions between poorly educated and highly educated women partly reflects the general increase, in the 1980s and 1990s, of polarisation between double full-time households and one-earner-and-a-half households, and between high-status and low-status double full-time households. However, the evidence shows that the incidence of homogamy declined in the UK after the 1970s and did not substantially change in the 1990s (Halpin and Chan, 2003). Moreover, although during the 1980s and 1990s male unemployment, wage inequalities and thus intra-household inequalities increased, in the late 1990s and early 2000s New Labour reforms mainly benefited low- and middle-income families. It is therefore likely that the stronger attachment to paid work shown by young highly educated women in Britain also reflects a change in orientations and preferences.

[9] Indeed, unlike in the case of the first transition out of paid work (estimated jointly with the transition into first job), a bivariate probit model with selection for the first transition back into paid work (estimated jointly with the first transition out of paid work) is not significant. Using education and time of last job as selection variables, estimates obtained with uncorrected probit and corrected probit were in fact fairly similar in all cohorts.

[10] More precisely, from the second cohort onwards, education becomes relevant in differentiating between chances of re-entering employment if part-time/full-time work is removed and a control for sample selection is performed. As discussed in Chapter Three, in Britain, in fact, labour market segmentation has followed the part-time/full-time divide, and education has become a strong correlate of the female type of labour market participation. The link between part-time employment and family-care breaks is also evident when second transitions in and out of paid work are studied. Whereas the type of job did not make a difference in the first interruption, it influences the second one: British women who, after the first family-care break, re-enter the labour market on a part-time basis more frequently interrupt for the second time compared with those working full time. Part-time work also has a positive, although not significant, effect on the probability of re-entering the labour market after the first interruption (Solera, 2005, tables 6.7 and 6.8). This may be due to the lower opportunity cost of quitting a part-time job compared with a full-time job, and to the lower ability to restart on a full-time basis, given human capital and childcare constraints. However, *à la* Hakim (Hakim, 1991, 2000) , it may also be due to a long-term strategy adopted by those women who desire or expect to have many employment interruptions for childcare responsibilities. That is to say, the causal relationship may be the reverse: it is not that women leave and re-enter the labour market because they work or have worked part time; rather, they work part time because they expect to have more children and to move between employment and housework. Whatever the causal chain may be, it is indubitable that in Britain many women do not pursue continuous careers and alternate episodes of part-time paid work with episodes of full-time family care.

[11] Unlike Italy, in the case of Britain the Heckman control for sample selection (using as selection variables 'part-time full-time work' and 'education', variables that affect the chances of interrupting paid work but not of re-entering it, once interrupted) is significant in all cohorts with a Rho of roughly −0.30 in the first three cohorts and −0.70 in the last cohort ($p < 0.05$). However, estimates do not change substantially apart from the effect of marriage, which in the probit corrected for sample selection remains significant only in the last cohort, and the effect of having a child over three, which now significantly reduces chances of re-entering employment. This, again as in the case of Italy, suggests that among the unmeasured factors captured through Rho, family income and the partner's characteristics have a weight.

SIX

'Her' and 'his' education and class: new polarisations in work histories

Introduction

Everywhere, education is a strong discriminator of women's labour market supply and types of family–work combination. As discussed in Chapter Two, it gives access to higher job positions and wages, it mediates attitudes and identities and it furnishes greater bargaining power in adopting 'preferred' choices. Moreover, everywhere a woman's allocation of time between paid and unpaid work is negotiated within the household, and, because of either cognitive or instrumental rationality, it is influenced by her partner's symbolic and material resources. However, variations across countries in the link between education, motherhood and participation are still wide. This chapter focuses precisely on the family–work nexus and on its variation according first to the woman's education, and then to her partner's education and class. Do women with low educations behave differently from those with high educations when they get married or become mothers? In particular, is motherhood a social leveller, or does education overcome motherhood's typically negative effect on participation? Do women married to high-educated or high-class men behave differently from those whose husbands have a lower educational and occupational profile? And how has all this changed across generations?

Education and types of work history

Descriptive evidence

As evidenced by Figure 3.2, Italy records one of the widest gaps in participation between poorly educated and highly educated women in Europe. By using cross-sectional data, Bettio and Villa (1996, 2000) have found that nine out of 10 top-educated Italian women aged 20-39 are in the labour force when they do not have children. The participation rates of their lower-educated counterparts diminish by roughly a third. Motherhood reduces participation to a lesser extent, depending on the mother's level of education. While highly educated Italian women with children aged under 14 record a participation rate that is only six percentage points lower than that of highly educated childless women, low-educated mothers reduce their activity rates by 22 percentage points compared with their childless counterparts (Bettio and Villa, 1996, 2000). Indeed, in comparative terms, Italy also records one of the lowest child effects. Among less than upper-secondary-educated women, 55% with children, against 62% without children, were in continuous employment during the period 1994-98. The corresponding figures for Britain were 54% and 76% respectively. Among tertiary-educated women in Italy, contrary to their British counterparts, those with children are more often in continuous employment than those without children (OECD, 2002, table 2.8).

Similarly to the procedure in second section of Chapter Five, Figure 6.1 draws on the BHPS and the ILFI to show the distribution of women's types of work history by cohort and education. Figure 6.2 does likewise by explicitly including motherhood in the frame: that is, by distinguishing between mothers and non-mothers. Figure 6.3 breaks Italy down into regions, calculating the share, by cohort, education and motherhood, of different types of work history up until age 35 in the Centre-North and South of Italy. Finally, Figure 6.4 focuses only on women who have experienced discontinuous careers by age 35, and it shows the percentage of poorly educated or highly educated women who interrupt paid work at different stages of the family lifecourse.

The findings for Italy yield three insights. The first is rather as expected: education favours continuity and, in line with previous studies (Addabbo, 1999; Bettio and Villa, 2000), it seems that in Italy women's labour supply responds much more to education than to motherhood. Indeed, the gap between highly educated and poorly educated women in the share of continuous employment among those who have started a labour market career is no more than 30 absolute percentage points. Moreover, motherhood has a strong influence on work history continuity only at low levels of education – apart from the oldest cohort, where for both highly educated and poorly educated mothers the gap with respect to

Figure 6.1: Incidence of different types of work history up to age 35 in Italy and Britain, by birth cohort and education

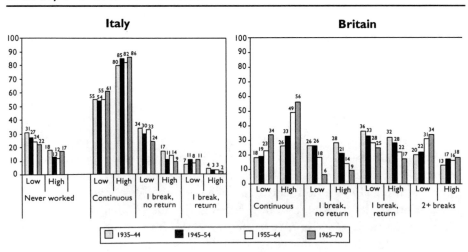

Notes: low-educated =up to lower-secondary; high-educated=upper-secondary or tertiary.
Source: ILFI, 2005; BHPS, 2005

Figure 6.2: Incidence of different types of work history up to age 35 in Italy and Britain, by birth cohort, education and motherhood

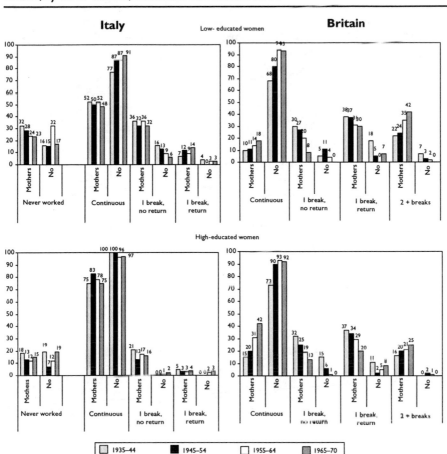

Notes: Low-educated =up to lower-secondary; High-educated=upper-secondary or tertiary.
Source: ILFI, 2005; BHPS, 2005

non-mothers is 25 absolute percentage points. However, childless Italian women tend to be more continuous than mothers among the less educated, whereas the impact of motherhood almost halves among women with intermediate or higher levels of education.

The second insight is that North–South divides are still marked in Italy. In the Centre-North, nearly all women start a labour market career; but once highly educated women have started, their careers are more frequently continuous and less affected by motherhood than those of low-educated women. Moreover, in the Centre-North, little has changed across cohorts. Only from the second cohort onwards has the impact of motherhood reduced for both highly educated and poorly educated women. In the South of Italy, differences between poorly educated and highly educated women emerge primarily from the first entry into paid work,

Figure 6.3: Incidence of different types of work history up to age 35 in Centre-North and South of Italy, by birth cohort, education and motherhood

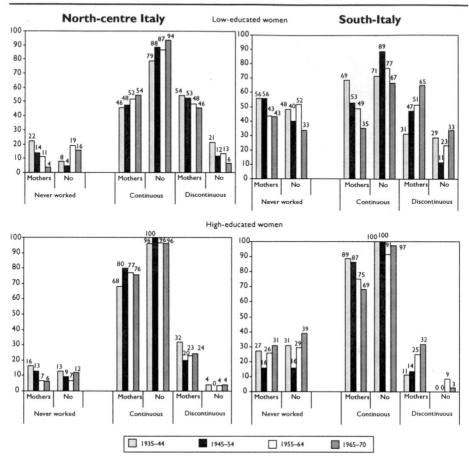

Notes: Low-educated =up to lower-secondary; High-educated=upper-secondary or tertiary.
Source: ILFI, 2005

given that nearly one in every two of the former is permanently excluded from the labour market, compared with one in three of the latter. Among those starting to work in the South, unlike in the Centre-North, continuous employment has decreased over time especially for mothers and in particular for poorly educated mothers. As in the Centre-North, the effect of motherhood is stronger for the poorly educated, although in the last cohort, and therefore in the 1880s and 1990s, continuous employment among southern highly educated mothers was 30 absolute percentage points less than among non-mothers, and the same gap was observable for the less educated.

The third insight arising from the Italian figures is that, as already noted, there is little difference between cohorts in the distribution of mothers' work histories at both lower and higher levels of education. This lends support to Schizzerotto et al's (1995) and Solera's (2004) finding that the increase in female participation

Figure 6.4: Incidence of different timings of interruptions (among women who interrupt by age 35) in Italy and Britain, by birth cohort and education

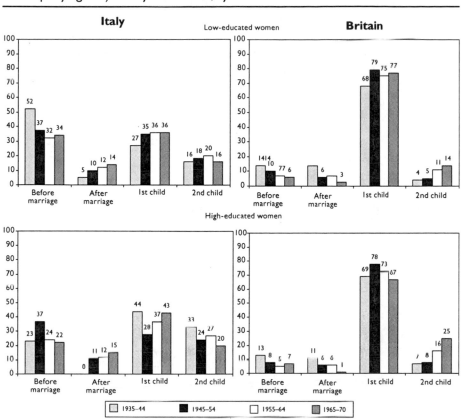

Notes: low-educated =up to lower-secondary; high-educated=upper-secondary or tertiary.
Source: ILFI, 2005; BHPS, 2005

in Italy during the post-war decades conceals a strong compositional effect. Only among the low educated does the impact of motherhood increase from the first to the second cohort, while among the most educated it decreases, and then increases again in the last cohort. This is the expected effect of the 'partial and selective' labour market deregulation in Italy discussed in Chapter Four.

In Britain, by contrast, women's labour supply seems to respond more to motherhood than to education. However, the impact of children is, as expected, stronger among the low educated, at least from the second cohort onwards. Indeed, in the post-war decades discontinuous employment was by far the most typical pattern both for low- and high-educated women: only about 20% of the former and 30% of the latter never interrupted by age 35 in the first and second cohort. In the youngest cohorts continuous employment increased for all, but especially for the most educated, whose gap with respect to the least educated rose from about 10 to 20 absolute percentage points. This signals, as expected, that polarisation has increased over time: while nearly 90% of mothers in the oldest cohort interrupted paid work regardless of their level of education, in the last cohort 80% of low-educated mothers had discontinuous careers, against 58% of the most educated.

Moreover, in Britain differences between highly educated and poorly educated women seem to concern more the rate than the timing of interruptions. As Figure 6.4 shows, women withdrawing from employment tend to do so around first childbirth, regardless of the level of education. Only in the last cohort does the share of highly educated women exiting at second, not first, child increase, which signals their tendency to remain attached to the labour market as long as possible. In Italy, differences between highly educated and poorly educated women seem, by contrast, to reside less in 'quantum' and more in 'timing'. As seen, around 60% of the low educated and 80% of the high educated have continuous careers once they have started to work. Yet among the few that interrupt their labour market participation, those who are low educated tend to do so earlier, before marriage. This was particularly the case in the post-war decades, when 52% of low-educated women interrupted before marriage, against 23% of those with higher educations. The latter, indeed, tended to postpone exits at first or second child.

These figures echo the findings of previous research. For example, on comparing the employment behaviour around childbearing of women born in 1946 and in 1958, Joshi and Hinde (1993) found little discrepancy between 'mothers' and 'daughters' in their exit rates if they had no or few qualifications. The biggest change occurred among the highly educated. Evidently, women in the 1958 generation with high earning potential in Britain were able to benefit most from the equal opportunity provisions enacted in the 1970s, and particularly from statutory maternity leave and employers' family-friendly practices, and could thus maintain employment continuity while raising children. Also low-educated women – if they fulfilled the criterion of continuous employment with the same employer – had access to maternity leave provisions. Yet, they nevertheless tended more to stay out of the labour market when children were young. This may have been out of 'choice', as Hakim (Hakim, 2000) argues, and as the significant effect of unobserved heterogeneity used in some studies signals (Dex et al, 1998), it may also have been due to necessity, since these women often could not afford private childcare arrangements. Indeed, many studies show (Ward et al, 1996; Dex et al, 1998; Davies and Joshi, 2001, 2002) that taking maternity leave is important in Britain, but it is not essential in ensuring women's employment continuity and the associated benefits. Even without maternity leave, highly educated mothers are more likely to have continuous work histories than are mothers with low earning potential who take maternity leave. Crucial is the ability to enter high-grade jobs – as highly educated women do more often – and thus be able to afford private childcare services. This was also evident in Table 5.3, where in all cohorts apart from the youngest, the effect of education on British women's chances of pursuing a continuous career disappears once class is introduced into the models. In Britain, educational qualifications and class also seem more important than the timing of first birth. Postponing childbearing, which is typical of highly educated women, allows the accumulation of human capital that favours a continuous full-time career. However, women with high qualifications and high-status jobs combine paid work and motherhood more frequently even when they become mothers in their early twenties (Joshi et al, 1996; Dex et al, 1998).

Also, the figures for Italy are in line with previous longitudinal research, which shows that in Italy education is a crucial driving force of both women's first entry into the labour market and subsequent attachment to it (Schizzerotto et al, 1995; Bison et al, 1996; Bernardi, 1999; Pisati, 2002; Schizzerotto, 2002a). However, to date no Italian longitudinal study has explicitly examined whether the factors pushing women out of and back into paid work are the same for low- and high-educated women, and whether differences between them have changed across cohorts. The following subsection is the first analysis of this aspect which is both longitudinal and historical.

Does the effect of marriage, children and class differ for high- and low-educated women?

Drawing on event-history models, Table 6.1 shows more clearly how the effect of marriage, children and class on women's employment transitions has changed across cohorts for poorly educated and highly educated women. Given the split into educational groups (and thus the smaller sample sizes), and the focus on the family–work nexus, these models contain fewer variables compared to those shown in Chapter Five. Mothers' work experience and the yearly unemployment rate have been dropped. The age of the youngest child is distinguished into fewer categories, with the months when the woman is pregnant and the youngest child is 0–3 being merged together. Moreover, part-time/full-time work is dropped because, as we have seen, it is irrelevant in the first transition out, while class is reduced to three categories: high class (service class, petty bourgeoisie and routine non-manual workers of high grade); middle class (routine non-manual employees of low grade); low class (manual workers). In order to capture how women with different levels of education are influenced by the characteristics of their jobs, a much more precise class schema is certainly needed in addition to labour market experience. Also required is a measure of 'quality': in terms not only of incomes and securities but also of satisfaction, tasks and responsibilities required, access to training, promotions, and, hence, in terms of overall attractiveness and social prestige. The Goldthorpe class schema partly captures such quality differences, but it does not enable a distinction to be drawn between them within the same category. Moreover, the introduction of its extended version, instead of the rough three-categorisation proposed here, would suffer from problems of multicollinearity with education. Indeed, although in Britain mobility is high, and although qualified people start their careers also in low classes, the numbers of highly educated women in manual positions and of poorly educated women in service positions are still quite low. Despite these caveats, it seems that this three-class schema, although clearly rough, captures broad differences in incomes

Table 6.1: Estimated rate of women's first transition out of and back into employment in Italy and Britain, by education (discrete time hazard rate models)

	Transition out				Transition back			
	Italy		Britain		Italy		Britain	
	Education		Education		Education		Education	
	Low	High	Low	High	Low	High	Low	High
Baseline birth cohort: 1935-1944								
1945-1954	**-0.05**	**-0.56****	-0.14*	-0.32**	0.24*	0.58	0.11	0.15
1955-1964	-0.06	-0.30*	**-0.43*****	**-0.69*****	0.26*	0.77*	0.43***	0.48***
1965-1974	**-0.10**	**-0.45****	-0.61***	-1.07***	0.83***	1.36***	0.93***	0.85***
Duration	**0.000**	**-0.003****	-0.01***	-0.01***	-0.01***	-0.01*	**-0.003*****	**-0.007*****
Previous LM exp					-0.003***	-0.002	**0.002****	**-0.001**
Baseline class: high								
middle	**0.62*****	**0.96*****	0.22***	0.45***	**-0.58*****	**0.57***	-0.12*	0.07
low	**0.45*****	**0.83*****	0.24***	0.43***	**-0.55*****	**0.32**	-0.21***	-0.19*
Baseline Region: North (England)								
Centre (Wales)	0.09	-0.13	0.13*	-0.08	-0.05	-0.25	**-0.21***	**0.05**
South (Scotland)	0.27***	0.04	-0.09	0.12	-0.96***	-1.55***	-0.06	0.11
Baseline marital status: not couple								
couple	**-0.25***	**0.26**	0.73***	0.52***	-0.83***	-0.69*	0.33***	0.19
Baseline child status: no children								
pregnant or yng child aged 0-3	1.71***	1.67***	**4.07*****	**4.37*****	-0.13	-0.85*	-0.64***	-1.12***
yng child aged 3+	0.47**	0.81**	2.51***	2.24***	**0.54***	**-0.37**	0.12	-0.07
Number of children	-0.52***	-0.49***	**-1.61*****	**-1.35*****	0.17**	0.14	0.07*	0.16***
Constant	-6.42***	-7.04***	-6.40***	-6.70***	-4.23***	-4.94***	-4.75***	-3.93***
Log-Likelihood	-4471.2	-1587.5	-5113.2	-2337.6	-1568.9	-440.2	-5608.3	-2186.6
Number of months-persons	241,305	209,584	196,272	123,014	87,283	23,187	103,242	32,972
Number of women	1,510	1,463	1,633	929	708	234	1,271	543
Number of transitions	668	210	1151	490	234	68	1,028	417

Notes: estimates using option « cluster »; Low-class=manual workers; Middle-class=routine non-manual workers, low grade; High-class=service, petty bourgeoisie, routine non-manual, high grade;
* $p < .10$; ** $p < .05$; ***$p < .01$; in **bold** = coefficients different between the low- and high-educated at least at .10 probability level.
Source: BHPS, 2005; ILFI, 2005

and, to some extent, in 'cultures' – as studies on 'doing gender' and 'doing class' have emphasised (see Chapter Two).

Figures 6.1 and 6.2 show that, in Britain, the gap between poorly educated and highly educated women in terms of the risk of employment interruptions first arose in the 1980s and 1990s, with the third birth cohort. Previously, the differences mainly concerned the probability and timing of women's return into employment once it had been interrupted. Indeed, Table 6.1 shows that, *ceteris paribus*, both highly and poorly educated women in the younger cohorts have reduced their tendency to withdraw from the labour market. Yet this reduction is more marked among the highly educated. Moreover, the timing of interruptions seems to differ slightly. As the stronger effect of having a young child signals, highly educated women tend to exit more around childbirth than around marriage. They also respond less to income or care needs due to having two or more children. Table 6.1 also shows that both highly educated and poorly educated women have increased their re-entries once they have exited. For the low educated, by contrast, re-entries seem more closely linked to previous labour market experience and to family-life phases. In fact, low-educated women tend to re-enter more, the longer they have worked previously, probably because they have developed a stronger work identity, or simply a larger amount of human capital to spend on finding a new job. They also appear less reluctant to re-enter when their children are young. Evidently, compared to well-educated mothers, more low-educated ones cannot afford to stay out of the labour market even when their children are aged under three.

Overall, these findings confirm that a polarisation by education took place among British women during the 1980s and 1990s. As other studies illustrate, this came about not only in the extent and duration of employment interruptions around childbearing but also in the income costs associated with them. For example, Davies and Joshi (2001, 2002) chose stylised illustrative situations and simulated their lifetime incomes (from earnings, pensions and other state transfers) to show that education reduced the earnings consequences of motherhood and the financial dependence on marriage. The gap widened especially in the 1990s, when the wage penalty of part-time employment increased and the proportion of mothers employed full time rose mainly among highly qualified women. Women with middle levels of education also increased their attachment to the labour market: they became more likely to spend most of the time when their children were young in employment, albeit on a part-time basis. As a result, the earnings costs of motherhood diminished for women with high earning power, and decreased or remained stable for women with average power, depending on the number of children. Instead, earnings costs tended to rise for the least educated. In the case of higher-educated women, who in the 1990s made increasing use of privately purchased childcare, it was more the direct cost of motherhood that rose. New Labour's reforms, with more explicit parenting policies and welfare-to-work policies, should have reduced class and education divides. However, as said, they have been too recently implemented for their effect to be captured in the fourth cohort of this study.

As in Britain so in Italy, polarisations among differently educated women have increased over time. In Italy, however, only highly educated women have, *ceteris paribus*, reduced their exit rates. As already shown by Figure 6.4, when highly educated women exit employment they tend do so later, not before marriage as in the case of the low educated. Moreover, their behaviour seems to be less geographically differentiated and driven more by cost-opportunity considerations: indeed, the labour market experience accumulated and the occupational class achieved matter more. By contrast, in the case of transition back into employment, low-educated women are more affected by the type of job held before interrupting and by the age of their youngest child. As just seen, the same applies to British low-educated women. Evidently, in both countries, when highly educated women decide to re-enter employment, they tend to do so regardless of their previous labour market history and their family-life phase.

As suggested by Solera and Negri (2008), in a study on mothers' labour market transitions in two non-metropolitan areas in the North of Italy, these findings indicate that the push to leave the labour market, or to remain in it over family formation, is mediated by different cognitive and cultural factors, which intersect with structural factors. Where and when maternal employment is less supported, given low demand for labour and poor family policies, and where and when it is less practiced and accepted, stopping work when children are born is considered to be 'normal', so that what a woman has accumulated so far in the labour market is less important. Similarly, the decision to re-enter appears to be more conditioned by family contingencies to do with either income or care. By contrast, where and when the working-mother model is more institutionally supported and more accepted and, to some extent, followed regardless of level of education and class, the mechanisms that guide women's transitions in and out of paid work are more in line with a 'rational' logic. That is to say, they seem more responsive to constraints, opportunities and cultural models that make working part of a woman's identity and her conception of welfare. This more 'rational' dimension leaves more room for the influence of factors not connected to the family sphere, such as previous labour market experience, type of job and occupational position. The next section examines to what extent, for whom and where women have become less influenced in their behaviour by their husband's resources as captured by his education and class.

Does 'his' education and class matter?

As discussed in Chapter Two, the family is a crucial locus for the production and redistribution of income and care. It is where consumption but also labour supply decisions are taken, and where gender and inter-generational models are defined and practsed. Within the couple, individual choices concerning employment, fertility and time for care are negotiated with those of the partner, with important outcomes in terms of actual but also future material and symbolic experiences and conditions. Such choices are also conditioned by the previous education, and the occupational and 'moral' histories, that each partner brings into the relationship. In lifecourse terminology, lives are interdependent across own multiple careers and others' multiple careers. It is thus of interest to consider how a woman's movements in and out of paid work are linked to her partner's education and class, controlling for her profile. This raises further issues concerning inequality to do with both gender and class. Indeed, 'his' and 'her' class and education are usually correlated through patterns of homogamy. The extent to which they still differentiate women's family–work combinations gives further insights into the question of 'choices' and 'constraints' in the development of individual lifecourses. As repeatedly stressed, the data available cannot be used to disentangle the weight of preferences and constraints and they do not allow differentiation between the monetary or non-monetary dimensions of class and education. However, they do make it possible to show whether women's behaviour has become more or less dependent on what their husbands do, and whether polarisation has assumed new forms.

There is evidence that British women's labour market decisions have become more autonomous, or at least more independent from the husband's resources. Similarly, there is evidence that polarisation has become more closely linked to 'her' rather than 'his' profile over time. For example, Joshi and Hinde (1993) argue that female employment growth in the post-war period was driven by the behaviour of women married to men in white-collar or high-level occupations. Between 1957 and 1980, the proportion of middle-class wives in employment by the time their youngest child was 11 years old rose from 45% to 86%. By 1981 the difference with respect to the wives of higher- and lower-class men had almost disappeared. Other studies also show that, whereas for women born just after the war the occupational position of their husbands and the region in which they lived were the main determinants of their employment behaviour, by the 1970s women's own characteristics had become much more important. In mainstream economic terms, the income effect weakened while the own-wage (real or potential) effect grew stronger. Indeed, in recent generations more women have acquired human capital through education, training and employment experience. These factors, rather than the husband's occupation, have increasingly differentiated among women. In turn, divisions have emerged between highly educated women who delay childbearing and once they become mothers take maternity leave and then return to full-time jobs, and women with low educational qualifications who have children earlier, take more and longer breaks and return to part-time work (Joshi, 1986; McRan et al, 1996; Dex et al, 1998; McCulloch and Dex, 2001).

In Italy, too, there is evidence that the effect of the partner's resources has weakened. For example, by using three pooled cross-sections of the Bank of Italy Surveys on Household Income and Wealth in 1987, 1989 and 1991, and by estimating a trivariate model of participation, fertility and wages, Di Tommaso

(1999) shows that the husband's wage has the expected negative sign on the wife's probability of being in the labour market, but its effect is much smaller than her own wage (individual probability elasticity is equal to −0.20 for the male wage against 2.82 for the female wage). This holds even when controlling for education, age and region in the wage equation, and for cohort, unearned income and wealth in the participation and fertility equation. Similarly, Bratti (2003) estimates a joint model of married women's fertility and participation on the basis of the 1993 Bank of Italy Survey on Household Income and Wealth and studies the effect of women's education, controlling, among other factors, for the husband's wage, education, job qualification and branch (the last three taken as a proxy for his life income profile), and for his age (which, together with education, is a proxy for his attitude to women's employment). Bratti finds that the husband's income has the usual negative effect but, all else being equal, a woman's education markedly increases her labour force participation, and especially its compatibility with motherhood. Further, Addabbo (1999) uses the same Bank of Italy dataset, but for 1995, to explore gender differences in labour supply, finding that, for women, the effect of the partner's income is significantly negative but very small. Besides income, Addabbo also looks at the husband's employment status. Specifically, she tests for the existence of an 'added worker effect' by studying whether wives of unemployed men have higher employment probabilities than do the wives of self-employed or employed husbands. Compared to an employee, a self-employed husband increases his wife's labour supply probability by 10%, whereas being unemployed makes no difference.

On the sociological side, it is only in recent decades that the issue of the effect of the partner's resources – with their various connotations – has fully entered the empirical research agenda. This has occurred within social stratification research when its focus has shifted from the conventional study of inter-generational social mobility to the analysis of homogamy and couples' careers in a lifecourse perspective. In Italy, Bernardi's (1999) pioneering study used life-history data for the first time to explicitly explore the effect of the husband on the wife's participation and outcome in the labour market; and emulating previous research by German and Dutch scholars (Bernasco, 1994; Blossfeld et al, 1996; Bernasco et al, 1998), Bernardi has tested the different hypotheses put forward by 'new home economics' theory and social capital theory. More specifically, Bernardi uses the Second National Survey on Fertility Control and Expectation carried out between the end of 1995 and the beginning of 1996 to examine the effect, using dynamic models, of the husband's education and occupational score at the time of marriage on his wife's transition out of and back into employment. He finds that economic and sociological theories apply to different aspects of women's careers: economic theory explains women's labour supply, while sociological theory accounts for women's occupational achievement. Although the husband's resources can help his wife to obtain a high-status job, they encourage them to move out of employment and discourage them from returning. Yet the negative effect of the husband's occupational status on his wife's labour supply is significant only for the upper positions and, in line with the 'income and wage effect' in the economic literature, it is outweighed by the positive effect of the wife's own resources. Hence, the significant positive sign of the 'comparative advantage in market work' dummy implies that the husband's disincentive effect operates only for couples where the husband has a higher occupational score than the wife. A subsequent study Blossfeld and Drobnic (2001), which examines the process of couples' careers within a cross-national comparative framework, shows that Bernardi's findings in Italy resemble those of other studies conducted in Germany and Spain. But they differ from those obtained in Denmark and Sweden, where the husband's occupational resources have a positive effect, and from those in Britain, where there is no effect. As argued by Blossfeld and Drobnic, cross-country differences in the effect of the partner's resources largely mirror types of welfare regime, which suggests that the decision-making process within couples also crucially depends on institutional settings and cultural traditions. Further evidence on the role of the macro context derives from an earlier cross-country study by Smits et al (1996), who studied how occupational status differences between spouses affected the wife's labour supply and her occupational achievement in the 12 member states of the European Union in 1990. They found that the differences were largely related to the country's dominant religion. The negative effect of occupational status differences on the wife's employment was stronger in Catholic countries than in non-Catholic ones.

A recent strand of sociological research has thus helped shed light on the mechanisms determining couples' decisions in regard to employment over the lifecourse, and on the financial and non-financial nature of educational and occupational resources. Yet, as is the case of most of the economic literature, it has not explicitly addressed changes across cohorts. Indeed, in Bernardi's work, as well as in most studies in other countries, the effect of the partner, in addition to other factors, is controlled for marriage cohorts, but no interaction terms are used to determine whether this effect differs across cohorts, and how. What little we know about changes over time in Italy comes from cross-sectional studies and bivariate figures. For example, Bellotti (1993) shows that, in the Veneto region in 1993, the activity rates of married women aged 41-49 varied greatly according to the occupational class of the husband. They grew by approximately 28 percentage points between the working class and the petty bourgeoisie, and declined only slightly between the routine non-manual middle class and the upper class. In the case of women aged 33-40, the gap between working-class and petty-bourgeoisie wives diminished, while the gap between petty-bourgeoisie and middle-class wives increased. The wives of upper-class husbands had almost the same activity rate as the wives of petty-bourgeois husbands. For younger women (those aged 25-32 in 1993), on the other hand, whether the husband worked in the middle class or in the upper class seems not to have made a difference (Bellotti, 1993). On the basis of repeated cross-sectional data, Saraceno (2003a) likewise argues that only in the late 1950s and early 1960s in Italy did the model of the stay-at-home housewife become the norm; that is, when Italy enjoyed the post-war economic boom and the first welfare policies in favour of wages and workers' rights were introduced. Yet, at that time, adherence to the model was not universal. Indeed, a large proportion of the population could not afford to rely on the male wage alone: neither in the South, where the primary labour market was smaller, so that not all male breadwinners had 'golden age' jobs, nor in the Centre-North among unskilled manual workers whose jobs, although well protected, were poorly paid. Since the late 1960s, with increasing investment in education and the parallel development of the tertiary sector and of some women-friendly social policies, women's decisions to work have become more independent from their husbands' class positions.

The next two subsections will look, using longitudinal data, at changes across generations in the effect of the partner's resources. As specified in Chapter Four, I shall focus only on first marriages, and only on husbands for whom the entire occupational history is available, from one year before the start of the marriage to its end, or to the interview date. Cohabitations are not considered. Indeed, in contexts where the diffusion of cohabitation is still at the beginning – such as in many parts of Italy still today or among older cohorts in Britain – cohabiting women and men have too specific characteristics and are subject to too specific mechanisms to be merged with marital couples. Moreover, I shall use as the indicator of the partner's (material and symbolic) resources his level of education and occupational class. As in previous sections, I shall first report bivariate descriptive figures on the incidence of different types of work history by age 35, and then multivariate event-history estimates on married women's risk of moving from employment to housework. In order to make the figures more straightforward, in the descriptive analyses the husband's class is differentiated into only two categories, manual versus non-manual workers, and is measured at the beginning of the observational window, that is, one year before marriage. In the regression analyses both 'his' and 'her' class are time-varying but, for sample size reasons, they are categorised into three groups: for women, manual workers, routine non-manual workers of low grade, higher positions (service, petty bourgeoisie, routine non-manual workers of high grade); for men, manual workers, routine non-manual workers of any grade, service or petty bourgeoisie. As discussed earlier in this chapter, this is certainly a rough distinction but it nevertheless makes it possible to capture interesting differences.

Descriptive evidence

In Italy, women married to husbands with different educational or class profiles differ first of all in terms of their permanent exclusion from the labour market. Wives of low-educated or manual workers have more frequently never experienced a job episode. This gap has widened over time. In the last cohort, 10% of wives of husbands from the manual class or with upper-secondary or tertiary educations have never started a labour market career against about 29% of wives of low-status husbands. In the oldest cohort the figures are 27% against 31%.[1]

Once women start to work, continuous employment is by far the most typical pattern quite independently of what the husband does and with little difference across cohorts, although women married to high-educated and non-manual workers less frequently interrupt their labour market participation, and although from the second cohort onwards it is mainly wives of highly educated men who have increased their attachment to paid work. Interestingly, even with the two-category distinction employed here, the incidence of different types of women's work histories are very similar if 'his' education or 'his' class are used, probably because of a strong association between the two features (Figure 6.5).

As already seen, in Britain the divide between women has moved, across generations, from whether and when paid work is re-entered to whether and when it is exited in the first place. This is also evident when the figures are broken

Figure 6.5: Incidence of different types of work history up to age 35 in Italy and Britain, by birth cohort, education and class of partner

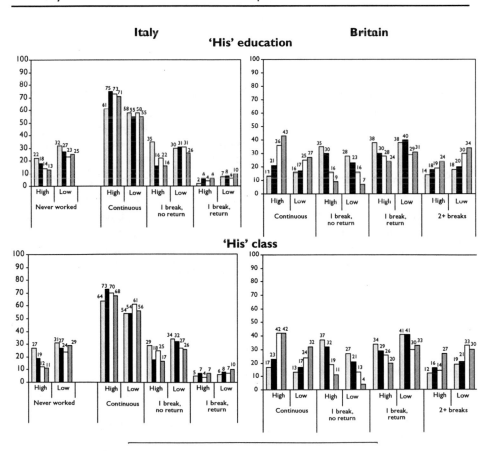

Notes: Low-educated =up to lower-secondary; High-educated=upper-secondary or tertiary; Low-class=manual workers; High-class=non manual workers.
Source: BHPS, 2005; ILFI, 2005

down on the basis of the husband's occupation. In fact, nearly all women from the older generation interrupted employment over family formation, regardless of their husbands' level of education and class. Differences emerged later, with wives of low-status men re-entering employment less once it had been interrupted, or more often experiencing two or more breaks. Women from subsequent generations, and in particular from the third generation onwards, exhibit different forms of attachment to the labour market. As was found when types of work histories were distinguished on the basis of her profile (her education, cohort and motherhood experience), wives of high-educated or high-class men have started to reduce their exits or, if they have exited, to increase their re-entries, even between births – as indicated by the growth of the 'two or more breaks' type of history (Figure 6.5). The same increase in labour market attachment is observable among wives of low-educated low-class men, although to a lesser extent.

All these descriptive figures largely confirm what was seen previously when types of work history were distinguished on the basis of the woman's profile, and they suffer from the same 'bivariate' limitation. There are many possible mechanisms responsible for such trends and numbers. Given the high degree of homogamy in mating selection and its relative stability over time, differences between highly educated and poorly educated women may conceal differences in their husbands' profiles, or vice versa. Moreover, if a partner effect operates and is not completely due to homogamy, it is impossible with my data to capture the extent to which it is an income or an efficiency or bargaining power effect, as economists argue, a social capital effect as many sociologists underline, or a gender norms effect as feminists have maintained. On moving from a bivariate to a multivariate environment, I still cannot disentangle these different monetary and non-monetary dimensions properly. Nevertheless, it is possible to determine whether the effect of 'his' class and education remains after controlling for 'her' class and education, and how this has changed across cohorts. This issue is analysed in the next subsection.

Evidence on women's transitions out of paid work

Table 6.2 shows the results of models on Italian married women's transitions from employment to housework for all cohorts together, and then cohort by cohort, with the addition, compared with Table 5.2, of the partner's level of education and class. As usual, highlighted in bold are the effects for the second, third and fourth cohorts, which differ significantly from the effects for the first cohort. Table 6.3 shows the results of the same models for Britain.

In line with the previous Italian findings mentioned above (Bellotti 1993; Addabbo, 1999; Di Tommaso, 1999; Bratti 2003), if the woman's educational and labour market profile is controlled for, the partner's occupation seems not to matter. As the models separated by cohort show, it did matter in the oldest cohort, when the wives of highly educated men more often interrupted employment than the wives of low-educated husbands. Indeed, in the immediate post-war

Table 6.2: Estimated rates of married women's first transition from employment to housework in Italy, by education and class of partner (discrete time hazard rate models)

	All	1935–44	1945–54	1955–64	1965-74
Her birth cohort: 1935-1944					
1945-1954	−0.14				
1955-1964	−0.14				
1965-1974	0.12				
Her duration in employment	−0.003***	−0.002*	−0.004***	−0.003**	-0.005**
Her education: up to lower-secondary					
upper-secondary or tertiary	−0.81***	−0.91***	−1.05***	−0.75***	−0.67***
Her class: service – petty bourgeo. routine non-manual workers, high					
routine non-manual workers, low	0.82***	0.47*	0.72***	0.96***	0.97***
manual workers	0.68***	0.63**	0.68***	0.72***	0.60**
Region: North					
Centre	0.13	−0.03	**0.37***	0.12	0.05
South	0.19*	−0.94***	**0.25**	**0.46***	**0.68***
Child status: no children					
pregnant or youngest child aged 0-3	0.41***	0.25	0.63***	0.27	0.39*
youngest child aged 3+	−0.49***	−1.41***	**−0.23**	**−0.42**	**−0.32**
Number of children	−0.46***	−0.56***	−0.61***	−0.23*	-0.26*
His education: up to lower-secondary					
upper-secondary or tertiary	0.12	0.58**	**0.07**	0.17	**-0.12**
His class: service - petty bourgeo.					
routine non-manual workers, low and high	−0.02	0.56*	**−0.13**	**−0.38***	0.03
manual workers	0.11	0.39*	0.20	**−0.03**	**-0.06**
Constant	−5.21***	−5.04***	−5.38***	−5.56***	−5.11***
Log-likelihood	−4878.7	−857.6	−1260.1	−1249.4	-666.3
Number of months-persons	204,134	39,733	69,642	69,905	24,854
Number of women	1,826	368	557	593	308
Number of transitions	642	143	200	190	109

Notes: estimates using option « cluster »; * p<.10; ** p<.05; ***p<.01; in **bold** = coefficients of second, third and fourth cohort that differ from the first cohort at least at .10 probability level.
Source: ILFI, 2005

decades the normative male–breadwinner model was still highly influential, but it could only be adopted by high–class, high-status couples. Within the cohorts since then, and in contrast with one of my hypotheses, the partner effect has not only attenuated but disappeared. Evidently, although in Italy, and especially in the South, women's entry into paid work has not become 'universal' as elsewhere; women's labour supply is now strongly dependent on their own profile, and no longer on their partners. This further reinforces the role performed in Italy by

Table 6.3: Estimated rates of married women's first transition from employment to housework in Britain, by education and class of partner (discrete time hazard rate models)

	All	1935-44	1945-54	1955-64	1965-74
Her Birth cohort: 1935-1944					
1945-1954	−0.31***				
1955-1964	−0.58***				
1965-1974	−0.85***				
Her duration in employment	−0.004***	−0.004***	**−0.001**	−0.005***	−0.008**
Her education: up to lower-secondary					
upper-secondary or tertiary	−0.26***	−0.26*	−0.19	−0.36**	−0.02
Her class: service − petty bourgeo.					
routine non-manual workers, high					
routine non-manual workers, low	−0.34***	0.17*	0.22	0.36**	**0.85****
manual workers	−0.36***	0.40***	0.23*	0.44**	0.62**
Region: England					
Wales	−0.06	−0.22	0.007	0.05	**0.68****
Scotland	0.07	1.10***	**−0.03**	**−0.26**	**−0.03**
Child status: no children					
pregnant or youngest child aged 0-3	3.54***	3.26***	**3.73****	**3.87****	3.69***
youngest child aged 3+	2.26***	1.17*	**2.68****	**2.97****	2.11***
Number of children	−1.38***	−1.89***	**−2.20****	**−1.05****	**−0.68****
His education: up to lower-secondary					
upper-secondary or tertiary	0.02	0.16	0.05	−0.11	−0.09
His class: unemployed					
service − petty bourgeo	−0.77***	−0.78*	−1.11**	−0.70**	−0.17
routine non-manual workers, low and high	−0.48**	−0.54	−0.61*	−0.58*	−0.36
manual workers	−0.61***	−0.65	−0.99**	−0.54*	−0.20
Constant	−4.46***	−4.18***	−4.70***	−5.34***	−6.22***
Log-likelihood	−3617.7	−860.9	−1043.7	−1196.2	−438.2
Number of months-persons	86,027	16,045	24,179	32,666	13,137
Number of women	1,193	274	344	405	171
Number of transitions	813	210	257	257	89

Notes: estimates using option « cluster »; * p<.10; ** p<.05; ***p<.01; in **bold** = coefficients of second, third and fourth cohort that differ from the first cohort at least at .10 probability level.
Source: BHPS, 2005

a woman's education in shaping her employment patterns. In a context where education is a *passepartout* for acceptance of a modern role of women and for entry into 'good' labour markets, such as those in the public sector which enable reconciliation, it is essentially her education that strongly polarises own attitudes, and others' supportive views, opportunities and choices.

As already pointed out in Chapter Five, in Britain class seems more important than education. Indeed, when both class and education are introduced into the model, not only the woman's education but also her partner's education matter less, if at all. Moreover, as found by other studies (Dex et al, 1995; Joshi et al, 1996; McGinnity, 2002), what seems to influence British women's labour supply more is not their partners' occupational class but their partners' employment status. Women whose husbands become unemployed tend to exit paid work more frequently than women whose husbands are in employment, regardless of the type of position. As widely argued, the reason for this lies in the British system of unemployment compensation. In countries where the unemployment benefit system is individual based, paid through either social insurance or social assistance programmes that do not apply means-tests based on a spouse's earnings, the wives of unemployed men do not have lower participation rates. Rather, in these countries, they seem not to be affected by their husbands' employment status, or they are affected in the other direction, through the so-called 'additive worker effect'. Put in another way, in order to supplement the lower and less stable family income, such women are more, not less, likely to enter employment when their husbands become unemployed. In Britain the opposite occurs. Since the majority of unemployed men do not receive insurance benefits but rely on schemes that are means tested on family income and offer very low earnings disregard for the spouse, the woman may find that working, and particularly working part time, does not make economic sense. This 'discouragement effect' has slightly changed across cohorts. It was absent in the immediate post-war decades and became more visible with the second and third cohort, that is, under the Conservative policies of the 1980s and 1990s. It has diminished under New Labour's reforms, as the loss of significance by the coefficients of class for the last cohort seems to suggest.

Conclusion

In Chapter Five we saw that, in both Italy and Britain, women's attachment to paid work has increased, either through a reduction in the share of women permanently excluded from paid work or a reduction in the number and duration of family-care breaks. Over time, women's divides on the basis of education levels have also increased. More specifically, in Italy, differences in first entries between highly educated and poorly educated women have markedly diminished from the third cohort onwards, whereas differences in exits once employment has been entered have remained quite constant, increasing only in the last cohort, probably due to Italy's 'partial and selective' deregulation. In Britain, once class has been controlled for, education appears irrelevant in differentiating among women's transitions out of paid work for many generations and decades, apart from the last one, when highly educated women exhibit a stronger attachment to paid work regardless of their occupational class. Since their chances of reconciling family with work responsibilities when holding relatively low-paid jobs are not particularly dissimilar to those of the low educated, this was interpreted as an 'attitude effect'.

By conducting separate analyses, first by women's education, and then by their partner's education and class, this chapter has added further elements to the issue of stratification and 'choice'.

Two insights emerge. The first is that, contrary to individuation-type arguments *à la* Beck or *à la* Hakim, both in Italy and Britain women's employment paths still differ by 'classic' stratification factors, such as education and class. The manner in which they differ, however, is peculiar. Italy is well known in Europe for having one of the widest participation gaps between poorly educated and highly educated women but also one of the lowest 'child effects'. My findings further confirm this phenomenon. In Italy, participation responds much more to education than to motherhood, and education differentiates first entry into paid work much more than subsequent permanence in it. Indeed, the gap between highly educated and poorly educated women in the share of continuous employment among those who have started a labour market career is low; and motherhood appears to have a strong influence on work-history continuity only at low levels of education, with the exception of the oldest cohort. Moreover, regional disparities were, and still are today, very marked. In the Centre-North, nearly all women start a labour market career, but once they have started, highly educated women are more frequently continuous and less affected by motherhood. In the South of Italy, differences between poorly educated and highly educated women are mainly apparent in the first entry into paid work. My findings also confirm that relatively little has changed across generations, lending support to the claim that the increase in female participation in Italy in the post-war decades conceals a strong compositional effect.

In Britain, the impact of motherhood is, as expected, stronger than in Italy; and, within Britain, it has been stronger from the second cohort onwards. Indeed, in the post-war decades discontinuous employment was by far the most typical pattern for both low- and high-educated women. In the youngest cohorts, continuous employment has increased for all, but especially for the most educated. Moreover, in Britain, differences between highly educated and poorly educated women seem to concern more the rate than the timing of interruptions. Indeed, when they interrupt, women tended to do so around marriage in older cohorts, or around first childbirth in younger cohorts, regardless of level of education. This suggests that opportunities and constraints have a weight in shaping women's choices. In a liberal regime like the British one, of crucial importance is the ability to enter high-grade jobs – as highly educated women more often do – and thus be able to afford private childcare. In Italy, by contrast, differences between highly educated and poorly educated women seem to be less in 'quantum' and more in 'timing'. Among the few women who interrupt, those with low educations tend to do so earlier than those with better qualifications. Since policies to support work–family reconciliation are 'equally' ungenerous, and the economic necessity to work should operate the other way round, inducing low-educated women to interrupt later rather than earlier, this can be interpreted as an 'attitude effect'. It may be that low-educated women have partners (and large segments of society) less supportive of the combination of work with family responsibilities. It may also be that they themselves are less work oriented, or less able to negotiate different choices – or it might even be that they simply 'get tired' of their jobs, given that they are generally low income and low quality.

Event-history multivariate models confirm the descriptive bivariate figures on the link between education, motherhood and participation. In Britain, all else being equal, across generations both highly educated and poorly educated women have reduced their tendency to withdraw from the labour market. Yet this reduction has been more marked among the highly educated. Moreover, although both highly educated and poorly educated women have increased their re-entries, once they have exited, in the case of the low-educated re-entries seem more closely linked with previous labour market experience and family-life phases. Overall, my findings confirm that polarisation by education occurred among British women during the 1980s and 1990s.

In Italy, too, polarisations among differently educated women have increased over time. However, it is only highly educated Italian women who have, *ceteris paribus*, reduced their exit rates. Moreover, their exit decisions seem less geographically differentiated and driven more by cost-opportunity considerations: that is, by the labour market experience accumulated and the occupational class reached. Both poorly educated and highly educated women have increased their transitions back into paid work. However, as in Britain, it is mainly the low educated who appear to be influenced by the type of job held before interrupting, and by the age of their youngest child. Evidently, in both countries, when highly educated women decide to re-enter, they tend to do so regardless of their previous history.

In line with previous research, the second insight emerging from the analyses reported throughout this chapter is that in both countries polarisation has become based much more on 'her' than 'his' profile, but again in distinctive ways. Bivariate descriptive figures show that women in Italy who are married to husbands with different educational or class profiles differ primarily in their permanent exclusion from the labour market. In other words, the wives of low-educated or manual workers have more often never experienced a job episode. Once women start to work, continuous employment is by far the most typical pattern, quite independently of the husband's occupation, and with little difference across cohorts. In Britain, the divide between women has changed across generations, from whether and when to re-enter paid work to whether and when to exit it in the first place. Indeed, nearly all women in British older generations interrupted employment over family formation, regardless of the level of education and the class of their husbands. Differences emerged later, with the wives of low-status men re-entering employment less once they had interrupted it. In younger generations, wives of high-educated or high-class men have started to reduce their exits, or if they have exited, to increase their re-entries, even between births. The same increase in labour market attachment is observable among the wives of low-educated, low-class men, albeit to a lesser extent.

Multivariate analyses, however, show that in both countries, if the woman's educational and labour market profile is controlled for, her partner's occupation seems not to matter. In Italy, only in the oldest cohort do wives of highly educated men interrupt employment more frequently than the wives of low-educated men. In subsequent cohorts, and in contrast with one of my hypotheses, the partner's effect has not only attenuated but disappeared. In Britain, in older cohorts as well, the partner's education and class has, all else equal, no influence. Rather, it is his employment status that matters. More precisely, women whose husbands become unemployed tend to exit paid work more frequently than women whose husbands are working, regardless of the type of position. As many authors have stressed, this discouragement effect is linked to the British system of unemployment protection, and it is particularly strong in the second and third cohort, that is, under the Conservative policies of the 1980s and 1990s.

As underlined several times, the data used here, like most longitudinal retrospective-type data, cannot be used to disentangle the weight of preferences and constraints because they do not enable differentiation between the monetary or non-monetary dimensions of class and education. It is thus not possible to state whether what has been observed, for her and him, is an income-wage effect or an efficiency or bargaining power effect as economists argue, a social capital effect as many sociologists underline, or a cultural or institutional effect as feminists have maintained. However, the analyses performed have made it possible to determine whether women's employment behaviour around marriage and children has become more or less dependent on education or on class, and on her or his education and class. The analyses have thus yielded new insights into 'old' and 'new' forms of polarisation, opening the way for causal narratives and policy implications. These will be proposed by the next and concluding chapter as it summarises the key findings of the book and suggests explanations in light of the theoretical and empirical approach described in Chapters One, Two and Four.

Note

[1] Obviously, this association between never entering paid work and education or class of the partner is difficult to interpret in causal terms. It is indeed likely that a woman takes the decision whether or not to enter employment before she meets her future husband and may actually base her partner selection on this decision, at least to some extent. Then, within marriage, this decision may be reinforced or, for various reasons, reversed (for example because of the need for income when the number of children increases or because a separation is anticipated).

Conclusions

It is a well-established fact that over the last 50 years women's labour market participation has increased in all the advanced countries. It is also well established that this increase has mainly concerned the behaviour of married women and mothers and has been due to a constellation of interrelated micro and macro factors. These include the rising demand for female labour, the increasing preference among women for non-domestic roles, the growing opportunity costs of homemaking as women's education and real wages have risen, and the welfare state's increasing support for work–family reconciliation. Also well documented is the cross-country variation in the timing, degree and type of such changing factors and in their implications for women's labour market involvement.

This book has explored changes in women's employment and work–family articulations over the lifecourse using a largely innovative approach, which is simultaneously longitudinal over the lifecourse, and comparative both across cohorts and across countries. Unlike most studies that have only focused on specific lifecourse transitions or on specific cohorts, it has considered the entire work careers of women from the time they leave full-time education until their forties, looking at changes across four birth cohorts in Italy and Britain in the incidence and determinants of first entry and subsequent exits from and re-entries into paid work. A variety of 'explanans' have been considered, including supply-side characteristics, gender-role and childcare norms, social policies, labour market regulation, and employment structure and opportunities. By combining insights from different theories, the analysis has been based on an integrated conceptual framework that views the lifecourse as both agency and structure and, in turn, considers how both women's preferences and the wide set of opportunities and constraints have changed from the 1950s to the 2000s in Italy and Britain.

The approach followed in this study has three distinctive features. First, it is based on retrospective longitudinal data, on long periods of individual lives, on a comparison across both time (generations) and space (countries) and on a very rich set of individual and familial covariates. All together, these features have yielded a better understanding of changes over time in women's lifecourses. Although preferences and constraints have not been measured directly, this complex approach has made it possible to suggest causal narratives, looking at the intersections of micro and macro foundations of women's behaviour and choices.

Second, the book has used the prism of inequality. Regardless of whether the polarisation of women's employment trajectories is an effect of changing preferences, changing opportunities or changing abilities to act upon preferences and overcome constraints, there is evidence that such polarisation has assumed new forms. This has to do with the 'classic' stratification factors of class, education and age. It has also importantly to do with gender. As feminists have pointed out, gender expectations embedded in family, labour market and social policy arrangements define both the material and symbolic contexts in which women negotiate their decisions and the extent and form taken by inequalities. Hence, if the intention is to explain women's employment and work–family articulations, the prism of gender is indispensable. The adoption of a gender perspective is the third distinctive feature of this book.

Using a micro–macro lifecourse model, and in particular within a (gendered) institutional rational-action framework, the book has sought to answer the following questions:

• How much and for whom have continuous careers increased?
• Who tends to exit from paid work?
• Who, once they have exited, tends to re-enter and when?
• Is polarisation among women based more on class or on education?
• On 'his' or on 'her' profile?
• How has all this changed across cohorts?

In the following sections I shall first delineate a synthetic comparative biography of the four cohorts studied in the two countries, evidencing inter-cohort continuities and discontinuities and cross-countries commonalities and differences, and then discuss the policy implications of my findings.

Summary of the main findings

Over the past 50 years, women's employment has increased markedly in all the developed countries, including those that still in the 1970s, like Italy, had the lowest women's activity and occupation rates. Compared with the members of their mothers' and grandmothers' cohorts, younger women have not only invested in education and entered the labour market on a more massive scale; they have also remained more frequently in the labour market when getting married or becoming mothers, exiting in much smaller numbers or shortening their breaks. They have also changed their family behaviours, starting to postpone if not reduce entry into marriage and motherhood. Women's lifecourses have thus become less structured around the family sphere and more closely centred on the work sphere. The experience of motherhood now occupies a shorter span of women's lifecourses; it is less connected with the experience of being part of a marriage or, generally, of a couple; while it is more interconnected with the experience of working. As many scholars underline, this has generated a new time structure for people's everyday and overall lives, new gender (and generational) relationships, and new interdependencies between male and female lifecourses. It has also given rise to differing access to the material and symbolic resources that define both viable and acceptable behaviours and which affect the differential power available to women and men in bargaining on their 'preferred' choices. However, differences across countries and among women in patterns of women's labour market attachment and in work–family articulations have been, and remain, significant.

My findings show that in both Italy and Britain, women from younger cohorts are more attached to the labour market, but also that the types and causes of this increasing attachment differ importantly. In Britain, women's employment has gradually expanded from exiting the labour market when marrying and re-entering on completion of childrearing, to exiting on first childbirth and re-entering more often between births and more quickly after childbearing. One in five women in the 1935-44 birth cohort had continuous careers from first job until the age of 35, but among mothers the figure was only one in 10. That is to say, women withdrew from the labour market regardless of their level of education, their occupational class and their labour market experience. Only women from the petty bourgeoisie and service class, or women whose mothers had been in paid work, showed a significant lower propensity to interrupt. Human capital investments and work orientations mattered later, in the decision on whether and when to re-enter paid work. In subsequent generations, women's employment behaviour has grown more differentiated. Discontinuous employment around childbearing has continued to be the typical pattern, but women have started to spend less time out of paid work by postponing exits for childbirth and by anticipating re-entries between one child and the next. Moreover, the human capital profile of women has begun to matter more, with re-entry rates becoming significantly dependent on past occupational class, labour market experience and education, while the number of children loses importance. Whereas in the oldest cohort 20% of poorly educated women and 26% of highly educated ones had continuous careers, in the youngest cohort the figures rise to 34% and 56% respectively. Contrary to individuation theory, polarisation continues to be mainly based on social class: once class is controlled for, the effect of education on women's chances of moving in and out of paid work disappears, except in the last cohort. Evidently in Britain, for a long time also highly educated women had to have entered good labour market positions if they were to be able to pursue continuous careers. In younger generations, class and previous labour market experience also started to exert greater weight on the transition back into work.

Women's divides have increased over time. The women's labour supply in Britain is well known for having one of the most marked motherhood effects and one of the widest educational gaps in Europe. Indeed, while in the post-war decades interrupting employment was the typical pattern for both poorly educated and highly educated women, in the youngest generations continuous employment has increased for all, but especially for the most educated. When low- and high-educated women interrupt, they tend to do so at similar stages: around marriage in the oldest cohorts, around childbirth in the youngest ones. Moreover, both highly educated and poorly educated women have increased their re-entries, once they have exited, but re-entries for the highly educated seem to occur regardless of previous labour market experience and family-life phase. Not only has polarisation increased over time, it has also become based much more on the woman's profile than on her partner's. Descriptive bivariate analyses show that nearly all women interrupted employment over family formation in the past, regardless of the level of education and the class of their husbands. Differences emerged later, with the wives of low-status men re-entering employment to a lesser extent once they had interrupted it. In younger generations, wives of high-educated or high-class men have started to reduce their exits, or if they have exited, to increase their re-entries, even between births. The same increase in labour market attachment is observable among the wives of low-educated low-class men, albeit to a lesser extent. However, multivariate analyses show that, in all cohorts, if the woman's educational and labour market profile is controlled for, her partner's education and class has no influence. Rather, it is his employment status that matters: in contrast with the 'additive worker effect', women tend to exit more when their husbands become unemployed, especially in the second and third cohort – that is, in the 1980s and 1990s.

In Italy, nearly one in four women in the 1935-44 birth cohort have never worked, and among those who have started to work, three in five have never stopped. One in five in the 1965-70 birth cohort have never worked, whereas nearly four in five have had continuous careers. Also in Italy, therefore, women's labour market attachment has increased over time. However, in both old and young cohorts, Italian women appear polarised in an 'opt-in/opt-out' participation pattern: either they remain lifelong housewives, never entering paid work or interrupting it around marriage or childbirth without ever re-entering, or they remain lifelong workers. Continuous participation was and still is by far the most typical pattern. Moreover, although the timing of interruptions has everywhere been progressively postponed and the timing of re-entries anticipated, in order to reduce the cost of long breaks, in Italy the relatively few women who interrupt tend to do so earlier than British women and the few who re-enter tend to do so later.

In old as in young cohorts, it is essentially education (and public employment) that distinguishes between 'insiders and outsiders'. As hypothesised, in Italy the post-war increase in women's employment seems to have been mainly compositional: the effect of education, occupational class, labour market position and marriage and children on exits from and re-entries into paid work remains largely constant. This means that since the late 1960s more women have started to work and enjoy full-time continuous careers because more women have acquired the characteristics that have always favoured their labour market involvement: high education, well-paid or family-convenient well-protected jobs such as those in the public sector, and a small number of children. Put more explicitly, in Italy the trade-off between family and work has long remained high. Faced with a persistent unfriendly context but new preferences, what women have changed in their choices is the pole of this trade-off: in order to ensure themselves entry and permanence in the labour market they have increasingly and intentionally invested in education, while delaying marriages and reducing fertility. Women's agency beyond institutional and cultural constraints also emerges from the attachment they show to paid work even when they have children and despite scarce childcare provision. Evidently, women who want both a family and a labour market career use all the formal and informal resources at their disposal to do so.

By international standards, Italy is also well known for the relatively low effect exerted by children, as regards both their age and number. This emerges from my data as well, and suggests that women who enter and remain in the labour market in Italy are a more select group than in other countries: they are well educated, they work in well-paid jobs or family-convenient jobs and sectors that allow them to 'buy' other people's time in order to substitute for the family work they cannot perform themselves. Moreover, they can rely on inter-generational solidarity for their income, but especially for their childcare needs. More than in other countries, education is a crucial resource for Italian women. My analysis shows that the higher the education level of women, the more determinedly they look for a job and the more they finally obtain one. Once employment has been entered, the higher the woman's level of education, the lower her risk of exiting it, regardless of the type of job. Put otherwise, as expected, in Italy, unlike in Britain, well-educated women remain in employment over the family formation phase also when they are not in the primary labour market. International data on gender-role attitudes also show that, both in the past and today, education in Italy strongly discriminates the support for maternal employment and for new gender roles. Thus, in Italy, women's involvement in paid work has not become 'universal', cutting across regions, levels of education and social classes. Rather, polarisation in Italy has assumed partly new forms: geographical disparities have increased in the first entry into paid work, while disparities between highly educated and poorly educated women have diminished; and both geographical and educational gaps have sharpened in the permanence over family formation. Moreover, in all cohorts, women married to low-educated men or manual workers more frequently never start a labour market career. Once they have started to work, only in the oldest cohort – that is, in the immediate post-war decades – have wives of low- and high-educated men behaved differently. Subsequently, and contrary to my hypotheses, labour market transitions over family formation have become independent from the partner's profile. Moreover, in the last cohorts, exits around childbirth have decreased, whereas re-entries have become more closely affected by the gender models within which women have grown up, and less by increasing numbers of children.

Regional disparities in the Italian scenario are very marked. Indeed, the 'opt-in/opt-out' participation pattern and the compositional nature of women's employment growth apply much more to the South than to the Centre-North of Italy. In the Centre-North, 19% of women from the 1935-44 birth cohort have never worked, against 48% in the South. In later cohorts, only 8% are permanently out of the labour market in the Centre-North, against 35% in the South. Moreover, in the Centre-North, the proportion of continuous careers among women who start to work increases from 56% in the oldest cohort to 81% in the youngest. In the South of Italy the proportion was already 75% in the oldest cohort, and declines in the youngest cohort, for which employment opportunities in the primary labour market, above all in the public sector, have worsened. In other words, fewer southern women enter paid work compared to northern women, but those who do so in both old and young cohorts are a rather selective privileged group. The large majority of them are highly educated with strong work orientations; they obtain jobs in the primary labour market; and they pursue continuous careers regardless of unemployment rates, family responsibilities and their partner's characteristics. This also means that if only the Centre-North is considered, Italy appears more similar to Britain, and especially in the youngest cohorts, when British women's initial decisions become more crucial and women's work histories more polarised on education, as has always been the case in Italy. Since the deregulatory measures introduced in Italy during the late 1990s and early 2000s, without any substantial improvement in caring services and economic support for families, British and northern Italian younger cohorts have grown even more similar.

The issue of inequality and 'choice': structural constraints, preferences and individual agency

As discussed throughout Chapter Two, women's choices in the labour market, like other types of choices, reflect the complex interplay between own preferences, 'other significant' preferences, moral and socially negotiated views, overall cultural models, and institutional and economic opportunities. Both preferences and opportunities/constraints are socially structured. They differ by gender, education and class; and they develop over lifecourse and historical time. They are also strongly intertwined, as changing preferences may induce new behaviours and demands for new norms and institutions. For their part, norms and policies, by making certain behaviours more convenient and viable while at the same time defining them as more or less appropriate, affect gender normality models, identities and preferences. Indeed, and to put it in rational choice language, rationality can be both instrumental and cognitive. Rationality can take the form of a cost-benefit calculation intended to maximise current or lifelong incomes, or it may stem from a cultural model where work and the employment–care combination is central to a woman's identity and conception of welfare. As the 'doing gender' perspective has highlighted, differences between middle-class or working-class women in mothering do not necessarily respond to individual self-maximisation and to different sets of opportunities and constraints affecting both actors' goals and their capacities to achieve them. They also respond to moral rationalities created at a micro relational level through the development of careers as identities, and of moral and social views on what is proper behaviour negotiated with partners and within social networks. These gendered moral rationalities are stratified by education and class.

Because of these various interdependencies between preferences and constraints, the micro and the macro, the institutional, the cultural and the material, it is very difficult to determine empirically and analytically the extent to which women's observed employment behaviours are 'agency' or 'structure' effects. It is even more difficult if the data available do not contain information on subjective dimensions, such as attitudes, preferences and intentions, as my data and most longitudinal retrospective data do. However, with the adoption of a micro–macro lifecourse perspective, and in particular of a (gendered) institutional/rational-action framework, it is 'legitimate' to advance causal narratives. These narratives are closely linked to welfare and gender regimes. As many institutional-oriented sociologists and especially feminists have pointed out, how and to what extent women's employment is polarised (by education, class and generation) and how and to what extent this polarisation reflects preferences or constraints strongly depend on the gender division of domestic labour, gender and childcare norms, and welfare policies. For example, the effect of social class or education on women's labour market transitions is much stronger in those countries where both defamilialisation and decommodification are relatively low; or where the choice of leaving the labour market in concomitance with marriage or children depends closely on the public support given to maternal employment in terms of income, time and services, and on the prevalent, also institutionalised, gender ideology. Where policies are more 'universal', more supportive of maternal employment but also of paternal care, not only behaviours but also attitudes (or, in a less rational-choice language, identities and moral rationalities) appear to be less stratified by education and class. Moreover, since preferences are not exogenous to institutions, even if women's behaviours are found to reflect women's orientations more than their constraints, still unexplained is why women, from that country or that generation, have more or less work-centred attitudes and choose different combinations of family with paid work. As Nussbaum (2000, p 114) puts it, 'a critical scrutiny of preference and desire would reveal the many ways in which habit, fear, low expectations and unjust background conditions deform people's choices and even their wishes for their own lives'. Starting from this debate on the tension between 'agency' and 'structure', in the following part of this section I shall link my main findings on changes across cohorts in women's employment trajectories with the changes that occurred in the two countries in normative, economic and institutional configurations from the 1950s to the 2000s.

In Britain, women's employment has gradually expanded from exiting the labour market when marrying and re-entering on completion of childrearing, to exiting on first childbirth and re-entering more often between births and more quickly after childbearing. Indeed, in Britain, where the service economy and, in particular, part-time work have increased since the 1940s and 1950s, and where a relatively deregulated labour market has always allowed for easy entries and re-entries into the labour market, also women in the oldest cohort have not had difficulties in gaining access to the labour market. Yet, the post-war cultural norm of incompatibility between the roles of wife-mother and paid worker and the parallel male-breadwinner welfare state prevented most of them from continuous labour market participation. In line with the hypotheses outlined in Chapter Four, as the marriage bar declined, gender-role attitudes became less traditional, and after maternity leave was introduced in 1978, women's employment behaviour became more differentiated.

The biggest change occurred with the third cohort, that is, in the 1980s and 1990s, when heterogeneity and polarisation increased. With the further decline of the traditional male-breadwinner norm and the increasing approval of maternal employment, the divide shifted from whether and when to re-enter employment to whether and when to interrupt it in the first place. However, without a parallel improvement in work–family reconciliation policies and in the terms and conditions of the labour market, women's ability to act upon preferences and overcome constraints were strongly dependent on their type of job, labour market experience and family income. Indeed, the neoliberal governments of the 1980s and 1990s removed the institutional support for the wage floor, resisted greater support for out-of-home affordable childcare services, and weakened employment and social security protections for short part-timers and non-continuous employees, including maternity leaves. Further, in an attempt to reduce public spending and reservation wages for the unemployed, they cut benefit levels and expanded family-based means-tested benefits, which notably penalised the wife's earnings. As argued by many feminists, these policies have not only reinforced the tendency towards a low-skill, low-wage production system and towards class inequalities; they have also maintained the male-breadwinner gender contract of the Beveridgean post-war welfare state, albeit in the modernised version of the 'one-and-a-half-earner family'. Indeed, they have left responsibility for childcare to private arrangements, ultimately to women, and they have stimulated the growth of the low-wage, unregulated part-time sector, which largely relies on mothers. As a result, the polarisation has widened. Only highly educated women, who typically enter the primary labour market, and can thus enjoy the most generous maternity leave schemes and afford to pay private childcare arrangements, tend to remain in employment around childbirth or take short breaks, rapidly returning into full-time jobs. The other women, those who are less educated, more family oriented or who would prefer to keep working but do not have well-paid, well-protected jobs, do not remain in the labour market during pregnancy or when their children are under school age. Moreover, although they try to reduce the cost of employment interruptions by re-entering more often between births and more quickly after childbearing, these women have more frequent and longer breaks compared with women in good jobs, and they more often re-enter paid work on a part-time basis. Furthermore, they more often lose occupational status, earning power and access to good pensions schemes.

In Britain, differences between highly educated and poorly educated women seem to concern more the rate than the timing of interruptions. Indeed, when they interrupt, women tend to do so around marriage in older cohorts, or around first childbirth in younger cohorts, regardless of level of education. Moreover, on controlling for class, such differences disappear. This further suggests that structural constraints have a weight: of crucial importance in a liberal regime like the British one is the ability to enter high-grade jobs – as highly educated women more often do – and thus be able to afford private childcare and pursue continuous careers, if desired. The reforms introduced under New Labour – with the intention of promoting an adult-worker family model comprising an expansion of leaves and of employee-friendly flexibility, support for childcare costs, a minimum wage and incentives for welfare-to-work transition – have contributed to reducing poverty traps, welfare dependency and women's exits from paid work. Indeed, women in the last cohort exhibited a reduced tendency to exit paid work when their partners become unemployed, which was mainly the effect of the family-based system of unemployment protection of the 1980s and 1990s. Also the effect of motherhood has slightly diminished, for both highly educated and poorly educated women. At the same time, however, because these reforms have focused on stimulating demand rather than supply, on promoting childcare in disadvantaged areas, and on easing the cost of childcare on the basis of parents' income and employment status, they have not greatly changed divisions between better-off highly educated mothers and poor ones. Moreover, the refusal to reduce normal working hours schedules, as the European Union Working Time Directive prescribed, has made it difficult for both mothers and fathers to find time for care.

In Italy, the demand for female labour shifted in favour of women only in the early 1970s, but it has never reached the level in Britain. Caring services, personal services linked to domestic activities and consumer-oriented financial services have remained largely 'internalised' within the extended family. Hence, since the second cohort, which built families and careers in the 1970s when public employment and protection for dependent workers grew rapidly, more women have started labour market careers in Italy. Yet, women's increasing labour supply has clashed with fiscal crisis and sluggish private-sector job growth, and with expansion in the informal, autonomous and black-market employment used by firms to circumvent regulatory rigidities. Women have been increasingly trapped in unemployment and black-market employment and have been discouraged from participation, especially in the South.

In the Italian welfare regime, the family – with its strong kinship and inter-generational solidarity extending well beyond the boundaries of the nuclear family – has continued to perform crucial welfare roles, largely compensating for disparities between 'protected' and 'unprotected' segments of the labour market, for the high price of rents or mortgages, for insufficient or unaffordable out-of-home caring services, and for the direct economic cost of children. Indeed, the male-breadwinner/familistic welfare regime built in the post-war decades remained substantially untouched during the 1980s and 1990s. Universal family allowances and general unemployment or safety-net schemes were not introduced, nor did the provision of **infant** services increase, while the time scheduling of universal preschool services and especially of schools remained unfriendly to full-time working parents. Also, maternity/parental leave arrangements continued to favour employed versus self-employed parents and, de facto, public versus private employees. Likewise, until the mid-1990s, no serious reforms modified the strong labour market regulation introduced in the 1970s to guarantee a lifelong family wage for core (essentially male) full-time breadwinners. Moreover, and clearly in tandem with this factor, traditional gender-role attitudes remained widespread. Still persistently widespread were the beliefs that the best locus for childcare is the family (and therefore women), and that parents' obligations towards children extend far beyond the end of compulsory schooling until they have formed families and built their careers. Compared to norms that disapprove of women's employment only when they have preschool children and define family obligations only within household boundaries, such as those in Britain, these 'extended inter-generational' care norms constrain women's career choices to a greater extent. Indeed, although on the one hand young Italian mothers can more often rely on the help of their parents or parents-in-law (particularly grandmothers), on the other they are themselves expected to spend a great deal of time with their children, support them throughout their entire educational and early labour market career, and, later, take care of their grandchildren and their elderly parents and parents-in-law. Put differently, compared to Britain, in Italy longer phases of women's lifecourses are taken up with intensive caring demands. As some authors argue, these 'extended inter-generational' care norms not only constrain women's labour supply but also women's fertility, because they further raise the cost of children.

Since the late 1990s, reforms of both labour market regulation and family policies have been introduced in Italy. Law 53/2000 on maternity and parental leaves clearly defined childcare as a parental, not just maternal, responsibility: fathers have become entitled to leave on their own account, irrespective of the wife's right, and they have been explicitly encouraged to take time off for childcare. Since 1997, a variety of atypical employment relationships, such as fixed-term contracts, subcontracting and pseudo-self-employment, work on call, weekend work contracts and part-time work, have been allowed or encouraged. However, as numerous authors have pointed out, because of cultural barriers but also because of insufficient income protection during optional leave, the take-up rate by fathers has remained very low. Moreover, the deregulation – which has been described as 'partial and selective' because it is only focused on labour market outsiders (namely young people and women) – has not greatly changed either the performance or the distortions of the Italian labour market. It has progressively eroded employment protection for new entrants, but the levels of unemployment and labour market segmentation have been left virtually unaffected. Wide labour force divides persist between self-employment and employment, the public and private sector, big and small firms, the official and the informal sector. And gender and generational divides have increased. In particular, entry and entrapment in atypicality affects the process of family formation, which tends to be postponed or reduced. It also affects women's movements in and out of paid work over family formation because, in Italy, strong maternity and parental leave provisions only apply to employees. Hence, an increasing number of young Italian women are faced with family–work combinations with few or no guarantees in terms of either social rights or employment prospects. This makes them more similar to their British sisters, who are accustomed to coping with a deregulated 'liberal' labour market outside the 'flexisecurity' model, but who can rely less extensively on family support to maintain their attachment to paid work when their children are young, and more extensively on re-entry chances when work has been interrupted. Young Italian women are also, in some respects, more similar to their 'grandmothers' than to their 'mothers', since the latter entered the labour market during the 'golden age', while the former did so in more precarious economic and institutional conditions. However, compared to their 'grandmothers', younger Italian women are better educated and less constrained by male-breadwinner norms and policies. Moreover, they more often have partners who participate in domestic and childcare work, albeit to a lesser extent than in other European countries. In line with many 'non-evolutionary' accounts, this suggests that social change is not linear. It also suggests that Italian and British women are becoming 'more convergent' but institutional and cultural models still make them 'divergent'. Indeed, as many authors argue, although common trends are observable, change is path-dependent.

The outcomes of the above-described set of opportunities and constraints for Italian women's employment are as expected. In a context where the official rigid labour market reduces the range of working-time options and makes entry and re-entries into the labour market difficult, and where the extended family largely compensates for the lack of public childcare, work histories over the family lifecourse differ little. The crucial decisions for Italian women occur at an earlier stage, when they choose how much to invest in education, whether or not to enter the labour market and for how long, and in which sector to look for a job. And indeed, women's employment in Italy has essentially expanded through an increase in first entry into the labour market, and in continuous careers once entered, rather than in rates and speeds of re-entries, as in Britain. Only in the last cohort, and contrary to my hypotheses, has the gap between highly educated and poorly educated women widened, while exits around childbirth have diminished. Moreover, in the last cohorts, re-entries have become more affected by the gender models within which women have grown up, and less by increasing numbers of children. Overall, these findings suggest that, in more recent times, preferences and gender identities have started to count also in work patterns over family formation. These findings are also consistent with accounts of the effect of post-1997 Italian deregulation policies. In the face of 'partial and selective' deregulation targeted on new entrants, offering few social protections and not accompanied by general welfare reforms, highly educated women have more individual and familial resources on which they can draw to cope with uncertainty.

Both in Italy and Britain the divide between highly educated and poorly educated women has always been wide, and it has even increased in the last cohorts. However, unlike in Britain, in Italy this divide does not disappear when controlling for class. This is likely to reflect the interplay between different structural and normative factors. In Britain, where a highly deregulated labour market has allowed for a wide spread of earnings and where a residualist welfare state has induced reliance on the private sphere (market and family) but where informal help from the extended family is weak, class is more important than education. Even highly educated mothers need to have long work experience or high-class jobs in order to enjoy some maternity protection or sufficient incomes to purchase care. In Italy, instead, education seems more important than class. As in Britain and as everywhere else, education facilitates access to good jobs and to the career ladder. However, Italian women can more often rely on generous maternity leaves and on informal childcare services. Hence, they are, *class paribus*, less influenced by age and number of children. Furthermore, unlike in 'deregulated' Britain, in Italy women face a higher risk of permanent exclusion if they exit paid work. Clearly, for women who have invested in education this is very costly. Also, in Italy, where traditional gender-role norms and 'extended' care norms are stronger, education pays off with higher legitimacy to work. Work by women who have invested in education is more accepted even when the wage returns are relatively small and/or working times are incompatible with family responsibilities. These norms, like most norms, probably influence both preferences and constraints: that is, they are internalised by women who choose to invest in education. They are also internalised by the significant others who may, more or less directly, support their decisions or, conversely, may pressure lower-educated women to stop work or not to start working at all, unless their families need an extra source of income.

Differences in structural and cultural factors also play a crucial role in explaining Italy's persistent North–South divide. In the South, both industrialisation and tertiarisation have arrived later, and to a rather limited extent. In particular, tertiarisation in the South has essentially meant public sector jobs; and with the decline of agriculture, low-educated women have been the main losers. Indeed, in the face of higher male competition for low-qualified jobs in the public sector, and of scarcer job opportunities outside it, southern poorly educated women have had fewer chances of finding jobs than their northern counterparts. Moreover, amid more persistent traditional norms that view married women as the 'natural' caregivers and men as entitled to the scarce jobs available, southern poorly educated women have been more discouraged even from looking for jobs. As typically happens, these norms, preferences and existing options reinforce each other. Highly educated women are more legitimated to work as full earners because they, and their families, do not want to waste the investment made. It is also likely that they are more legitimated to work because they have greater access to family-convenient, well-protected jobs that do not substantially threaten traditional gender roles, or they are able to enter high-grade jobs that are sufficiently 'high' to justify deviation from these roles, especially in a context of high unemployment where income is pooled between a large range of relatives. At the same time, in these economic and cultural circumstances, it is mainly women with strong work preferences who choose to invest in education, look determinedly for jobs, and keep them over family formation. As in the Centre-North so in the South, the proportion of work-oriented women has increased across cohorts. Indeed, many studies show that in the last decades, increasing numbers of Italian women have invested in education, wanted paid work, and been ready to face long unemployment spells before obtaining 'proper' paid work in the regular market. However, unlike in the Centre-North, in the South of Italy it is still mainly high-educated women who succeed in getting such work, although in the 1990s (that is, in our fourth cohort) their position also worsened. The others either do not try to find a job or give up the search, to remain in the grey area of informal paid work or discouraged domestic work, especially if they are middle educated or unsuccessful highly educated.

Policy implications: a lifecourse approach combining time with income, decommodification with defamilialisation, at-home with outside-home gender equality

As widely acknowledged and discussed, work–family incompatibility entails high individual and social costs. At the individual level, it means lower fertility or lower household incomes and higher risks of poverty. It also means, for women, depreciation of human capital investments, loss of economic independence and medical costs related to childbirths postponed beyond the optimal biological age. At the societal level, it implies a waste of human capital and, above all, a threat to welfare state and economic sustainability. As also widely acknowledged and discussed, policies can do a great deal in reducing, maintaining or exacerbating work–family incompatibility. By comparing across time and space, this book, data limitations notwithstanding, has shed further light on the role of policies.

The results of the comparative analysis suggest that both social and labour market policies are important in shaping women's lifetime employment patterns. In particular, they suggest that flexible working is not per se a 'win-win' strategy to combine employment and family life, as presented in much discourse on post-industrial welfare state dilemmas. In Italy, where generous maternity and parental leave provisions are combined with poor childcare services and family allowances, and with strong labour market regulation or a 'partial and selective' deregulation producing an 'insider–outsider' divide and limiting the development of employee-friendly flexibility, the outcome is the well-known low-fertility/low-participation equilibrium. The outcome for women is also, especially in the South, entrapment in the informal market. In Britain, where poor maternity leave and childcare services have gone together, until very recently, with the absence of parental leave, with family-based means-tested income transfers, with strong wage deregulation, and with a large but unprotected part-time sector (the functional equivalent of informal employment in Italy), the outcome has been, at the aggregate level, a low-skill, cheap labour equilibrium combined; at the individual level, the risk of fragmented careers and of entrapment in the secondary labour market and/or in welfare assistance. As much research shows, in countries such as the Scandinavian ones where there is a mix of generous leaves, extended to fathers as well, of generous childcare services and of a good protection for – mostly temporary – part-time jobs, it is easier for women to combine working and caring and to have (formally) uninterrupted work careers, although at the price of occupational gender segregation. Moreover, among those who prefer or need to work part time or to stay at home while children are young, more women are able to re-enter and move into full-time work. They thus pay a relatively low penalty in terms of downward occupational mobility and lifetime incomes.

Consequently, in order to sustain women's attachment to paid work without threatening levels of fertility, poverty, gender and class equality, and overall economic and societal sustainability, of crucial importance is a package of policies developed around three pillars. First, as many feminists have argued, decommodification and defamilialisation should be combined. The state should give women the right to be commodified not only through good employment opportunities but also through redistribution of the caring burden from the family to the state (or the market), and within the family, from women to men. At the same time, the state should also guarantee a certain degree of individual decommodification, thereby enabling women to survive and support their children without being forced either to work or to marry. Universal and less income- or labour market-based entitlements also prevent or reduce class inequalities – primarily material inequalities but also symbolic ones. Second, only if the commodification of women is accompanied by the familialisation of men can gender equality become really achievable. As suggested by Fraser (1994), this can be done by 'making men more similar to women', that is, by promoting a 'dual-earner/dual-carer society'. This would affect both 'opportunities/constraints' and 'preferences', changing the concrete possibilities to take time off for care but also the expectations and moral definitions concerning who should do so. Behind this lies the issue of a new equilibrium between employment and care at the societal and individual as well as couple level. The issue of giving a new definition to citizenship also arises, for these policies imply a logic shift: not only should money and economic life be considered rights, but also time, care and political, social and family life. Third, if besides income and care, time is also important, not only parental leaves and childcare services but also parent-friendly working time regulation should be promoted. As Crompton (2006, p 218) argues in conclusion to her book and referring particularly to the British case:

> [C]ontrols over working hours would make a major contribution to a reconfiguration of employment and family life. If working hours were shorter, men would be enabled to increase their contribution to the work of caring, and women would be better enabled to avoid the 'mummy track' of part-time work (although the example of France suggests that changes in working hours need to be matched by changes within the family as well).

Ultimately, such policy implications relate to a lifecourse perspective. As the lifecourse develops, income and care needs change, and so does the desired and necessary time for paid work, domestic and childcare work, education and leisure. In the new employment and family scenario – that of the increasing entry and permanence of women in paid work but also of increasing instability in both the labour market and the family – two exigencies must be reconciled: guaranteed 'flexisecurity' and guaranteed work–family reconciliation. This requires superseding the traditional industrial citizenship models that based protection against social risks on the status of worker and on employee open-ended contracts, and which assumed female unpaid care work within the couple (or the kinship network). It also requires superseding an individualistic logic when policies are designed. Although rights should be individual rather than family based, the attention should focus on interdependencies between individuals and between different life spheres, and in particular on couples rather than single workers; that is, on changing needs in regard to the balance between care and income, and among time for training and education, for paid work, unpaid work, and spare time. In other words, promoting women's employment and robust dual-earner families, without threatening fertility, poverty and gender equality, requires a gendered lifecourse policy.

References

Abbott, A. and Hrycak, A. (1995) 'Measuring Resemblance in Sequence Data: an Optimal Matching Analysis of Musicians "Careers"', *American Journal of Sociology*, 96 (1): 144-85.

Addabbo, T. (1997) 'Part-Time Work in Italy', in H.P. Blossfeld and C. Hakim (eds) *Between Equalization and Marginalization: Women Working Part-Time in Europe and the United States of America*, Oxford: Oxford University Press.

Addabbo, T. (1999) 'Labour Supply and Employment Probabilities in Italy: A Gender Analysis in a Regional Perspective', *Economia e Lavoro*, 33 (3-4): 189-207.

Adsera, A. (2005) 'Where Are the Babies? Labour Market Conditions and Fertility in Europe', *IZA Discussion Paper No. 1576*, Bonn: IZA.

Albrecht, J.W., Edin, P.A. and Vroman, S.B. (2000) 'A Cross-Country Comparison of Attitudes Towards Mothers Working and their Actual Labour Market Experience', *Labour*, 14 (4): 591-608.

Allison, P.D. (1982) 'Discrete Time Methods for the Analysis of Event Histories', in S. Lienhardt (ed) *Sociological Methodology*, San Francisco, CA: Jossey-Bass.

Allison, P.D. (1984) *Event History Analysis: Regression for Longitudinal Event Data*, Beverly Hills, CA: Sage Publications.

Alwin, D.F., Braun, M. and Scott, J. (1992) 'The Separation of Work and the Family: Attitudes Towards Women's Labour-Force Participation in Germany, Great Britain, and the United States', *European Sociological Review*, 8 (1): 13-37.

Anttonen, A. and Sipilä, J. (1996) 'European Social Care Services: Is it Possible to Identify Models', *Journal of European Social Policy*, 6 (2): 87-100.

Arosio, L. (2002) 'Percorsi Tipici di Mobilità: Una Nuova Prospettiva per lo Studio delle Carriere Lavorative', *Polis*, 1 (April): 75-100.

Arosio, L. (2004) *Gli Opposti si Respingono? Scelte di Coppia e Stabilità Coniule in Italia*, Rome: Aracne Editrice.

Balbo, L. (1978) 'La Doppia Presenza', *Inchiesta*, 32: 3-6.

Ball, S.J. (2003) *Class Strategies and the Education Market: The Middle Classes and Social Advantage*, London: RoutledgeFalmer..

Ballestrero, M.V. (1993) 'Maternità', *Digesto*, Torino: UTET.

Barbagli, M. (1988) *Sotto Lo Stesso Tetto*, Bologna: Il Mulino.

Barbagli, M. and Saraceno, C. (1998) *Separarsi in Italia*, Bologna: Il Mulino.

Barbera, F. (2004) *Meccanismi Sociali: Elementi di Sociologia Analitica*, Bologna: Il Mulino.

Barbieri, P. and Scherer, S. (2005) 'Le Conseguenze Sociali della Flessibilizzazione del Mercato del Lavoro in Italia', *Stato e Mercato*, 74 (2): 56-90.

Barbieri, P. and Scherer, S. (2007) 'Vite Svendute: Uno Guardo Analitico alla Costruzione Sociale delle Prossime Generazioni di Outsider', *Polis*, 3: 431-60.

Barbieri, P. and Scherer, S. (2008) 'Flexibilizing the Italian Labor Market: Unanticipated Consequences of Partial and Targeted Labor Market Deregulation', in H. Blossfeld, S. Buchholz, E. Bukodi and K. Kurz (eds) *Young Workers, Globalization and the Labor Market: Comparing Early Working Life in Eleven Countries*, Cheltenham, Northampton, MA: Edward Elgar.

Barrell, R. (1994) *The UK Labour Market: Comparative Aspects and Institutional Developments*, Cambridge: Cambridge University Press.

Battistoni, L. (ed) (2003) *I Numeri delle Donne: Partecipazione Femminile al Mercato del Lavoro: Caratteri, Dinamiche e Scenari, Quaderni SPINN, No 4*, Rome: Ministero del lavoro e delle politiche sociali.

Battistoni, L. (ed) (2005) *I Numeri delle Donne, Quaderni SPINN, No 17*, Rome: Ministero del lavoro e delle politiche sociali.

Beck, U. (1992) *Risk Society: Towards a New Modernity*, London: Sage Publications.

Beck, U. and Beck-Gernsheim, E. (2002) *Individualization: Institutionalized Individualism and its Social and Political Consequences*, London: Sage Publications.

Becker, G.S. (1975) *Human Capital: A Theoretical and Empirical Analysis with Special Reference to Education*, New York: NBER.

Becker, G.S. (1981) *A Treatise on the Family*, Cambridge: Harvard University Press.

Becker, G.S. (1996) *Accounting for Tastes*, Cambridge, MA: Harvard University Press.

Bellotti, V. (1993) 'La Partecipazione al Lavoro delle Donne Coniugate', *Polis*, 7 (2): 301-20.

Bernardi, F. (1999) 'Does the Husband Matter? Married Women and Employment in Italy', *European Sociological Review*, 15 (3): 285-300.

Bernardi, F. (2001) 'The Employment Behaviour of Married Women in Italy', in H.-P. Blossfeld and S. Drobnic (eds) *Careers of Couples in Contemporary Societies: From Male Breadwinner to Dual Earner Families*, Oxford: Oxford University Press.

Bernardi, F. and Nazio, T. (2005) 'Globalisation and the Transition to Adulthood in Italy', in H.-P. Blossfeld, E. Klijzing, M. Mills and K. Kurz (eds) *Globalization, Uncertainty and Youth in Society*, London: Routledge, pp 349-74.

Bernardi, F., Layte, R., Schizzerotto, A. and Jacobs, S. (2000) 'Who Exits Unemployment? Institutional Features, Individual Characteristics and Chances of Getting a Job', in D. Gallie and S. Paugam (eds) *Welfare Regimes and the Experience of Unemployment in Europe*, Oxford: Oxford University Press.

Bernasco, W. (1994) *Coupled Careers: The Effects of Spouse's Resources on Success at Work*, Amsterdam: Thesis Publishers.

Bernasco, W., De Graaf, P. and Ultee, W. (1998) 'Coupled Careers: Effects of Spouse's Resources on Occupational Attainment in the Netherlands', *European Sociological Review*, 1: 15-31.

Bertolini, S. and Rizza, R. (eds) (2005) 'Atipici?', *Sociologia del Lavoro*, 97, Milano: Franco Angeli.

Bettio, F. (1988a) 'Sex-Typing of Occupations, the Cycle and Restructuring in Italy', in J. Rubery (ed) *Women and Recession*, London: Routledge and Kegan Paul.

Bettio, F. (1988b) 'Women, the State and the Family in Italy: Problems of Female Participation in Historical Perspective', in J. Rubery (ed) *Women and Recession*, London: Routledge and Kegan Paul.

Bettio, F. (2008) 'Occupational Segregation and Gender Wage Disparities in Developed Economies: Should We Still Worry?', in F. Bettio and A. Vershchagina (eds) *Frontiers in the Economics of Gender*, London: Routledge.

Bettio, F. and Plantenga, J. (2004) 'Comparing Care Regimes in Europe', *Feminist Economics*, 10 (1): 85-113.

Bettio, F. and Villa, P. (1996) 'Trends and Prospects for Women's Employment in the 90s: Italy', *Report for EC Network on the Situation of Women in the Labour Market*, Manchester: UMIST.

Bettio, F. and Villa, P. (1998) 'A Mediterranean Perspective on the Breakdown of the Relationship between Participation and Fertility', *Cambridge Journal of Economics*, 22: 137-71.

Bettio, F. and Villa, P. (2000) 'To What Extent Does it Pay to be Better Educated? Education and the Work Market for Women in Italy', in M.J. Gonzalez, T. Jurado and M. Naldini (eds) *Gender Inequalities in Southern Europe: Women, Work, and Welfare in the 1990s*, London: Frank Cass: 150-170 .

Bettio, F., Rubery, J. and Smith, M. (1996) *Gender, Flexibility and New Employment Relations in the European Union*, Torino: ILO.

Beveridge, W., Sir (1942) *Social Insurance and Allied Services*, London: HMSO.

Billari, F., Philipov, D. and Baizan, P. (2001) 'Leaving Home in Europe: The Experience of Cohorts Born around 1960', *International Journal of Population Geography*, 7 (5): 311-38.

Bimbi, F. (1992) 'Tre Generazioni di Donne: Le Trasformazioni nei Modelli di Identità Femminile', in S. Ulivieri (ed) *Educazione e Ruolo Femminile*, Firenze: la Nuova Italia: Nis Ed.

Bimbi, F. (1995) 'Metafore di Genere tra Lavoro non Pagato e Lavoro Pagato: Il Tempo ei Rapporti Sociali di Sesso', *Polis*, 9: 379-400.

Bimbi, F. (1997) 'Lone Mothers in Italy: A Hidden and Embarrassing Issue in a Familist Welfare Regime', in J. Lewis (ed) *Lone Mothers in European Welfare Regimes: Shifting Policy Logics*, London: Jessica Kingsley Publishers.

Bison, I.., Pisati, M. and Schizzerotto, A. (1996) 'Disuguaglianze di Genere e Storie Lavorative', in S. Piccone Stella and C. Saraceno (eds) *Genere: La Costruzione Sociale del Femminile e Maschile,* Bologna: Il Mulino.

Bison, I. (2006) 'Intergenerational Transmissions: Cultural, Economic or Social Resources? When She Helps Him to the Top', Paper presented at the RC28 spring meeting, Nijmegen, 11-14 May.

Bittman, M., England, P., Folbre, N. and Matheson, G. (2001) *When Gender Trumps Money: Bargaining and Time in Household Work*, Chicago, IL: Joint Center for Poverty Research, Northwestern University/University of Chicago.

Blossfeld, H.-P. (ed) (1995) *The New Role of Women: Family Formation in Modern Societies*, Boulder, CO: Westview Press.

Blossfeld, H.-P. and Drobnic, S. (2001) *Careers of Couples in Contemporary Societies: From Male Breadwinner to Dual Earner Families*, Oxford: Oxford University Press.

Blossfeld, H.-P. and Hakim, C. (1997) *Between Equalization and Marginalization: Women Working Part-Time in Europe and the United States of America*, Oxford: Oxford University Press.

Blossfeld, H.-P. and Prein, G. (eds) (1998a) *Rational Choice Theory and Large-Scale Data Analysis*, Boulder, CO: Westview Press.

Blossfeld, H.-P. and Prein, G. (1998b) 'The Relationship Between Rational Choice Theory and Large-Scale Data Analysis – Past Developments and Future Perspectives', in H.-P. Blossfeld and G. Prein (eds) *Rational Choice Theory and Large-Scale Data Analysis*, Boulder, CO: Westview Press.

Blossfeld, H.-P. and Rower, G. (1995) *Techniques of Event History Modeling: New Approaches to Causal Analysis*, Hillsdale, NJ: Lawrence Erlbaum Associates.

Blossfeld, H.-P. and Shavit, Y. (1993) *Persistent Inequality: Changing Educational Attainment in Thirteen Countries*, Boulder, CO: Westview Press.

Blossfeld, H.-P., Drobnic, S. and Rower, G. (1996) *Employment Patterns: A Crossroad between Class and Gender*, Bremen: Sonderforschungsbereich 186.

Blossfeld, H.-P., Manting, D. and Rower, G. (1993) 'Patterns of Change in Family Formation in the Federal Republic of Germany and the Netherlands: Some Consequences for Solidarity between Generations', in H.A. Becker and P.L.J. Hermkens (eds) *Solidarity of Generations: Demographic, Economic and Social Change, and Its Consequences*, Amsterdam: Thesis Publishers, pp 175-96.

Blossfeld, H.-P., Klijzing, E., Mills, M. and Kurz, K. (eds) (2005) *Globalization, Uncertainty and Youth in Society*, London: Routledge.

Blossfeld, H.-P., Klijzing, E., Pohl, K. and Rower, G. (1999) 'Why Do Cohabiting Couples Marry? An Example of a Causal Event History Approach to Interdependent Systems', *Quality & Quantity*, 33 (3): 229-42.

Boje, T.P. and Leira, A. (eds) (2000) *Gender, Welfare State and the Market: Towards a New Division of Labour*, London: Routledge.

Bozzon, R. (2008) 'Modelli di partecipazione delle donne al mercato del lavoro. Un'applicazione dell'analisi delle sequenze alle storie lavorative femminili', *Stato e Mercato*, 83 (2): 217-50.

Bourdieu, P. (1972) 'La trasmissione dell'eredità culturale', in Barbagli, M (ed) *Scuola, potere e ideologia*, Bologna: Il Mulino, pp 131-61.

Bourdieu, P. (1979) La *distinction*, Paris : Éditions de Minuit

Boudon, R. (1998) 'Limitations of Rational Choice Theory', *American Journal of Sociology*, 104 (3): 817-28.

Boudon, R. (2001) 'Which Rational Action Theory for Future Mainstream Sociology: Methodological Individualism or Rational Choice Theory?', *European Sociological Review*, 17 (4): 451-7..

Boudon, R. (2003) 'Beyond Rational Choice Theory', *Annual Review of Sociology*, 29: 1-21.

Bound, J., Brown, C. and Mathiowetz, N. (2001) 'Measurement Errors in Survey Data', in J.J. Heckman and E. Learner (eds) *Handbook of Econometrics*, vol 5, New York: Elsevier, pp 3705-843.

Bratti, M. (2003) 'Labour Force Participation and Marital Fertility of Italian Women: The Role of Education', *Journal of Population Economics*, 16: 525-54.

Bratti, M., Del Bono, E. and Vuri, D. (2004) *New Mothers' Labour Force Participation in Italy: The Role of Job Characteristics*, Bonn: Institute for the Study of Labor.

Breen, R. (ed) (2004) *Social Mobility in Europe*, Oxford and New York: Oxford University Press.

Breen, R. and Garcia-Penalosa, C. (2002) 'Bayesian Learning and Gender Segregation', *Journal of Labor Economics*, 20 (2): 899-922..

Brewster, K. L. and Rindfuss, R.R. (2000) 'Fertility and Women's Employment in Industrialised Nations', *Annual Review of Sociology*, 26: 271-96.

Brines, J. (1993) 'The Exchange Value of Housework', *Rationality and Society*, 5 (3): 302-40.

Brown, M. and Scott, J. (1998) 'Multidimensional Scaling and Equivalence: Is Having a Job the same as working?', ZUMA-Nachrichten Spezial, January.

Brückner, H. and Mayer, K.U. (2005) 'The De-Standardization of the Life Course: What it Might Mean and if it Means Anything Whether it Actually Took Place', *Advances in Life Course Research*, 9: 27-54.

Bruegel, I. (1979) 'Women as a Reserve Army of Labour: A Note on Recent British Experience', *Feminist Review*, 3: 12-33.

Bruegel, I. and Perrons, D. (1998) 'Deregulation and Women's Employment: The Diverse Experiences of Women in Britain', *Feminist Economics*, 4 (1): 103-25.

Brynin, M. and Schupp, J. (2000) 'Education, Employment, and Gender Inequality in the Family', *European Sociological Review*, 16 (4): 349-65.

Burchell, B, Dale, A. and Joshi, H. (1997) 'Part-Time Work among British Women', in H.-P. Blossfeld and C. Hakim (eds) *Between Equalization and Marginalization: Women Working Part-Time in Europe and the United States of America*, Oxford: Oxford University Press.

Caracciolo di Torella, E. (2007) 'New Labour, New Dads: The Impact of Family Friendly Legislation on Fathers, *The Industrial Law Journal*, 36: 318-28.

Casavola, P. (1994) 'Occupazione e Disoccupazione: È Cambiato il Mercato del Lavoro Italiano?', mimeo, Banca d'Italia, April.

Castells, M. (1996) *The Rise of Network Society*, Oxford: Blackwell.

Castiglioni, M., Dalla Zuanna, G. (2008) 'Marital and Reproductive Behavior in Italy after 1995: Bridging the Gap with Western Europe?', *European Journal of Population*, 25(1): 1-26.

Chan, T.W. (1995) 'Optimal Matching Analysis: A Methodological Note on Studying Career Mobility', *Work and Occupations*, 22 (4): 467-90.

Chiesi, A. (1998) 'La Specificità della Terziarizzazione in Italia Un'Analisi delle Differenze Territoriali della Struttura Occupazionale', *Quaderni di Sociologia*, XLII (17): 41-64.

Christofides, L.N. (2000) 'Social Assistance and Labour Supply', *Canadian Journal of Economics*, 33 (3): 715-41.

Clarke, J., Langan, M. and Williams, F. (2001) 'The Construction of the British Welfare State, 1945-1975', in A. Cochrane (ed) *Comparing Welfare States*, London: Sage Publications.

Coleman, J.S. (1981) *Longitudinal Data Analysis*, New York: Basic Books.

Coleman, J.S. (1990) *Foundations of Social Theory*, Cambridge, MA: Belknap Press.

Coltrane, S. (2000) 'Research on Household Labour: Modelling and Measuring the Social Embeddedness of Routine Family Work', *Journal of Marriage and the Family*, 64 (4): 208-33.

Commissione di Indagine Sulla Povertà e l'Emarginazione (1995) *Verso Una Politica Di Lotta Alla Povertà: L'Assegno Per i Figli e Il Minimo Vitale*, Rome: Presidenza del Consiglio dei Ministri.

Conaghan, J. (2002) 'Women, Work, and Family: A British Revolution?', in J, Conaghan, R.M. Fischl and K. Klare (eds) *Labour Law in an Era of Globalization*, Oxford: Oxford University Press, pp 53-74.

Connell, R.W. (1987) 'Gender Regimes and Gender Order', in R.W. Connell, *Gender and Power*, Stanford, CA: Stanford University Press, pp 23-66.

Conti, M. and Sette, E. (2007) 'Job Security and Fertility: Evidence from Italy', Mimeo, University of Genova.

Cooke, K. (1987) 'The Withdrawal from Paid Work of the Wives of Unemployed Men: A Review of Research', *Journal of Social Policy*, 16: 371-82.

Corbetta, P. (1999) *Metodologie e Tecniche Della Ricerca Sociale*, Bologna: Il Mulino.

Council of Europe (2004) *Recent Demographic Developments in Europe*, Strasbourg: Council of Europe Publishing.

Cousins, C. (1994) 'A Comparison of the Labour Market Position of Women in Spain and the UK with Reference to the "Flexible" Labour Debate', *Work, Employment and Society*, 8 (1): 45-67.

Crompton, R. (2006) *Employment and the Family: The Reconfiguration of Work and Family Life in Contemporary Societies*, Cambridge: Cambridge University Press.

Crompton, R. and Harris. F. (1998) 'Explaining Women's Employment Patterns: "Orientation to Work" Revisited', *British Journal of Sociology*, 49 (1): 118-49.

Crouch, C. (1990) 'United Kingdom: The Rejection of Compromise', in G. Baglioni and C. Crouch (eds) *European Industrial Relations: The Challenge of Flexibility*, London: Sage Publications.

Crouch, C. (1999) *Social Change in Western Europe*, Oxford: Oxford University Press.

Davies, H. and Joshi, H. (2001) 'Who has Borne the Cost of Britain's Children in the 1990s?', in K. Vleminckx and T.M. Smeeding (eds) *Child Well-Being, Child Poverty and Child Policy in Modern Nations: What Do We Know?*, Bristol: The Policy Press.

Davies, H. and Joshi, H. (2002) 'Women's Incomes over a Synthetic Lifetime', in E. Ruspini and A. Dale (eds) *The Gender Dimension of Social Change: The Contribution of Dynamic Research to the Study of Women's Life Courses*, Bristol: The Policy Press.

De Henau, J., Meulders, D. and O'Dorchai, S. (2007) 'Parents' Care and Career: Comparing Parental Leave Policies across EU-15', in D. Del Boca and C. Wetzels (eds) *Social Policies, Labour Markets and Motherhood: A Comparative Analysis of European Countries*, Cambridge: Cambridge University Press.

de Lillo, A. and Schizzerotto, A. (1985) *La Valutazione Sociale Delle Occupazioni*, Bologna: Il Mulino.

De Sandre, P., Pinnelli, A. and Santini, A. (eds) (1999) *Nuzialità e Fecondità in Trasformazione: Percorsi e Fattori Del Cambiamento*, Bologna: Il Mulino.

De Sandre, P. (1991) 'Contributo Delle Generazioni Ai Cambiamenti Recenti Nei Comportamenti e Nelle Forme Familiari', in P. Donati (ed) *Secondo Rapporto Sulla Famiglia in Italia*, Turin: Ed. Paoline.

Deakin, S. and Wilkinson, F. (1991) 'Social Policy and Economic Efficiency: The Deregulation of the Labour Market in Britain', *Critical Social Policy*, 33: 40-61.

Del Boca, D. (1993) *Politiche Pubbliche e Offerta di Lavoro*, Rome: La Nuova Italia Scientifica: Rome.

Del Boca, D. (2002) 'The Effect of Child Care and Part Time Opportunities on Participation and Fertility Decisions in Italy', *Journal of Population Economics*, 15 (3): 549-73..

Del Boca, D. and Pasqua, S. (2005) 'Labour Supply and Fertility in Europe and the U.S.', in T. Boeri, D. Del Boca and C. Pissarides (eds) *Women at Work: An Economic Perspective*, Oxford: Oxford University Press.

Del Boca, D and Saraceno, C. (2005) 'Le Donne in Italia tra Famiglia e Lavoro', *Economia & Lavoro*, 1: 125-39.

Del Boca, D. and Wetzels, C. (eds) (2007) *Social Policies, Labour Markets and Motherhood: A Comparative Analysis of European Countries*, Cambridge: Cambridge University Press.

Del Boca, D., Locatelli, M.. and Pasqua, S. (2000) 'Employment Decisions of Married Women: Evidence and Explanations', *Labour*, 14 (1): 35-52.

Del Boca, D., Pasqua, S., Pronzato, C. and Wetzels, C. (2007) 'An Empirical Analysis of the Effects of Social Policies on Fertility, Labour Market Participation and Earnings of European Women', in D. Del Boca and C. Wetzels (eds) *Social Policies, Labour Markets and Motherhood: A Comparative Analysis of European Countries*, Cambridge: Cambridge University Press.

Della Sala, V. (2002) '"Modernization" and Welfare-State Restructuring in Italy: The Impact on Child Care', in S. Michel and R. Mahon (eds) *Child Care Policy at the Crossroads: Gender and Welfare State Restructuring*, New York: Routledge.

Den Dulk, L. (2001) *Work-Family Arrangements in Organisations: A Cross-National Study in the Netherlands, Italy, the United Kingdom, and Sweden*, Amsterdam: Rozenberg.

Dex, S., Gustafsson, S., Smith, N. and Callan, T. (1995) 'Cross-National Comparisons of the Labour-Force Participation of Women Married to Unemployed Men', *Oxford Economic Papers*, 47: 611-35.

Dex, S., Joshi, H., Macran, S. and McCulloch, A. (1998) 'Women's Employment Transitions around Childbearing', *Oxford Bulletin of Economics and Statistics*, 60 (1): 79-100.

Di Tommaso, M.L. (1999) 'A Trivariate Model of Participation, Fertility and Wages: The Italian Case', *Cambridge Journal of Economics*, 23: 623-40.

Dickens, L. and Hall, M. (1995) 'The State: Labour Law and Industrial Relations', in P. Edwards (ed) *Industrial Relations: Theory and Practice in Britain*, Oxford: Blackwell.

Drobnic, S. (2000) 'The Effects of Children on Married and Lone Mothers' Employment in the United States and (West) Germany', *European Sociological Review*, 16 (2): 137-57.

Duncan, G., White, M., Cheng, Y. and Tomlinson, M. (1998) *Restructuring the Employment Relationship*, Oxford: Clarendon Press.

Duncan, S. (2005) 'Mothering, Class and Rationality', *Sociological Review*, 53 (1): 50-76.

Easterlin, R.A. (1976) 'The Conflict between Aspirations and Resources', *Population and Development Review*, 2 (3-4): 417-25.

Easterlin, R.A., Macdonald, C. and Macunovich, D.J. (1990) 'How have American Baby Boomers Fared? Earnings and Economic Well-Being of Young Adults, 1964-1987', *Journal of Population Economics*, 3 (4): 277-90.

EEIG European Opinion Research Group (2004) *Eurobarometer - Europeans' Attitudes to Parental Leave*, Brussels: EEIG European Opinion Research Group.

Eisenhower, D., Mathiowetz, N.A. and Morganstein, D. (1991) 'Recall Errors: Sources and Bias Reduction Techniques', in P.P. Biemer, R.M. Groves, L. Lyberg, N.A. Mathiowetz and S. Sudman (eds) *Mesurements Errors in Surveys*, New York: John Wiley, pp 127-44..

Elder, G. (1975) 'Age Differentiation and the Life Course', *Annual Review of Sociology*, 1: 165-90.

Elder, G.H. (ed) (1985) *Life Course Dynamics: Trajectories and Transitions, 1968-1980*, Ithaca, NY: Cornell University Press..

Elder, G.H. (1994) 'Time, Human Agency and Social Change: Perspectives on the Life Course', *Social Psychology Quarterly*, 57 (1): 4-15.

Elder, G.H.. (1998) 'The Life Course as Developmental Theory', *Child Development*, 69: 1-12.

Elliott, J. (2002) 'Longitudinal Analysis and the Constitution of the Concept of Gender', in E. Ruspini and A. Dale (eds) *The Gender Dimension of Social Change: The Contribution of Dynamic Research to the Study of Women's Life Courses*, Bristol: The Policy Press.

Elliott, J., Dale, A. and Egerton, M. (2001) 'The Influence of Qualifications on Women's Work Histories, Employment Status and Earnings at Age 33', *European Sociological Review*, 17 (2): 145-68.

Emerson, M. (1988) 'Regulation or Deregulation of the Labour Market: Policy Regimes for the Recruitment & Dismissal of Employees in the Industrialized Countries', *European Economic Review*, 32: 775-817.

Engelhardt, H., Kögel, T. and Prskawetz, A. (2001) *Fertility and Female Employment Reconsidered: A Macro-Level Time Series Analysis*, Rostock: Max Planck Institute for Demographic Research.

England, P. (1993) 'The Separative Self: Androcentric Bias in Neoclassical Assumptions', in M.A. Ferber and J.A. Nelson (eds) *Beyond Economic Man: Feminist Theory and Economics*, Chicago, IL: University of Chicago Press.

Erikson, R. and Goldthorpe, J.H. (1992) *The Constant Flux: A Study of Class Mobility in Industrial Societies*, Oxford: Clarendon Press.

Ermisch, J. and Francesconi, M. (2000) 'Patterns of Household and Family Formation', in R. Berthoud and J. Gershuny (eds) *Seven Years in the Lives of British Families: Evidence on the Dynamics of Social Change from the British Household Panel Survey*, Bristol: The Policy Press.

Esping-Andersen, G. (1990) *The Three Worlds of Welfare Capitalism*, Cambridge: Polity Press.

Esping-Andersen, G. (1996a) *Welfare States in Transition: National Adaptations in Global Economies*, London: Sage Publications.

Esping-Andersen, G. (1996b) 'Welfare States Without Work: The Impasse of Labour Shedding and Familialism in Continental European Social Policy', in G. Esping-Andersen (ed) *Welfare States in Transition: National Adaptations in Global Economies*, London: Sage Publications.

Esping-Andersen, G. (1999) *Social Foundations of Postindustrial Economies*, Oxford: Oxford University Press.

Esping-Andersen, G. (2000) 'Who is Harmed by Employment Regulation?', in G. Esping-Andersen and M. Regini (eds) *Why De-Regulate Labour Markets?*, Oxford: Oxford University Press.

Esping-Andersen, G. and Regini, M. (eds) (2000) *Why De-Regulate Labour Markets?*, Oxford: Oxford University Press.

European Childcare Network (1994) *Leave Arrangements for Workers with Children: A Review of Leave Arrangements in the Member States of the European Community and Austria, Finland, Norway and Sweden*, Report Prepared for the Equal Opportunities Unit (DGV). Brussels: European Commission.

European Commission (2000) *Employment in Europe 2000*, Brussels.

European Observatory on National Family Policies (1992) *National Family Policies in EC-Countries in 1991*, Brussels: European Commission.

Fagan, C. and O'Reilly, J. (1998a) *Part-Time Prospects: International Comparison of Part-Time Work in Europe, North-America and the Pacific Rim*, London: Routledge.

Fagan, C. and O'Reilly, J. (1998b) 'Conceptualising Part-Time Work: The Value of an Integrated Comparative Perspective', in C. F. and J. O'Reilly (eds) *Part-Time Prospects: International Comparison of Part-Time Work in Europe, North-America and the Pacific Rim*, London: Routledge: 1-32.

Fagan, C. and Rubery, J. (1996) 'The Salience of the Part-Time Divide in the European Union', *European Sociological Review*, 12 (3): 227-50.

Fagnani, J. (1996) 'Family Policies and Working Mothers: A Comparison of France and West Germany', in M.D. Garcia-Ramon and J. Monk (eds) *Women of the European Union: The Politics of Work and Daily-Life*, London: Routledge.

Ferber, M.A. and Nelson, J.A. (eds) (1993) *Beyond Economic Man: Feminist Theory and Economics*, Chicago, IL: University of Chicago Press.

Ferrera, M. (1996) 'Il Modello Sud-Europeo di Welfare State', Rivista Italiana Di Scienza Politica, 1: 67-101.

Finch, J. and Mason, J. (1993) *Negotiating Family Responsibilities*, London: Routledge.

Firebaugh, G. (1997) *Analysing Repeated Surveys*, Thousand Oaks, CA: Sage Publications.

Flinn, C.J. and Heckman, J.J. (1982a) 'Models for the Analysis of Labour Force Dynamics', *Advances in Econometrics*, 1: 35-95.

Flinn, C.J. and Heckman, J.J.. (1982b) 'New Methods for Analyzing Individual Event Histories', *Sociological Methodology*, 13: 99-140.

Fraser, N. (1994) 'After the Family Wage: Gender Equity and the Welfare State', *Political Theory*, 22: 591-618.

Gauthier, A.H. (1996) *The State and the Family: A Comparative Analysis of Family Policies in Industrialised Countries*, Oxford: Clarendon Press.

Gavio. F. and Lelleri, R. (2005) 'La Fruizione dei Congedi Parentali in Italia: Monitoraggio dell'Applicazione della Legge n. 53/2000 Negli Anni 2002 e 2003', in P.P. Donati (Osservatorio Nazionale sulla Famiglia) *Famiglie e Politiche di Welfare in Italia: Interventi e Pratiche*, Vol II, Bologna: Il Mulino.

Geist C. (2005) 'The Welfare State and the Home: Regime Difference in the Domestic Division of Labour', *European Sociological Review*, 21: 23-41.

Gershuny, J. (1997) 'Sexual Divisions and the Distribution of Work in the Household', in G. Dench (ed) *Rewriting the Sexual Contract*, London: Institute of Community Studies, pp 141-52.

Giddens, A. (1991) *Modernity and Self-Identity: Self and Society in the Late Modern Age*, Cambridge: Polity Press.

Giele, J.Z. and Elder, G.H., Jr (1998) *Methods of Life Course Research: Qualitative and Quantitative Approaches*, Thousand Oaks, CA: Sage Publications.

Ginsburg, N. (1992) *Divisions of Welfare*, London: Sage Publications.

Glass, J. and Riley, L. (1998) 'Family Responsive Policies and Employee Retention Following Childbirth', *Social Forces*, 76: 1401-35.

Goldthorpe, J.H. (1996) 'Class Analysis and the Reorientation of Class Theory: The Case of Persisting Differentials in Educational Attainment', *British Journal of Sociology*, 47 (3): 481-512.

Goldthorpe, J.H. (2000) *On Sociology: Numbers, Narratives, and the Integration of Research and Theory*, Oxford: Oxford University Press.

Goldthorpe, J.H. (2001) 'Causation, Statistics, and Sociology', *European Sociological Review*, 17 (1): 1-20.

Goldthorpe, J.H. and McKnight, A. (2003) *The Economic Basis of Social Class*, Working Paper No 2003-05, Oxford: Department of Sociology, University of Oxford.

Gornick, J. and Jacobs, J. (1998) 'Gender, the Welfare State and Public Employment: A Comparative Study of Seven Industrialized Countries', *American Sociological Review*, 63: 688-710.

Gornick, J.C. and Meyers, M.K. (2003) *Families that Work: Policies for Reconciling Parenthood and Employment*, New York: Russell Sage Foundation.

Gornick, J., Meyers, M.K. and Ross, K. (1997) 'Supporting the Employment of Mothers: Policy Variation across Fourteen Welfare States', *Journal of European Social Policy*, 1: 45-70.

Gottardi, D. (1999) 'I Congedi Parentali nell'Ordinamento Italiano', *Lavoro e Diritto*, 3: 497-527.

Gottardi, D. (2001) 'La Disciplina del Congedo di Maternità e Paternità', *Guida al Lavoro*, 19: 16-23.

Gregory, A. and Windebank, J. (2000) *Women's Work in Britain and France: Practice, Theory and Policy*, London: Macmillan.

Groppi, A. (1996) *Il Lavoro delle Donne*, Rome-Bari: Laterza.

Grubb, D. and Wells, W. (1993) 'Employment Regulation and Patterns of Work in EC Countries', *OECD Economic Studies*, 21: 7-58.

Gustafsson, S. (1994) 'Childcare and Types of Welfare States', in D. Sainsbury (ed) *Gendering Welfare States*, London: Sage Publications.

Gustafsson, S. (1995) 'Public Policies and Women's Labour Force Participation: A Comparison of Sweden, Germany and the Netherlands', in T.P. Schultz (ed) *Investment in Women's Human Capital*, Chicago, IL: University of Chicago Press.

Gustafsson, S. (2001) 'Optimal Age at Motherhood: Theoretical and Empirical Considerations on Postponement of Maternity in Europe', *Journal of Population Economics*, 14: 225-47.

Gustafsson, S., Kenjoh, E. and Wetzels, C. (2003) 'Employment Choices and Pay Differences Between Non-standard and Standard Work in Britain, Germany, Netherlands and Sweden', in S. Houseman and M. Osawa (eds) *Nonstandard Work In Developed Economies: Causes and Consequences*, Kalamazoo, Michigan: W.E. Upjohn Institute for Employment Research, pp 215-67.

Haas, B., Steiber, N., Hartel, M. and Wallace, C. (2006) 'Household Employment Patterns in an Enlarged European Union', *Work, Employment and Society*, 20: 751-71.

Hakim, C. (1991) 'Grateful Slaves and Self-Made Women: Fact and Fantasy in Women's Work Orientations', *European Sociological Review*, 7 (2): 101-21.

Hakim, C. (2000) *Work-Lifestyle Choices in the 21st Century: Preference Theory*, Oxford: Oxford University Press.

Halleröd, B. (2005) 'Sharing of Housework and Money among Swedish Couples: Do they Behave Rationally?', *European Sociological Review*, 21 (3): 273-88.

Halpin, B. and Chan, T.W. (1998) 'Class Careers as Sequences: An Optimal Matching Analysis of Work-Life Histories', *European Sociological Review*, 14: 111-30.

Halpin, B. and Chan, T.W. (2003) 'Educational Homogamy in Ireland and Britain: Trends and Patterns', *British Journal of Sociology*, 54 (4): 473-96.

Han, S.-K.. and Moen, P. (2001) 'Coupled Careers: Pathways Through Work and Marriage in the United States', in H.-P. Blossfeld and S. Drobnic (eds) *Careers of Couples in Contemporary Societies: From Male Breadwinner to Dual Earner Families*, Oxford: Oxford University Press.

Harkness, S. and Waldfogel, J. (2003) 'The Family Gap in Pay: *Evidence from Seven Industrialized Countries'*, Research in Labor Economics, 22: 369-414.

Heath, A. and Cheung, S.Y. (1998) 'Education and Occupation in Britain', in Y. Shavit and W. Müller (eds) *From School to Work*, Oxford: Clarendon Press.

Heckman, J.J. (1976) 'The Common Structure of Statistical Models of Truncation, Sample Selection, and Limited Dependent Variables and a Sample Estimator for Such Models', *The Annals of Economic and Social Measurement*, 5: 475-92.

Heckman, J.J. (1979) 'Sample Selection Bias as a Specification Error', *Econometrica*, 47: 153-61.

Heckman, J.J. and Borjas, G.J. (1980) 'Does Unemployment Cause Future Unemployment? Definitions, Questions and Answers from a Continuous Time Model of Heterogeneity and State Dependence', *Economica*, 47: 247-83.

Heckman, J.J. and Singer, B. (1982a) 'The Identification Problem in Econometric Models for Duration Data', in W. Hildebrand (ed) *Advances in Econometrics*, Cambridge: Cambridge University Press.

Heckman, J.J. and Singer, B. (1982b) 'Population Heterogeneity in Demographic Models', in K. Land and A. Rogers (eds) *Multidimensional Mathematical Demographic*, New York: Academic Press.

Hernes, H. (1987) *Welfare State and Woman Power*, Oslo: Norwegian University Press.

Hobson, B., Lewis, J. and Siim, B. (eds) (2002) *Contested Concepts in Gender and Social Politics*, Cheltenham: Edward Elgar.

Holt, D., Mc Donald, J.W. and Skinner, C.J. (1991) 'The Effect of Measurement Error on Event History Analysis', in P.P. Biemer, R.M. Groves, L. Lyberg, N.A. Mathiowetz and S. Sudman (eds) *Measurement Errors in Surveys*, New York: John Wiley, pp 665-86.

Humphries, J. (1983) 'The "Emancipation" of Women in the 1970s and 1980s: From the Latent to the Floating', *Capital and Class*, 20 (Summer): 6-28.

Inglehart, R. (1977) *The Silent Revolution*, Princeton, NJ: Princeton University Press.

Inglehart, R. (1990) *Culture Shift in Advanced Industrial Society*, Princeton, NJ: Princeton University Press.

Irwin, S. (2003) 'Interdependencies, Values and the Reshaping of Difference: Gender and Generation at the Birth of Twentieth-Century Modernity', *British Journal of Sociology*, 54 (4): 565-84.

ISTAT (2000) *Rapporto Annuale 1999*, Rome: ISTAT.

ISTAT (2006) *Avere un Figlio in Italia: Alcuni Approfondimenti Tematici dell'Indagine Campionaria sulle Nascite, Anno 2002*, Rome: ISTAT.

Jacobs, S. (1995) 'Changing Patterns of Sex Segregated Occupations Throughout the Life-Course', *European Sociological Review*, 11 (2): 157-71.

Jacobs, S. (1997) 'Employment Changes over Childbirth: A Retrospective View', *Sociology*, 31 (3): 577-90.

Jacobs, S. (1999) 'Trends in Women's Career Patterns and in Gender Occupational Mobility in Britain', *Gender, Work and Organisation*, 6 (1): 32-46.

Jones, R.K. and Brayfield, A. (1997) 'Life's Greatest Joy? European Attitudes Toward the Centrality of Children', *Social Forces*, 75 (4): 1239-70.

Joshi, H. and Hinde, P.R. (1993) 'Employment after Childbearing in Post-War Britain: Cohort-Study Evidence on Contrasts Within and Across Generations', *European Sociological Review*, 9 (3): 203-27.

Joshi, H., Macran, S. and Dex, S. (1996) 'Employment after Childbearing and Women's Subsequent Labour Force Participation: Evidence from the British 1958 Birth Cohort', *Journal of Population Economics*, 9: 325-48.

Joshi, H. (1986) 'Participation in Paid Work: Evidence From the Women and Employment Survey', in R. Blundell and I. Walker (eds) *Unemployment, Search and Labour Supply*, Cambridge: Cambridge University Press, pp 217-42.

Jurado-Guerrero, T. and Naldini, M. (1996) 'Is the South So Different? Italian and Spanish Families in Comparative Perspective', *South European Society and Politics*, 3 (1): 42-66.

Kabeer, N. (1999) 'Resources, Agency, Achievements: Reflections on the Measurement of Women's Empowerment', *Development and Change*, 30 (3): 435-64.

Kamerman, S. and Kahn, A. (2001) 'Child and Family Policies in an Era of Social Policy Retrenchment and Restructuring', in K. Vleminckx and T.M. Smeeding (eds) *Child Well-Being, Child Poverty and Child Policy in Modern Nations: What Do We Know?*, Bristol: The Policy Press.

Kan, M.Y. (2007) 'Work Orientation and Wives' Employment Careers: An Evaluation of Hakim's Preference Theory', *Work and Occupations*, 34 (4): 430-62.

Kaufmann, F.-H., Kuijsten, A., Schulze, H.J. and Strohmeier, K.P. (eds) (1997) *Family Life and Family Policies in Europe*, Oxford: Clarendon Press.

Kempeneers, M. and Lelievre, E. (1991) *Employment and Family within the Twelve*, Brussels: European Commission.

Kiernan, K..E. and Lelievre, E. (1995) 'Great Britain', in H.-P. Blossfeld (ed) *The New Role of Women*, Boulder, CO: Westview Press.

Kilkey, M. (2000) *Lone Mothers between Paid Work and Care: The Policy Regime in Twenty Countries*, Aldershot: Ashgate.

Kilkey, M. (2006) 'New Labour and Reconciling Work and Family Life: Making it Fathers' Business?', *Social Policy and Society*, 5: 167-175.

Killingsworth, M.R. (1983) *Labor Supply*, Cambridge: Cambridge University Press.

Knudsen, K. and Waerness, K. (2001) 'National Context, Individual Characteristics and Attitudes on Mothers' Employment: A Comparative Analysis of Great Britain, Sweden and Norway', *Acta Sociologica*, 44: 67-79.

Kohli, M. (2001) 'Organizzazione Sociale e Costruzione Soggettiva del Corso della Vita', in C. Saraceno (ed) (2001) *Età e Corso della Vita*, Bologna: Il Mulino.

Kohli, M. (2007) 'The Institutionalization of the Life Course: Looking Back to Look Ahead', *Research in Human Development*, 4: 253-71.

Kreps, D.M. (1997) 'Intrinsic Motivation and Extrinsic Incentives', *The American Economic Review*, 87 (2): 359-64.

Künzler, J. (2002) 'Paths Towards a Modernization of Gender Relations, Policies, and Family Building', in F.X. Kaufmann, A. Kuijsten, H.-J. Schulze and K.P. Strohmeier (eds) *Family Life and Family Policies in Europe*, vol 2, Oxford: Oxford University Press: 252-98.

La Valle, I., Arthur, S., Millward, C., Scott, J. and Clayden, M. (2002) *Happy Families? Atypical Work and its Influence on Family Life*, York: Joseph Rowntree Foundation.

Lareau, A. (2002) 'Invisible Inequality: Social Class and Childrearing in Black Black Families and White Families,' *American Sociological Review*, 67 (October): 747-76.

Laslett, P. and Wall, R. (eds) (1972) *Household and Family in Past-Time*, Cambridge: Cambridge University Press.

Leibfried, S. (1992) 'Towards a European Welfare State? On Integrating Poverty Regimes into the European Community', in Z. Ferge and J.E. Kolberg (eds) *Social Policy in a Changing Europe*, Frankfurt am Main: Campus Verlag.

Leitner, S. (2003) 'Varieties of Familialism: The Caring Function of the Family in Comparative Perspective', *European Societies*, 5: 353-75.

Lena, B. (2002) 'La Condizione della Donna Nella Famiglia e le Nuove Politiche Familiari', in Nazionale sulle Famiglie e le Politiche Locali di Sostegno alle Responsabilità Familiari, *Famiglie: mutamenti e politiche sociali*, Vol 1, Bologna: Il Mulino, pp 329-43

Lesthaeghe, R. (1995) 'The Second Demographic Transition: An Interpretation', in K. Oppenheim Mason and A.-M. Jensen (eds) *Gender and Family Change in Industrial Countries*, Oxford: Clarendon Press.

Lesthaeghe, R. and Moors, G. (2000) 'Recent Trends in Fertility and Household Formation in the Industrialised World', *Review of Population and Social Policy*, 9: 121-70.

Lewis, J. (1992) 'Gender and the Development of Welfare Regimes', *European Social Policy*, 2 (3): 159-73.

Lewis, J. (2002) 'Gender and welfare state change', *European Societies*, 4 (4): 331–57.

Lewis, J. (2003) 'Developing Early Years Childcare in England, 1997-2002: The Choices for (Working) Mothers', *Social Policy and Administration*, 37: 219–38.

Lewis, J. (2006) 'Employment and Care: The Policy Problem, Gender Equality and the Issue of Choice', *Journal of Comparative Policy Analysis*, 8 (2): 103–14.

Lewis, J. and Campbell, M. (2007) 'UK Work/Family Balance Policies and Gender Equality, 1997-2005', *Social Politics*, 14 (1): 4–30.

Lewis, J. and Ostner, I. (1995) 'Gender and the Evolution of European Social Policies', in S. Leibfried and P. Pierson (eds) *European Social Policy: Between Fragmentation and Integration*, Washington, DC: Brookings Institution, pp 159–193.

Lewis, J., Campbell, M. and Huerta, C. (2008) 'Patterns of Paid and Unpaid Work: Gender, Commodification, Preferences and the Implications for Policy', *Journal of European Social Policy*, 18 (1): 21–37.

Livi Bacci, M. (2001) 'Too Few Children and Too Much Family', *Daedalus*, 130: 139–55.

Lucchini, M., Saraceno, C.. and Schizzerotto, A. (2007) 'Dual-earner and dual-career couples in contemporary Italy', *Zeitschrift fuer FamilienForschung*, 3 (3): 290–310.

Lück, D (2006) 'The Impact of Gender Role Attitudes on Women's Life Courses', in H.-P. Blossfeld and H. Hofmeister (eds) *Globalization, Uncertainty and Women's Careers: An International Comparison*, Northampton: Edward Elgar, pp 405–32.

McCulloch, A. and Dex, S. (2001) 'Married Women's Employment Patterns in Britain', in H.-P. Blossfeld and S. Drobnic (eds) *Careers of Couples in Contemporary Societies: From Male Breadwinner to Dual Earner Families*, Oxford: Oxford University Press.

McDonald, P. (2000) 'Gender Equity in Theories of Fertility transition', *Population and Development Review*, 26: 427–39.

McDonald, P.K., Bradley, L.M. and Guthrie, D. (2006) 'Challenging the Rhetoric of Choice in Maternal Labour-Force Participation: Preferred Versus Contracted Work Hours', *Gender, Work & Organization*, 13 (5): 470–91.

McGinnity, F. (2002) 'The Labour-Force Participation of the Wives of Unemployed Men: Comparing Britain and West Germany Using Longitudinal Data', *European Sociological Review*, 18 (4): 473–88.

McIntosh, M. (1978) 'The State and the Oppression of Women', in A. Kuhn and A. Wolpe (eds) *Feminism and Materialism*, London: Routledge & Kegan Paul.

McLaughlin, E. and Glendinning, C. (1994) 'Paying for Care in Europe: Is There a Feminist Approach?', in L. Hantrais and S. Morgan (eds) *Family Policy and the Welfare of Women, Cross-National Research Papers*, 3rd series, Loughborough: European Research Centre, University of Loughborough).

McRae, S. (1991) 'Occupational Change Over ChildBirth', *Sociology*, 25 (4): 589–606.

McRae, S. (2003) 'Choice and Constraints in Mothers' Employment Careers: McRae Replies to Hakim', *British Journal of Sociology*, 54 (4): 585-92.

McRae, S. and Daniel, W.W. (1991) *Maternity Rights: The Experience of Women and Employers*, London: Policy Studies Institute.

Mcran, S., Joshi, H. and Dex, S. (1996) 'Employment After Childbearing: A Survival Analysis', *Work, Employment and Society*, 10(2): 273-96.

Magnusson, D., Bergman, L.R., Rudinger, G. and Torestal, B. (eds) (1991) *Problems and Methods in Longitudinal Research: Stability and Change*, Cambridge: Cambridge University Press.

Mandel, H. and Semyonov, M. (2006) 'A Welfare State Paradox: State Interventions and Women's Employment Opportunities in 22 Countries', *American Journal of Sociology*, 111 (6): 1910-49.

Mannheim, K. (1952) 'The Problem of Generations', in P. Kecskemeti (ed) *Essays on the Sociology of Knowledge*, New York: Routledge & Kegan Paul.

Mapelli, B. (2005) 'Giovani Donne e Maternità: Tempo, Servizi e Lavoro: la Relazione Ambigua con i Buoni Padri', in E. Ruspini (ed) *Donne e Uomini che Cambiano: Relazioni di Genere, Identità Sessuali e Mutamento Sociale*, Milan: Guerini Associati.

Maré, D. (2006) 'Constructing Consistent Work-life Histories: A guide for users of the British Household Panel Survey', ISER working papers 2006-39, Colchester: Institute for Social and Economic Research.

Marini, M.M. (1992) 'The Role of Models of Purposive Action in Sociology', in J.S. Coleman and T.J. Fararo (eds) *Rational Choice Theory: Advocacy and Critique*, Newbury Park, CA: Sage Publications.

Marini, M.M. and Singer, B.. (1988) 'Causality in the Social Sciences', in C.C. Clogg (ed) *Sociological Methodology*, San Francisco, CA: Jossey-Bass, pp 347-409.

Marsh, A. (2001) 'Helping British Lone Parents Get and Keep Paid Work', in J. Millar and K. Rowlingson (eds) *Lone Parents, Employment and Social Policy*, Bristol: The Policy Press.

Maucher, M. and Bahle, T. (eds) (2000) *Family Policy Database*, Mannheim: MZES.

Mayer, K.U. (1991) 'Life Courses in the Welfare State', in W.R. Heinz (ed) *Theoretical Advances in Life Course Research*, vol 1, Weinheim: Deutscher Studienverlag, pp 171-86.

Mayer, K.U. (1997) 'Notes on a comparative political economy of life courses', *Comparative Social Research*, 16: 203-26.

Mayer, K.U. (2009) 'Life Courses and Life Chances in a Comparative Perspective', in S. Svallfors (ed) *Analyzing Inequality: Life chances and Social Mobility in Comparative Perspective*, Stanford, CA: Stanford University Press.

Mayer, K.U. and Huinink, J. (1990) 'Age, Period, and Cohort in the Study of the Life Course: A Comparison of Classical A-P-C-Analysis with Event History Analysis or Farewell to LEXIS?', in D. Magnusson and L.R. Bergman (eds) *Data Quality in Longitudinal Research*, Cambridge, MA: Cambridge University Press, pp 211-32.

Mayer, K.U. and Schöpflin, U. (1989) 'The state and the life course', *Annual Review of Sociology*, 15: 187-209.

Menard, S. (1991) *Longitudinal Research*, London: Sage Publications.

Micheli, G.A. (2006) 'Svantaggi e Benefici del Lavoro Atipico nel Confronto tra Domanda e Offerta', *Stato e Mercato*, 78: 437-72.

Millar, J. (1999) 'Obligations and Autonomy in Social Welfare', in R. Crompton (ed) *Restructuring Gender Relations and Employment: The Decline of the Male Breadwinner*, Oxford: Oxford University Press.

Millar, J. and Rowlingson, K. (eds) (2001) *Lone Parents, Employment and Social Policy: Cross-National Comparisons*, Bristol: The Policy Press.

Millar, J. and Warman, A. (1996) *Family Obligations in Europe*, London: Family Policy Studies Centre.

Millar, J. and Warman, A. (1997) 'Family/State Boundaries in Europe', *Social Policy Review*, 9: 276-89.

Mincer, J. and Polachek, S. (1974) 'Family Investments in Human Capital: Earnings of Women', in T.W. Schultz (ed) *Economics of the Family*, Chicago, IL: University of Chicago Press.

Mingione, E. (1995) 'Labour Market Segmentation and Informal Work in Southern Europe', *European Urban and Regional Studies*, 2: 121-43.

Ministero del Lavoro e della Previdenza Sociale (2000) *Rapporto Di Monitoraggio Sulle Politiche Occupazionali e Del Lavoro*, Rome: Ministero del Lavoro e della Previdenza Sociale.

MISSOC (Mutual Information System on Social Protection in the European Union) (various years) *Social Protection in the Member States of the European Union*, Luxembourg: European Commission.

Mitchell, B.R. (1975) *European Historical Statistics 1750-1970*, London: Macmillan.

Molyneux, M. (1979) 'Beyond the Domestic Labour Debate', *New Left Review*: 116.

Monteduro, M.T. (1998) 'Unemployment, Discouraged Workers and Female Labour Supply: An Empirical Study in Italy', Ferrara: *Quaderni del Dipartimento di Economia, Istituzioni, Territorio No 4*, Universita Degli Studi di Ferrara.

Moors, G. (2001) 'Family Theory: The Role of Changing Values', in N.J. Smelser and P.B. Baltes (eds) *International Encyclopedia of the Social and Behavioural Sciences*, Oxford: Pergamon Press.

Mortimer, J.T.. and Shanahan, M.J. (eds) (2003) *Handbook of the Life Course*, New York: Kluwer Academic/Plenum Publishers, pp 23-50.

Mosley, H., O'Reilly, J. and Schömann, K. (eds) (2002) *Labour Markets, Gender and Institutional Change: Essays in Honour of Günther Schmid*, Cheltenham: Edward Elgar.

Moss, P. and O'Brien, M. (eds) (2006) 'International Review of Leave Policies and Related Research', Employment Relations Research Series No. 57, London: Department for Trade and Industry.

Münch, R. (1992) 'Rational Choice Theory: A Critical Assessment of its Explanatory Power', in J.S. Coleman and T.J. Fararo (eds) *Rational Choice Theory: Advocacy and Critique*, Newbury Park, CA: Sage Publications.

Naldini, M. (2003) *The Family in the Mediterranean Welfare States*, London: Frank Cass.

Naldini, M. (2006) *Le Politiche Sociali in Europa: Trasformazioni dei Bisogni e Risposte di Policy*, Rome: Carocci.

Naldini, M. and Jurado, T. (2008) 'The Changing South European Family' paper presented at the conference, Equalsoc Midterm Conference Famnet session, Berlin, 11-12 April.

Nazio, T. and MacInnes, J. (2007) 'Time Stress, Wellbeing and the Double Burden', in G. Esping-Andersen (ed) *Family Formation and Family Dilemmas in Contemporary Europe*, Barcelona: FBBVA, pp 155-84.

Negri, N. and Saraceno, C. (1996) *Le Politiche Contro la Povertà in Italia*, Bologna: Il Mulino.

Neugarten, B.L. (ed) (1968) *Middle Age and Aging*, Chicago, IL: University of Chicago Press.

Nussbaum, M.C. (2000) *Women and Human Development*, Cambridge: Cambridge University Press.

O'Connor, J.S. (1993) 'Gender, Class and Citizenship in the Comparative Analysis of Welfare State Regimes: Theoretical and Methodological Issues', *British Journal of Sociology*, 44: 502-18.

O'Connor, J.S. (ed) (1996) 'From Women in the Welfare State to Gendering Welfare State Regimes', *Special Issue of Current Sociology*, 44 (2):

O'Connor, J.S., Orloff, A. and Shaver, S. (1999) *States, Markets, Families: Gender, Liberalism and Social Policy in Australia, Canada, Great Britain and the United States*, Cambridge: Cambridge University Press.

O'Reilly, J.., I Cebrian, and M. Lallement, (eds) (2000) *Working-Time Changes: Social Integration Through Transitional Labour Markets*, Cheltenham: Edward Elgar.

OECD (Organisation for Economic Co-operation and Development) (1999) *Employment Outlook*, Paris: OECD.

OECD (2001a) *OECD Historical Statistics 1970-2000*, Paris: OECD.

OECD (2001b) 'Balancing Work and Family Life: Helping Parents into Paid Employment', *Employment Outlook 2001*, Paris: OECD.

OECD (2002) 'Women At Work: Who Are They and How Are They Faring?', *Employment Outlook 2002*, Paris: OECD.

OECD (2006) *OECD in Figures 2006*, Paris: OECD.

Olagnero M., Saraceno C. (1993) *Che vita è. L'uso dei materiali biografici nell'analisi sociologica*, La Nuova Italia Scientifica, Roma

ONS (Office for National Statistics) (2007) 'Report: Live Births in England and Wales, 2006: Area of Residence', *Population Trends*, 128: 71-8.

Oppenheim Mason, K. and Jensen, A.M. (eds) (1995) *Gender and Family Change in Industrial Countries*, Oxford: Clarendon Press.

Oppenheimer, V.K. (1988) 'A Theory of Marriage Timing', *American Journal of Sociology*, 94 (3): 563-91.

Oppenheimer, V.K. (1994) 'Women's Rising Employment and the Future of the Family in Industrial Societies', *Population and Development Review*, 20 (2): 293-342.

Orloff, A. (1993) 'Gender and Social Rights of Citizenship: The Comparative Analysis of Gender Relations and Welfare States', *American Sociological Review*, 58: 303-28.

Ortega y Gasset, J. (1933) *The Modern Theme*, New York: Norton.

Palmer, T. (2004) *Results of the First Flexible Working Employee Survey, Employment Relations Occasional Papers 04/703*, London: Department of Trade and Industry.

Palomba, R. (1995) 'Italy: The Invisible Change', in R. Palomba and H. Moors (eds) *Population, Family, and Welfare: A Comparative Survey of European Attitudes*, vol 1, Oxford: Clarendon Press.

Pateman, C. (1988) 'The Patriarchal Welfare State', in A. Gutmann (ed) *Democracy and the Welfare State*, New Jersey, NJ: Princeton University Press.

Pfau-Effinger, B. (1999) 'The Modernisation of Family and Motherhood', in R. Crompton (ed) *Restructuring Gender Relations and Employment: The Decline of the Male Breadwinner*, Oxford: Oxford University Press.

Pfau-Effinger, B. (2004) 'Socio-Historical Paths of the Male Breadwinner Model: An Explanation of Cross-National Differences', *British Journal of Sociology*, 55 (3): 377-99.

Piccone Stella, S. and Salmieri, L. (2007) 'Foto di Coppia con Bambino', in S. Piccone Stella (ed) *Tra un Lavoro e l'Altro: Vita di Coppia nell'Italia Post-Fordista*, Rome: Carocci.

Pisati, M. (2002) 'La Transizione alla Vita Adulta', in A. Schizzerotto (ed) *Vite Ineguali: Disuguaglianze e Corsi di vita Nell'Italia Contemporanea*, Bologna: Il Mulino.

Pisati, M. and Schizzerotto, A. (1999) 'Pochi Promossi, Nessun Bocciato: La Mobilità Di Carriera in Italia in Prospettiva Comparata e Longitudinale', *Stato e Mercato*, 56: 249-79.

Pisati, M. and Schizzerotto, A. (2003) 'The Italian Mobility Regime: 1985-1997', in R. Breen (ed) *National Patterns of Social Mobility, 1970-1999: Divergence or Convergence?*, Oxford: Oxford University Press.

Plantenga, J. and Remery, C. (2005) *Reconciliation of Work and Private Life: A Comparative Review of Thirty European Countries*, Luxembourg: Office for Official Publications of the European Communities.

Polachek, S. (1981) 'Occupational Self-Selection: A Human Capital Approach to Sex Differences in Occupational Structure', *Review of Economics and Statistics*, 63: 60-9.

Ponzellini, A. (2006) 'Work–Life Balance and Industrial Relations in Italy', *European Societies*, 8 (2): 273–94.

Power, M. (1983) 'From Home Production to Wage Labor: Women as a Reserve Army of Labor', *Review of Radical Political Economics*, 15 (1): 71–91.

Prein, G. (1998) 'Modelling Rational Action: A Longitudinal Approach', in H.-P. Blossfeld and G. Prein (eds) *Rational Choice Theory and Large-Scale Data Analysis*, Boulder, CO: Westview Press.

Price, S.J., McKenry, P.C. and Murphy, M.J. (eds) (2000) *Families across Time: A Life Course Perspective*, Los Angeles, CA: Roxbury.

Pronzato, C. (2007) *Return to Work after Childbirth: Does Parental Leave Matter in Europe?*, ISER Working Paper 2007-30, Colchester: Institute for Social and Economic Research.

Purcell, K., Hogarth, T. and Simm, C. (1999) *Whose Flexibility?*, York: Joseph Rowntree Foundation.

Ragin, C. (1991) 'Introduction: The Problem of Balancing Discourse on Cases and Variables in Comparative Social Science', in C. Ragin (ed) *Issues and Alternatives in Comparative Social Research*, Leiden: E.J. Brill.

Randall, V. (2002) 'Child Care in Britain, or, How Do You Restructure Nothing?', in S. Michel and R. Mahon (eds) *Child Care Policy at the Crossroads: Gender and Welfare State Restructuring*, New York: Routledge.

Reyneri, E. (2002) *Sociologia del Mercato del Lavoro*, Bologna: Il Mulino.

Reyneri, E. (2009) 'Il Lavoro delle Donne', in E. Reyneri, P. Manacorda and G. Indiretto (eds) 'Offerta di Lavoro e Occupazione Femminile' *Contributo Tematico a Commissione di Indagine sul Lavoro, Il Lavoro che Cambia. Contributi Tematici e Raccomandazioni*, Roma: CNEL, www.portalecnel.it/Portale/IndLavrapportiFinali.nsf/vwCapitoli?OpenView&Count=40

Riley, M.W., Johnson, M. and Foner, A. (1972) *Ageing and Society, Vol 3: A Sociology of Age Stratification*, New York: Russell Sage Foundation.

Ringen, S. (1997) 'Great Britain', in S. Kamerman and A. Kahn (eds) *Family Change and Family Policies in Great Britain, Canada, New Zealand and the United States*, Oxford: Clarendon Press: 29–102.

Risman, B.J. (2004) 'Gender as a Social Structure: Theory Wrestling with Social Change', *Gender & Society*, 18 (4): 429–50.

Robinson, R. and Bell, W. (1978) 'Equality, Success and Social Justice in England and the United States', *American Sociological Review*, 43: 115–43.

Robinson-Pant, A. (2004) 'Education for Women: Whose Values Count?', *Gender and Development*, 13 (4): 473–89.

Romano, M.C. and Sabbadini, L.L. (2007) 'Principali Trasformazioni dell'Uso del Tempo in Italia', in M.C. Bellloni (ed) *Andare a Tempo: Il Caso Torino: Una Ricerca sui Tempi della Città*, Milan: Franco Angeli, pp 35–54.

Rosen, S. (1986) 'The Theory of Equalizing Differences', in O. Ashenfelter and R. Layard (eds) *Handbook of Labor Economics*, Amsterdam: Elsevier Science Publishers, pp 641–92.

Rosina, A. and Saraceno, C. (2008) 'Interferenze Asimmetriche: Uno Studio sulla Discontinuità Lavorativa Femminile', *Economia & Lavoro*, XLII (2): 149-67.

Rubery, J. (ed) (1988a) *Women and Recession*, London: Routledge & Kegan Paul.

Rubery, J., Smith, M., Fagan, C. and Grimshaw, D. (1998) *Women and European Employment*, London: Routledge.

Ruspini, E. (2008) *La Ricerca Longitudinale*, Milan: Franco Angeli.

Sabbadini, L.L. (2002) 'La Rete di Aiuti Informali', in *Osservatorio Nazionale sulle Famiglie e le Politiche Locali di Sostegno alle Responsabilità Familiari*, Famiglie: Mutamenti e Politiche Sociali, vol II, Bologna: Il Mulino.

Sainsbury, D. (ed) (1994a) *Gendering Welfare States*, London: Sage Publications.

Sainsbury, D. (1994b) 'Women's and Men's Social Rights: Gendering Dimensions of Welfare States', in D. Sainsbury (ed) *Gendering Welfare States*, London: Sage Publications.

Sainsbury, D. (1996) *Gender, Equality and Welfare States*, Cambridge: Cambridge University Press.

Samek Lodovici, M. (2000) 'Italy', in G. Esping-Andersen and M. Regini (eds) *Why Deregulate Labour Markets?*, Oxford: Oxford University Press.

Santini, A. (1997) 'La Fecondita', in M. Barbagli and C. Saraceno (eds) *Lo Stato delle Famiglie in Italia*, Bologna: Il Mulino.

Saraceno, C. (1984) 'Shifts in Public and Private Boundaries: Women as Mothers and Service Workers in Italian Day-Care', *Feminist Studies*, (Spring): 7-30.

Saraceno, C. (1992) *Pluralità e Mutamento: Riflessioni sull'Identità al Femminile*, Milan: Franco Angeli.

Saraceno, C. (1993) 'Elementi per una Analisi delle Trasformazioni di Genere Nella Società Contemporanea e delle Loro Conseguenze Sociali', *Rassegna Italiana di Sociologia*, 1: 19-56.

Saraceno, C. (1994) 'Una Politica di Sostegno alle Responsabilità Familiari', *Il Mulino*, 3: 459-69.

Saraceno, C. (2001) 'Introduzione: Dalla Sociologia dell'Età alla Sociologia del Corso della Vita', in C. Saraceno (ed) *Età e Corso della Vita*, Bologna: Il Mulino.

Saraceno, C. (ed) (2002) *Social Assistance Dynamics in Europe: National and Local Poverty Regimes*, Bristol: The Policy Press.

Saraceno, C. (2003a) *Mutamenti della Famiglia e Politiche Sociali in Italia*, Bologna: Il Mulino.

Saraceno, C. (2003b) 'La Conciliazione di Responsabilità Familiari e Attività Lavorative in Italia: Paradossi e Equilibri Imperfetti', *Polis*, 17 (2): 199-228.

Saraceno, C. (2005) 'Le Differenze che Contano tra i Lavoratori Atipici', in S. Bertolini and R. Rizza (eds) *Atipici?*, Milan: Angeli.

Saraceno, C. and Piccone Stella, S. (1996) 'Introduzione: La Storia di un Concetto e di un Dibattito', in C. Saraceno, S. Piccone Stella (eds) *Genere: La Costruzione Sociale del Femminile e del Maschile*, Bologna: Il Mulino, pp 7-37.

Saurel-Cubizolles, M.-J., Romito, P., Escriba-Agüir, V., Lelong, N., Mas Pons, R. and Ancel, P.-Y. (1999) 'Returning to Work after Childbirth in France, Italy, and Spain', *European Sociological Review*, 15 (2): 179-94.

Savage, M. (2000) *Class Analysis and Social Transformation*, Buckingham: Open University Press.

Scheiwe, K. (1994) 'Labour Market, Welfare State, and Family Institutions: The Links to Mothers' Poverty Risks', *Journal of European Social Policy*, 4 (3): 201-24.

Scherer, S. and Steiber, N. (2007) 'Family and Work in Conflict? Evidence from Six European Countries', in D. Gallie (ed) *Employment Regimes and the Quality of Work*, Oxford: Oxford University Press, pp 137-78.

Schizzerotto, A. (ed) (2002a) *Vite Ineguali: Disuguaglianze e Corsi di Vita nell'Italia Contemporanea*, Bologna: Il Mulino.

Schizzerotto, A. (2002b) 'La Ricerca di un Impiego', in A. Schizzerotto (ed) *Vite Ineguali: Disuguaglianze e Corsi di Vita nell'Italia Contemporanea*, Bologna: Il Mulino.

Schizzerotto, A. and Cobalti, A. (1998) 'Occupational Returns to Education in Contemporary Italy', in Y. Shavit and W. Müller (eds) *From School to Work*, Oxford: Clarendon Press: 253-86.

Schizzerotto, A. and Lucchini, M. (2002) 'La Formazione di Nuove Famiglie in Italia e Gran Bretagna: Un'Analisi Longitudinale', in *Osservatorio Nazionale sulle Famiglie e le Politiche Locali di Sostegno alle Responsabilità Familiari,* Famiglie: Mutamenti e Politiche Sociali, vol 1, Bologna: Il Mulino: 63-93.

Schizzerotto, A., Bison, I. and Zoppe, A. (1995) 'Disparità di Genere nella Partecipazione al Mondo del Lavoro e Nella Durata delle Carriere', *Polis*, 9 (1): 91-112.

Scott, J. (1999a) 'European Attitudes towards Maternal Employment', *International Journal of Sociology and Social Policy*, 19 (9-10-11): 151-86.

Scott, J. (1999b) 'Family Change: Revolution or Backlash in Attitudes?', in S. McRae (ed) *Changing Britain: Families and Households in the 1990s*, Oxford: Oxford University Press.

Scott, J. (2000) 'Class and Stratification', in G. Payne (ed) *Social Divisions*, London: Macmillan.

Scott, J., Alwin, D.F. and Braun, M. (1996) 'Generational Changes in Gender-Role Attitudes: Britain in a Cross-National Perspective', *Sociology*, 30 (3): 471-92.

Sen, A. (1985) *Commodities and Capabilities*, Oxford: North-Holland.

Sen, A. (1992) *Inequality Re-examined*, Oxford: Oxford University Press.

Sen, A. (1999) *Development as Freedom*, New York: Knopf.

Sigle-Rushton, W. (2008) 'England and Wales: Stable Fertility and Pronounced Social Status Differences', *Demographic Research*, 19 (15): 455-502.

Sjöberg, O. (2004) 'The Role of Family Policy Institutions in Explaining Gender-Role Attitudes: A Comparative Multilevel Analysis of Thirteen Industrialized Countries', *Journal of European Social Policy*, 14 (2): 107-23.

Smith A. and Williams, D.R. (2007) 'Father-Friendly Legislation and Paternal Time Across Western Europe', *Journal of Comparative Policy Analysis*, Spring, 9(3): 175-92.

Smith, A.J. (2004) *Who Cares? Fathers and the Time They Spend Looking After Children*, Working Paper No 2004-05, July, Oxford: Department of Sociology, University of Oxford.

Smith, M. (2005) 'Dual Earning in Europe: Time and Occupational Equity', *Work, Employment and Society*, 19 (1): 131-9.

Smits, J., Ultee, W. and Lammers, J. (1996) 'Effects of Occupational Status Differences between Spouses on the Wife's Labor Force Participation and Occupational Achievement: Findings from 12 European Countries', *Journal of Marriage and the Family*, 58: 101-15.

Sobotka, T. (2004) 'Is Lowest-Low Fertility Explained by the Postponement of Childbearing?', *Population and Development Review*, 30 (2): 195-220.

Solera, C. (2001) 'Income Transfers and Support for Mothers' Employment: the Link to Family Poverty Risks', in K.Vleminckx and T.M. Smeeding (eds) *Child Well-Being, Chid Poverty and Child Policy in Modern Nations: What Do We Know?*, Bristol: The Policy Press, pp 459-84.

Solera, C. (2004) *Changes across Cohorts in Women's Work Histories: To What Extent are they Due to a Compositional Effect? A Comparison of Italy and Great Britain*, IUE Working Paper No 9, Fiesole: Istituto Universitario Europeo.

Solera, C. (2005) 'Women's Employment Over the Life Course: Changes across Cohorts in Italy and Great Britain', PhD thesis, European University Institute, Florence.

Solera, C. and Bettio, F. (2007) *Women's Work Histories in Italy: Education as Investment in Reconciliation and Legitimacy?*, DemoSoc Working Paper No 19, Barcelona: University of Pompeu Fabra.

Solera, C. and Negri, N. (2008) 'Conciliazione Famiglia-Lavoro: Strategia Ex-Ante o Ex-Post? Una Analisi su Coppie Vulnerabili nel Canavese', in W. Rinaldi (ed) *Giustizia e Povertà: Universalismo, Cittadinanza, Capabilities*, Bologna: Il Mulino.

Sørensen, A. (1994) 'Women's Economic Risk and the Economic Position of Single Mothers', *European Sociological Review*, 2: 173-88.

Sørensen, A. and McLanahan, S. (1987) 'Married Women's Economic Dependency, 1940-1980', *American Journal of Sociology*, 93: 659-87.

Sorrentino, C. (1990) 'The Changing Family in International Perspective', *Monthly Labour Review*, 113 (3): 41-58.

Spiess, K.C., Lacovou, M., Robson, K.L. and Uunk, W.J.G. (2004) 'Family Effects on Employment', in R. Berthoud and M. Lacovou (eds) *Social Europe: Living Standards and Welfare States*, Cheltenham: Edward Elgar, pp 69-98.

Staat, M. and Wagenhals, G. (1996) 'Lone Mothers: A Review', *Journal of Population Economics*, 9 (2): 131-40.

Stier, H. and Lewin-Epstein, N. (2001) 'Welfare Regimes, Family-Supportive Policies, and Women's Employment along the Life-Course', *American Journal of Sociology*, 106 (6): 1731-60.

Stier, H. and Lewin-Epstein, N. (2007) 'Policy Effect on the Division of Housework', *Journal of Comparative Policy Analysis*, 9 (3): 235-59.

Tam, T. (1997) 'Sex Segregation and Occupational Sex Inequality in the United States: Devaluation or Specialised Training?', *American Journal of Sociology*, 102 (6): 1652-93.

Theobald, H. and Maier, F. (2002) 'Women between Labour Market Integration and Segregation: Germany and Sweden Compared', in H. Mosley, J. O'Reilly and K. Schömann (eds) *Labour Markets, Gender and Institutional Change: Essays in Honour of Günther Schmid*, Cheltenham: Edward Elgar, pp 212-41.

Thornton, A. (1985) 'Changing Attitudes toward Separation and Divorce: Causes and Consequences', *American Journal of Sociology*, 90: 856-72.

Tilly, C. (1984) *Big Structures, Large Processes, Huge Comparisons*, New York: Sage Publications.

Todesco, L. (2008) 'Caratteristiche Demografiche e Sociali dei Coniugi', in A. Urbano (ed) *Evoluzione e Nuove Tendenze dell'Instabilità Coniugale, Argomenti No 34*, Rome: Istat, pp 73-85.

Treas, J. and Widmer, E.D. (2000) 'Married Women's Employment Over the Life Course: Attitudes in Cross-National Perspective', *Social Forces*, 78 (4): 1409-36.

Trifiletti, R. (1999) 'Southern European Welfare Regimes and the Worsening Position of Women', *Journal of European Social Policy*, 9 (1): 49-64.

Trussell, J. and Richards, T. (1985) 'Correcting for Unmeasured Heterogeneity in Hazard Models Using the Heckman-Singer Procedure', *Sociological Methodology*, 15: 242-76.

Uunk, W., Kalmijn, M. and Muffels, R. (2005) 'The Impact of Young Children on Women's Labour Supply: A Reassessment of Institutional Effects in Europe', *Acta Sociologica*, 48 (1): 41-62.

Van de Kaa, D. (1987) 'Europe's Second Demographic Transition', *Population Bulletin*, 42 (1): 1-57.

Van Putten, A.E., Dykstra, P.A. and Schippers, J.J. (2008) 'Just Like Mom? The Intergenerational Reproduction of Paid Labor', *European Sociological Review*, 24 (4): 435-49.

Villa, P. (2004) 'La diffusione del modello di famiglia a doppia partecipazione nei paesi europei e in Italia', *Inchiesta*, v. XXXIV, 146, pp 6-20.

Vlasblom, J.D. and Schippers, J. (2006) 'Changing Dynamics in Female Employment around Childbirth: Evidence from Germany, the Netherlands and the UK', *Work, Employment & Society*, 20: 329-47.

Walker, J. (1988) 'Women, the State and the Family in Britain: Thatcher Economics and the Experience of Women', in J. Rubery (ed) *Women and Recession*, London: Routledge & Kegan Paul.

Walters, S. (2005) 'Making the Best of a Bad Job? Female Part-Timers' Orientations and Attitudes to Work', *Gender, Work and Organization*, 12: 193-216.

Ward, C., Dale, A. and Joshi, H. (1996) 'Combining Employment with Childcare: An Escape from Dependency?', *Journal of Social Policy*, 25: 223-47.

West, C. and Zimmerman, D. (1987) 'Doing Gender', *Gender & Society*, 1: 125–51.

Wetzels, C. (2007) 'Motherhood and Wages', in D. Del Boca and C. Wetzels (eds) *Social Policies, Labour Markets and Motherhood: A Comparative Analysis of European Countries*, Cambridge: Cambridge University Press, pp 225-68.

Wetzels, C. and Tijdens, K. (2002) 'Dutch Mothers' Return to Work and the Re-Entry Effect on Wage', *Economic Review*, 45 (2): 169-89.

Wincott, D. (2006) 'Paradoxes of New Labour Social Policy: Toward Universal Child Care in Europe's "Most Liberal" Welfare Regime?', *Social Politics*, 13 (2): 286-312.

Yamaguchi, K. (1991) *Event History Analysis*, London: Sage Publications.

Table A1: Key characteristics of family and childcare allowances in Italy and Britain

Name of Programme	Year of major regulations	Type of Benefit	Main eligibility conditions and monthly amount in 2002
Italy			
Assegni Familiari	1937	Contributory	*All employees in private sector* Different schemes according to sector. Paid for each dependent child, but with an increasing rate for each additional child
	1940	Employers' contributory	*Extension to other dependent family members* (spouse, parents and parents in law)
	1944		Paid at the same rate for each child
	1967-77		*Extension to farmers, unemployed, part-time workers in agriculture*
	1988		Only for children, brothers and sisters, nephews and nieces of specific employment categories (such as farmers, sharecroppers)
Assegni per il nucleo familiare	1988 (replace of AF)	Employers' contributory and means tested	*For low-income families of all employees or former employed* persons (pensioners and persons on social security benefits) Rate depending not on sector, but on family size (spouse, children < 18, disabled relatives) and family income.
	1994		Supplement for each child after the first
	1999		*Extended to self-employed, free professionals, cococo (employer-coordinated freelance workers)*
	Amount in 2002		Example of a family with 4 members (without handicap): Annual income up to € 11,422.98: € 250.48 per month; Annual income between € 27,693.04 and € 30,403.39: € 38.73 per month. Income over € 43,962.05: no benefit.
Assegni di maternità	1999	Means tested	*New mothers in low-income families* not employed or employed but not insured for maternity leave provisions.
	Amount in 2002		€ 265.20 per month and paid only for five months after the child's birth or adoption.
No childcare allowances			
Britain			
Family Allowance + Child Tax Allowance	1948	Universal	*Child/ren < 16 y old, except first* If parents work, tax exemptions for each child
Child Benefit	1976 (replace FA)	Universal	*Child/ren < 16 or < 19 if in FT education,* all at same rate
	1991		Higher rate for elder or eldest child
	Amount in 2002		Eldest qualifying child of a couple: GBP 68.25 per month (€ 105). Each other child: GBP 45.72 per month (€ 70).
Childcare Tax Credit	2003	Means tested	Linked to entitlement to *Working Tax Credit* (*Working Family Tax Credit* from 1999 to 2003) for low-income workers. Those with children can claim up to 70% of their registered childcare costs up to a maximum of GBP 135 per week for 1 child, GBP 200 for 2+.

Source: Missoc (various years); Saraceno (2003a); Del Boca and Wetzels (2007)

Table A2: Key characteristics of maternity and parental leaves in Italy and Britain

Year of major regulations	Type of benefit	Main eligibility conditions	Maximum duration	Financial support
Italy				
		Maternity leave provisions		
1971	Contributory	*Insured employees irrespective of length of service; compulsory* 2 months before the expected confinement date, 3 months after	22 weeks	80% of earnings (some collective agreements require employers to pay an extra 20%; 100% for civil servants)
1987		*Extension to self-employed workers* depending on strict contribution requirements; not compulsory	22 weeks	80% of minimum wage of agricultural labourers or routine non-manual workers
1990		*Extension to free professionals* depending on strict contribution requirements; not compulsory	22 weeks	80% of 5/12 of declared yearly income
2000	Contributory	*Insured employees irrespective of length of service, compulsory* 5 months to be taken flexibly, at least 4 weeks before the birth	20 weeks	80% of earnings (some collective agreements require employers to pay an extra 20%; 100% for civil servants)
		Self-employed persons with social security membership, not compulsory	20 weeks	80 % of minimum wage of agricultural labourers or routine non-manual workers
		Free professionals, not compulsory	20 weeks	80% of 5/12 of declared yearly income
2000		*Extension to co.co.co* (employer-coordinated freelance workers) if 3 months contributions paid in previous year	20 weeks	80% of earnings in previous year
2003		*Extension to co.pro* (project work contracts) if 3 months contributions paid in previous year		
		Paternity leave No provision		
		Parental leave provisions		
1971	Contributory	*Insured employee, only for mothers, irrespective of length of service.*	6 months within 1st year of child	30% of earnings
1977		Extension of optional leave to insured employee *fathers,* who may benefit instead of the mother (if married)	10 months (o 11) within 8th year of child	
2000	Contributory	*Insured employee mothers and fathers irrespective of length of service and self-employed with social security membership.* Family right but individual entitlement to 6 months each. Total amount of leave not more than 10 months (11 months if the father takes at least 3 months of his quota). Leave is fractionable, and can be taken also in the form of vertical part-time		30% of earnings of first 6 months within child's 3rd birthday. Then means tested Self-employed replaced at work receive tax relief of €1693 (2004)

Year of major regulations	Type of benefit	Main eligibility conditions	Maximum duration	Financial support
		Self-employed with social security membership, but only mothers	3 months within child's 1st birthday	30% conventional earnings
		Leave for family reasons		
1971	Contributory	*Insured employee mothers with children < 3, irrespective of length of service*	Unlimited, within child's 3rd birth day	Unpaid
1977		*Extension to insured employee fathers, who may benefit instead of the mother*		
2000	Contributory	*Insured employee mothers and fathers, irrespective of length of service*	Unlimited, within child's 3rd birthday. 5 days a year per parent for a 3-8 year child	Unpaid

Britain

Year of major regulations	Type of benefit	Main eligibility conditions	Maximum duration	Financial support
		Maternity grant		
1978	Contributory	*Insured women, whether employee, self-employed or without employment*	Lump sum	£25 (1972 amount)
1986	Means tested	Maternity Payment from the Social Fund	Lump sum	
		Maternity allowance		
1978	Contributory	*Insured women, employee or self-employed: a minimum of 6 months of insured employment during the previous year*	18 weeks	£6 per wk (1972 amount) + increase for dependants
		Statutory maternity pay		
1986 (replace MA for continuous employees)	Contributory	*Only insured employees with 2 yrs FT or 5 yrs PT of continuous insured employment with same employer.*	40 weeks	90% earnings for first 6 weeks/flat-rate benefit next 12 weeks/unpaid last 22 weeks

Year of major regulations	Type of benefit	Main eligibility conditions	Maximum duration	Financial support
1994		*All pregnant insured employees qualify for a minimum of 14 wks, irrespective of length of service*	Minimum of 14 weeks	Flat-rate benefit (Level of Statutory Sick Pay)
		Qualifying for a further 26 wks are women with 1 yr of continuous insured employment with same employer (26 wks up to the qualifying week, that is, the 15th wk before expected week of confinement)	40 weeks	90% earnings for first 6 wks/flat-rate benefit next 12 wks/ unpaid last 22 wks
1999		*All pregnant insured employees qualify for a minimum of 26 wks of Paid Ordinary Maternity Leave, irrespective of length of service*	Minimum of 26 weeks	90% earnings for first 6 wks/ flat-rate benefit next 20 wks
		Qualifying for a further 26 wks are women with 1 yr of continuous insured employment with same employer (26 wks up to the qualifying week, that is, the 15th wk before expected week of confinement)	Extra 26 weeks	Unpaid

Paternity leave

Year of major regulations	Type of benefit	Main eligibility conditions	Maximum duration	Financial support
2002		*Male employees with 1 yr of continuous insured employment with same employer*	2 wks within first 8th weeks of life child	112 GBP (€150), a week or 90% of average weekly earnings if he earns less than 112 GBP

Parental leave provisions

Year of major regulations	Type of benefit	Main eligibility conditions	Maximum duration	Financial support
1999	Contributory	*Insured employees mothers and fathers with at least 1 yr of continuous employment with same employer.* Individual (non transferable) entitlement. *Leave can be taken at once, by means of reduced working hours, or in blocks depending on workplace arrangements*	13 weeks for each parent within child's 5th birthday	Unpaid (left to employer's discretion)

Leave for family reasons

Year of major regulations	Type of benefit	Main eligibility conditions	Maximum duration	Financial support
1999	Contributory	*Employee may ask for a 'reasonable' amount of time off work to deal with unexpected or sudden emergencies, such as illness of a dependent or breakdown of care arrangements*	'reasonable'	Unpaid

Source: Missoc (various years); Moss and O'Brien (2006); Gottardi (1999, 2001); Conaghan (2002)

Table A3: The family dimension of the taxation system in Italy and Britain

Year of major regulations	Units of taxation	Tax reliefs for spouses or cohabiting	Tax reliefs for children
Italy			
Before 1977	Families		
1977	Individuals	Tax credits or tax allowances (depending on the year) for dependent spouse	Tax credits or tax allowances (depending on the year) for dependent children. Both parents are entitled to the exempt
Amount in 2002		None for two-earner couples. Means-tested refundable tax-credit for dependent spouse	Refundable tax credit, not means-tested up to 3rd child. Min €285 max €516 per child, depending on income bands. From 4th child €516. No relief for lone parents. No relief for childcare or education costs
Britain			
Before 1990	Families	*Married Men's Allowance* Income Tax exemption for husbands on top of single person's income tax exemption	Since 1976 (Introduction of *Child Benefit*)
1988 (replace MMA; implementation 1990)	Individuals (with non-transferable personal exemptions)	*Married Couple's Allowance* Income Tax exemption for married couples on top of single person's income tax exemption; since 1993 allocable all to one spouse or split equally. *Additional Personal Allowance* For unmarried parents (lone parents or cohabiting) on top of single person's income tax exemption; claimable by both cohabiting parents; equivalent in value to MCA	No
Amount in 2002		Tax unit is the individual but tax credits depend on joint income and access to means-tested *Working Tax Credit* (WTC) and *Child Tax Credit* (CTC), the latter not conditional on being in work. Max amounts for CTC are €788 per family, plus €788 if child < 1yr (as *family element*), €2,089 per child (as *child element*). Max amounts of WTC+CTC for joint Y <€7,317, then WTC and child element reduced at a rate of 37% for joint Y < €72,300, then family element reduced to 0 at a rate of 15%. The WTC comprises a *childcare element* for children <3 in registered childcare facilities: 70% of max €10,180 for 1 child and 70% of max €15,082 for 2 children	

Source: European Observatory of National Family Policies (1992); Ringen (1997); Del Boca and Wetzels (2007)

Table A4: Family-friendly flexibility in Italy and Britain (early 2000s)

Type of Measure		Italy	Britain
Possibility to take leave of absence for family reasons		Unlimited, within child's third birthday Unpaid	'reasonable' amount of time Unpaid
Possibility to reduce working hours for family reasons		2 hrs/day for the mother until the child's 1st birthday. Fathers may benefit instead of the mother. Parents of a child aged under 18 have the right to apply to their employers for work flexibility.	Parents of a child aged under 6 have the right to apply to their employers for reduced working hours or work flexi-time.
Freedom in scheduling working time		Yes (but not family specific)	No (only some initiatives by some private companies)
Normal work schedules:	*Full-time*	36 hrs on average	40 hrs or more
	Part-time	About 50 % of full-time schedule	Wide variation: median far less than 20 hrs
Work–family arrangements provided by firms (1995-96)		For women employees with a child<15: 81%	
Extra-statutory maternity leaves		69%	61%
Extra-statutory parental leaves		5%	28%
Provision of child day-care		19%	10%
Working flexi-time		11%	32%
Voluntary part-time work		11%	30%

Source: OECD (2001b); Moss and O' Brien (2006)

Index